# SHORT PAPERS
## Volume 1

# Short Papers

*by*

C. H. MACKINTOSH

*Reprinted from*
THINGS NEW AND OLD

## Volume 1

*Published by*

BELIEVERS BOOKSHELF
P.O. Box 261
Sunbury, Penna. 17801

SHORT PAPERS
OF C. H. MACKINTOSH

Library of Congress Catalog Card No. 75-29527

PRINTED IN UNITED STATES OF AMERICA BY
Theo. Gaus' Sons, Inc., BROOKLYN, N. Y.

# Editor's Preface to the First Volume

C. H. Mackintosh lived 1820-1896, and was one of those great and godly men who were leaders in what is called the "Plymouth Brethren" movement. For 21 years he edited a monthly magazine called "Things New and Old." Many of the articles which he wrote for this periodical are found in the six-volume set of his "Miscellaneous Writings," which, by the mercy of God, has been in print ever since it was first issued in the last century. But many of the articles written for "Things New and Old" are not included in the "Miscellaneous Writings," and it is the purpose of the present series to bring these back into print, for the edification of the Lord's people.

Inasmuch as Mackintosh published the majority of these articles anonymously, it is due to the reader to say that the only way by which it is known that many of them were written by him, is that the style of the writing is his. This casts no uncertainty upon their authorship, since C. H. M.'s style is quite peculiar to himself, and easily recognized by anyone who is familiar with his writings; and, I suppose that any such person could readily verify that C. H. M. is the author of these. However, if any mistake has been made in this matter, the responsibility for it rests solely upon the editor.

Also, inasmuch as it is the habit of some, in reprinting old writings, to revise and abridge them as they will, the editor will take this opportunity to assure the reader that all of these articles are reprinted exactly as their author originally published them, the editor deeming it, first of all, unnecessary, but more than that, unjust, to make any changes, except for the occasional correction of errors and omissions in spelling and punctuation. The occasional references to particular issues of "Things New and Old" have not been deleted: they may prove interesting or useful to some, and they certainly need not be irksome to any.

The articles are not arranged in any particular order, except that those articles which naturally fall together are placed together. In some of these there is some repetition, but there is enough that is distinct in each article that the reader may bear with the repetition.

Finally, the editor wishes to say that he does not endorse every sentiment expressed in these writings by C. H. M. The writings are sound and edifying in the main, but the reader must be cast on the scriptures alone as to whether any particular point in them is the truth. This is not to cast a slight upon them. I endorse *heartily* the doctrine and spirit of them in general, it being just that which I have learned myself from God, through the scriptures. Hence my labor to have them reprinted. But *I* need not to commend these writings, being fully persuaded that they will commend themselves to all who are taught of God.

May God be pleased to use these writings abundantly for the instruction and edification of His beloved people, to His own glory and praise.

July, 1972                                          Glenn Conjurske
Madison, Wisconsin

# TABLE OF CONTENTS
## VOLUME 1

# SHORT PAPERS
## Volume 1

# A WORD TO OUR READERS

Dearly Beloved in the Lord,

Ere closing our volume for the year 1875, we desire to offer you a few earnest words on a subject which we deem to be of commanding interest and importance; it is this: *The divine sufficiency and supreme authority of holy scripture; and the urgent need of submitting ourselves absolutely to its guidance in all things.*

And, in thus stating our thesis, we would not have you to suppose, for a moment, that we undervalue human writings, in their proper place. Nothing is further from our thoughts. Indeed it would ill become us, as the conductors of a monthly magazine, to speak disparagingly of a branch of christian ministry so largely used of God in all ages of His church's history, and specially in this our own day.

No, beloved, we prize human writings more than we can attempt to say. We receive them as streams from the fountain head. And, further, we would add that we have rarely met anyone who affected to despise christian writings, on the plea of reading nothing but the Bible, that was not crude, shallow, and contracted. We might just as well say that we would not listen to a brother speaking to us in the assembly, as refuse to read what God had given him to write, provided we had time to do so. How often has a book or tract been made a rich blessing to the soul, either in bringing one to Christ, or building up or helping on in Him! How often may we have read some passage of scripture and seen nothing in it until the Lord had used some paragraph in a human writing to unlock its treasures to our hearts! We are, none of us, self-sufficient. We are dependent one on another. We grow by that which every joint supplieth. We need all the "helps" which God has set in the body for our common profit and blessing.

But having said thus much to guard against misunderstanding, and to put human writings in their right place, we return to our special object in this brief address.

There is but one supreme and paramount authority, and that is the word of God. All human writings are interesting as references, valuable as aids, but they are worthless, yea mischievous as authority. Scripture is all-sufficient. We want absolutely nothing, in the way of guidance and authority, beyond what we possess in the sacred canon of scripture. No doubt, it is only by the Holy Ghost we can understand, appreciate, or be guided by scripture; and, moreover, God may use a human voice or a human pen to help us; but scripture is divinely sufficient. It can make a child wise unto salvation; and it can make a man perfect unto all good works. See 2 Timothy iii. 15-17.

Now, having such a guide, such an authority, what becomes us as Christians—as children of God and servants of Christ? Why, clearly, to submit ourselves absolutely and unreservedly to its teaching, in all things. We are bound, by every argument and every motive which can possibly sway the heart, to test everything in which we are engaged, or with which we stand associated, by the holy standard of the word of God; and, if we find aught, no matter what, which will not stand that test, to abandon it at once and for ever.

And it is precisely here that we feel there is such serious failure in the professing church. As a rule, we do not find the conscience under the immediate action and government of the word. Human opinions bear sway. Human creeds and confessions of faith govern the heart and form the religious character. Human traditions and habits of thought are allowed a formative influence over the soul. If it be merely a question of personal salvation, profit, or blessing, scripture will be listened to. People are glad and thankful to hear how they can be saved and blessed. Everything that bears upon the individual conditions and destiny will meet a welcome.

But the moment it becomes a question of Christ's authority over us, in spirit, soul, and body; when the word of God is brought to bear upon our entire practical career, upon our personal habits, our domestic arrangements, our commercial pursuits, our religious associations, our ecclesiastical position, then, alas! it becomes apparent how completely the authority of holy scripture is virtually thrown overboard. In point of fact, the enemy seems to succeed as completely in robbing professing Christians of the real value, power, and authority of the word of God, as when, during that long and dreary period of the middle ages, it was wrapped in the shroud of a dead language, and buried in the dark cloisters of Rome. It is perfectly appalling, when one comes in contact with the actual condition of things amongst professing Christians, to observe the ignorance of scripture and the carelessness about it. Nor can any thoughtful person doubt but that the latter is the producing cause of the former. "If any man *will* do his will, he shall know of the doctrine." But if the word of God be neglected and practically ignored, as an authority, need we marvel when we find people ignorant of its precious contents?

We have been much struck, of late, in our intercourse with christian professors, in noticing the little moral weight which scripture seems to possess. You will rarely meet with any one who is prepared to start with this one grand point, that the voice of the Holy Ghost in scripture is absolutely conclusive, that it admits of no appeal, that it closes all discussion. We speak not now of man's interpretation of scripture—of anything in which it can be said, "*That is your opinion.*" We speak only of the written word of God which we possess, and to which we are individually responsible to submit ourselves, in all things. God has put his word into our hands, And He has put His Spirit into our hearts, and by that Spirit we can understand the word; and we are solemnly bound to be guided and governed by that word, in all the details of our practical career.

It is this we feel imperatively called upon to press home upon the hearts and consciences of our readers, in this our closing address. We have been earnestly waiting upon the Lord for a message, as we feel bound to do at all times. Indeed our constant cry is, "Lord, when the magazine ceases to be Thy messenger, let it cease to be altogether. Let it never outlive its freshness and usefulness." In looking then to Him for the very theme, we got this answer, "Press upon your readers, *the sufficiency and authority of holy scripture; and the necessity of absolute subjection to it in all things.*" This we have sought to do, according to our poor ability; and now we leave it with our readers to consider as before the

Lord, their personal responsibility in this weighty matter. We would entreat them, as they love the Lord Jesus Christ, to examine, in the light of scripture, their entire position and path; and, by the grace of God, and for His glory, to abandon, at once and for ever, all that is not in perfect accordance with that holy standard. Thus shall their path be as the shining light that shineth more and more unto the perfect day. Oh! may the true language of all our hearts be, "Speak, Lord; for thy servant heareth." "Lord, what wilt thou have me to do?" God grant it, for Christ's sake.

# HOW TO STUDY SCRIPTURE

## (An Extract from a Letter)

It is a very difficult thing for any one to attempt to prsecribe for another the proper method of studying scripture. The infinite depths of holy scripture, like the exhaustless resources that are in God, and the moral glories of the Person of Christ, are only unfolded to faith and need. This makes it so very simple. It is not cleverness, or intellectual power, we need, but the artless simplicity of a little child. The One who indited the holy scriptures must open our understandings to receive their precious teaching. And He will do so, if only we wait on Him in real earnestness of heart.

But we must never lose sight of the weighty fact, that it is as we act on what we know that our knowledge shall increase. It will never do to sit down like a bookworm to read the Bible. We may store our intellect with biblical knowledge, we may have the doctrines of the Bible and the letter of scripture at our finger-ends, without one particle of unction or spiritual power. We must go to scripture as a thirsty man goes to a well; as a hungry man goes to a meal; as a mariner goes to a chart. We must go to it because we cannot do without it. We go, not merely to study, but to feed. The instincts of the divine nature lead us naturally to the word of God, as the new-born babe desires the milk by which he is to grow. It is by feeding on the word that the new man grows.

Hence we may see how very real and practical is this question of how to study scripture. It is intimately connected with our entire moral and spiritual condition, our daily walk, our actual habits and ways. God has given us His word to form our character, to govern our conduct, and shape our course; and therefore, if the word has not a formative influence, and a governing power over us, it is the height of folly to think of storing up a quantity of scriptural knowledge in the intellect. It can only puff us up, and deceive us. It is a most dangerous thing to traffic in unfelt truth; it superinduces a heartless indifference, levity of spirit, insensibility of conscience, perfectly appalling to people of serious piety. There is nothing that tends so to throw us completely into the hands of the enemy as a quantity of head knowledge of truth, without a tender conscience, a true heart, an upright mind. The mere profession of truth which does not act on the conscience, and come out in the life, is one of the special dangers of the day in which our lot is cast. Better, by far, only know a little in reality and power, than profess a quantity of truth that lies powerless in the region of the understanding, exerting no formative influence upon the life. I would much rather be honestly in Romans vii., than fictitiously in chapter viii. In the former case I am sure to come right, but in the latter there is no telling what I may come to.

As to the question of making use of human writings to help us in the study of scripture, great caution is needed. No doubt the Lord may, and does, make use of the writings of His servants, just as He uses their oral ministry, for our instruction and edification. Indeed, in the present broken and divided state of the church, it is wonderful to mark the Lord's rich grace and tender care in feeding His beloved people with the writings of His servants.

But, we repeat, great caution is needed, earnest waiting on the Lord, that we may not abuse so precious a gift, that it may not lead us to trade on borrowed capital. If we are really dependent upon God, He will give us the right thing; He will put the right book into our hands; He will feed us with food convenient for us. Thus we receive it from Himself, and hold it in communion with Himself. It is fresh, living, powerful, formative; it tells on the heart, and shines in the life; and we grow in grace and in the knowledge of our Lord and Savior Jesus Christ. Precious growth! would there were more of it!

Finally, we have to remember that holy scripture is the voice of God, and the written word is the transcript of the living word. It is only by the Holy Spirit's teaching we can really understand scripture, and He reveals its living depths to faith and need. Let us never forget this.

# QUESTIONS; AND HOW TO MEET THEM

My Beloved Friend,                                              July, 1876

I have been very much interested of late in looking at the excellent way in which John the Baptist met the various questions which came before him; for, alas! there were questions in his day, as there are in ours.

What I specially refer to now is presented to us in chapters I and III of John's Gospel.

The first question which this dear and honoured servant of Christ was called to answer had respect to himself, and of this he makes very short work indeed. "This is the record of John, when the Jews sent priests and Levites from Jerusalem to ask him, Who art thou?"

It is ever unwelcome to any right-minded person to be asked to speak about himself. So, I doubt not, John found it. He readily told them that he was not the Messiah, that he was not Elias; yea, that he was not even the prophet. But they would have a positive answer. "They said unto him, Who art thou? that we may give an answer to them that sent us. What sayest thou of thyself?" Little indeed had he to say of himself. "I" had a very small place in John's thoughts. "A voice." Was this all? Yes; this was all. The Spirit in the prophet had spoken; John quotes the words, and there he leaves it. Blessed servant! Honoured witness! Would we had more of thy excellent spirit!—more of thy method of answering questions!

But these Pharisees were not satisfied. John's self-hiding spirit was entirely beyond them. "They asked him, and said unto him, Why baptizest thou then, if thou be not the Christ, nor Elias, neither the prophet?"

Here again the Baptist makes short work. "John answering them, saying, I baptize with water; but there standeth one among you whom ye know not. He it is who, coming after me, is preferred before me, whose shoe's latchet I am not worthy to unloose."

Thus, as to himself, he was merely a voice. And, as to his work, he baptized with water, and he was only too glad to retire behind that blessed One whose shoe's latchet he felt himself utterly unworthy to unloose.

This is uncommonly fine. I feel assured, my beloved friend, that the lovely spirit displayed by this most illustrious servant of Christ is what you earnestly covet for yourself. And I think I am one with you herein. I do long to know more and more of this self-hiding—this losing sight of self and its doings—this retiring spirit. Truly it is much needed in this day of egotistical boast and pretension.

But turn with me for a moment to John III. Here we have another kind of question. It is not now about himself or his work, but about purifying. "There arose a question among some of John's disciples and the Jews about purifying. And they came to John, and said unto him, Rabbi, he that was with thee beyond Jordan, to whom thou bearest witness, behold, the same baptizeth, and all come to him."

Now this was a mistake, for "Jesus himself baptized not, but his disciples." But this is not the point here. What strikes me is John's mode of settling all questions, right or wrong. He finds a perfect solution for all in the presence of his Lord. "John answered and said, A man can receive nothing except it be given him from heaven."

How true! How simple! How perfectly obvious! What a complete settlement of every question! If a man has anything at all, whence did it, whence could it, come? Surely only from heaven. What a perfect cure for strife, envy, jealousy, and emulation! "Every good gift and every perfect gift is *from above*, and *cometh down* from the Father of lights." What a tale this tells of earth and of man! What a record it bears to heaven and to God! Not one atom of good on earth but what comes from heaven. Not an atom of good in man but what comes from God. Why, then, should any one boast, or be jealous, or envious? If all goodness is from above, let there be an end of all strife, and let all hearts go up in praise to "the Father of lights."

Thus it was the Baptist met the questions of his day. He let all the questioners know that their questions had but little interest for him. And, more than that, he let them know where all his interests lay. This blessed servant found all his springs in the Lamb of God, in His precious work—in His glorious Person. The voice of the Bridegroom was enough for him, and, having heard that, his joy was full. The question of purifying might be interesting enough in its place, and no doubt, like all other questions, it had its right and its wrong side; but for John, the Bridegroom's voice was enough. In His presence he found a divine answer to every question—a divine solution of every difficulty. He looked up to heaven, and saw every good thing coming from thence. He looked into the Bridegroom's face, and saw every moral glory centered there. This was enough for him. Why trouble him with questions of any kind—questions about himself or his work, or about purifying? He lived far beyond the region of questions, in the blessed presence of his Lord, and there he found all his heart could ever need.

Now, my much loved friend, it seems to me that you and I would do well to take a leaf out of John's book as regards all this. I need not remind you that in this our day there are questions agitating men's minds. Yes, and some of us are called to account for not expressing ourselves more decidedly on some at least of these questions. But, for my part, I believe the devil is doing his utmost to alienate our hearts from Christ and from one another by questions. We ought not to be ignorant of his devices. He does not come openly, and say, "I am the devil, and I want to divide and scatter you by questions." Yet this is precisely what he is seeking to do.

Now, it matters not whether the question be right or wrong in itself; the devil can make use of a right question just as effectively as of a wrong one, provided he can succeed in raising that question into undue prominence, and causing it to come between our souls and Christ, and between us and our brethren. I can understand a difference in judgment, on various minor questions. Christians have differed about such for many long centuries, and they will continue to differ until the end of time. It is human weakness. But when any question is allowed to assume undue prominence, it ceases to be mere human weakness, and becomes a wile of Satan. I may have a very decided judgment on any given point, and so may you. But what I long for now is a thorough sinking of all questions, and a rejoicing together in hearing the Bridegroom's voice, and going on together in the light of His blessed countenance. This will confound the enemy. It will effectually deliver us from prejudice and partiality, from cliques and coteries. We shall then measure one another, not by our views of any particular question, but by our appreciation of the Person of Christ, and our devotion to His cause.

In a word, my beloved and valued friend, what I long for is that you and I, and all our dear brethren throughout the whole world, may be characterized by a deep-toned, thorough, devotion to the name, and truth, and cause of Christ. I long to cultivate broad sympathies, that can take in every true lover of Christ, even though we see not eye to eye on all minor questions. At best "we know but in part;" and we can never expect people to agree with us about questions. But if Christ be our one absorbing object, all other things will assume their right place, their relative value, their proper proportions. "Let us, therefore, as many as be perfect (as many as have Christ for their one object), be thus minded: and if *in anything* ye be otherwise (or differently, ἑτέρως) minded, God shall reveal even this unto you. *Nevertheless*, whereto we have already attained, let us walk by *the same rule* (Christ), and mind the same thing" (Christ). The moment anything else but Christ is introduced as a rule to walk by, it is simply the work of the devil. Of this I am as sure as that I hold this pen in my hand.

May the Lord keep us all close to Himself, walking together, not in sectarianism, but in true brotherly love, seeking the blessing and prosperity of all who belong to Christ, and promoting in every possible way His blessed cause, until He come!

Ever most affectionately yours,
C. H. M.

# EPAPHRODITUS

We want the reader to turn with us for a few moments to Philippians ii, and study the brief sketch of the interesting character of Epaphroditus. There is great moral beauty in it. We are not told very much about him, but, in what we are told, we see a great deal of what is truly lovely and pleasant—much that makes us long for men of the same stamp in this our day. We cannot do better than quote the inspired record concerning him; and may the blessed Spirit apply it to our hearts, and lead us to cultivate the same lovely grace which shone so brightly in that dear and honoured servant of Christ!

"I supposed it necessary," says the blessed apostle, "to send to you Epaphroditus, my brother and companion in labour, and fellow-soldier, but your messenger, and he that ministered to my wants. For he longed after you all, and was full of heaviness, because that ye had heard that he had been sick. For indeed he was sick nigh unto death; but God had mercy on him, and not on him only, but on me also, lest I should have sorrow upon sorrow. I sent him therefore the more carefully, that when ye see him again, ye may rejoice, and that I may be the less sorrowful. Receive him therefore in the Lord with all gladness; and hold such in reputation; because for the work of Christ he was nigh unto death, not regarding his life, to supply your lack of service toward me." Philippians ii. 25-30.

Now it is quite possible that some of us, on reading the above, may feel disposed to inquire if Epaphroditus was a great evangelist or teacher, or some highly gifted servant of Christ, seeing that the inspired apostle bestows upon him so many high and honorable titles, styling him his "brother, and companion in labour, and fellow-soldier."

Well, we are not told that he was a great preacher, or a great traveller, or a profound teacher in the church of God. All that we are told about him, in the above touching narrative, is that he

11

came forward in a time of real need to supply a missing link, to "stop a gap," as we say. The beloved Philippians had it upon their hearts to send help to the revered and aged apostle in his prison at Rome. He was in need, and they longed to supply his need. They loved him, and God had laid it upon their loving hearts to communicate with his necessities. They thought of him, though he was far away from them; and they longed to minister to him of their substance.

How lovely was this! How grateful to the heart of Christ! Hearken to the glowing terms in which the dear old prisoner speaks of their precious ministry. "But I rejoiced in the Lord greatly, that now at the last your care of me hath flourished again; wherein ye were also careful, but ye lacked opportunity. . . . Notwithstanding, Ye have well done that ye did communicate with my affliction. Now, ye Philippians, know also that in the beginning of the gospel, when I departed from Macedonia, no church communicated with me as concerning giving and receiving, but ye only. For even in Thessalonica ye sent once and again unto my necessity. Not because I desire a gift; but I desire fruit that may abound to your account. But *I have all, and abound; I am full,* having received of Epaphroditus the things from you, an odour of a sweet smell, a sacrifice acceptable, well pleasing to God."

Here we see the place which Epaphroditus filled in this blessed business. There lay the beloved apostle in his prison at Rome, and there lay the loving offering of the saints at Philippi. But how was it to be conveyed to him? These were not the days of cheque banks and post-office orders. No, nor of railway travelling. It was no easy matter to get from Philippi to Rome in those days. But Epaphroditus, that dear, unpretending, self-surrendering servant of Christ, presented himself to supply the missing link; to do just the very thing that was needed, and nothing more; to be the channel of communication between the assembly at Philippi and the apostle at Rome. Deep and real as was the apostle's need, precious and seasonable as was the Philippians' gift, yet an instrument was needed to bring them both together, and to apply the latter to the former; and Epaphroditus offered himself for the work. There was a manifest need, and he met it—a positive blank, and he filled it. He did not aim at doing some great showy thing, something which would make him very prominent, and cause his name to be blazed abroad as some wonderful person. Ah! no, Epaphroditus was not one of the pushing, self-confident, extensive class. He was a dear, self-hiding, lowly servant of Christ, one of that class of workmen to whom we are irresistibly attracted. Nothing is more charming than an unpretending, retiring man, who is content just to fill the empty niche; to render the needed service, whatever it is; to do the work cut out for him by the Master's hand.

There are some who are not content unless they are at the head and tail of everything. They seem to think that no work can be rightly done unless they have a hand in it. They are not satisfied to supply a missing link. How repulsive are all such! How we retire from them! Self-confident, self-sufficient, ever pushing themselves into prominence. They have never measured themselves in the presence of God, never been broken down before Him, never taken their true place of self-abasement.

Epaphroditus was not of this class at all. He put his life in his hand to serve other people; and when at death's door, instead of being occupied with himself or his ailments, he was thinking of others. "He longed after you all, and was full of heaviness"—not because he was sick, but—"because ye had heard that he had been sick." Here was true love. He knew what his beloved brethren at Philippi would be feeling when informed of his serious illness—an illness brought on by his willing-hearted service to them.

All this is morally lovely. It does the heart good to contemplate this exquisite picture. Epaphroditus had evidently studied in the school of Christ. He had sat at the Master's feet, and drunk deeply into His spirit. In no other way could he have learnt such holy lessons of self-surrender and thoughtful love for others. The world knows nothing of such things; nature cannot teach such lessons. They are altogether heavenly, spiritual, divine. Would that we knew more of them! They are rare amongst us, with all our high profession. There is a most humiliating amount of selfishness in all of us, and it does look so hideous in connection with the name of Jesus. It might comport well enough with Judaism, but its inconsistency with Christianity is terribly glaring.

13

But we must close; and, ere we do so, we shall just notice the very touching manner in which the inspired apostle commends Epaphroditus to the assembly at Philippi. It seems as if he could not make enough of him, to speak after the manner of men. "He longed after you all, and was full of heaviness, because that ye had heard that he had been sick. For indeed he was sick nigh unto death; but God had mercy on him, and not on him only, but on me also, lest I should have sorrow upon sorrow." How deeply affecting! What a tide of divine affection and sympathy rolled in upon that unpretending, self-sacrificing servant of Christ! The whole assembly at Philippi, the blessed apostle, and, above all, God Himself, all engaged in thinking about a man who did not think about himself. Had Epaphroditus been a self-seeker, had he been occupied about himself or his interests, or even his work, his name would never have shone on the page of inspiration. But no; he thought of others, not of himself, and therefore God, and His apostle, and His church, thought of him.

Thus it will ever be. A man who thinks much of himself saves others the trouble of thinking about him; but the lowly, the humble, the modest, the unpretending, the retiring, the self-emptied, who think of, and live for, others, who walk in the footsteps of Jesus Christ, these are the persons to be thought of and cared for, loved and honoured, as they ever will be, by God and His people.

"I sent him therefore the more carefully," says the beloved apostle, "that when ye see him again ye may rejoice, and that I may be the less sorrowful. Receive him therefore in the Lord with all gladness; and hold such in reputation. Because for the work of Christ he was nigh unto death, not regarding his life, to supply your lack of service toward me."

Thus it was with this most dear and honoured servant of Christ. He did not regard his life, but laid it at his Master's feet, just to supply the missing link between the church of God at Philippi, and the suffering and needy apostle at Rome. And hence the apostle calls upon the church to hold him in reputation, and the honoured name of Epaphroditus has been handed down to us by the pen of

14

inspiration, and his precious service has been recorded, and the record of it read by untold millions, while the name and the doings of the self-seekers, the self-important, the pretentious, of every age, and every clime, and every condition, are sunk—and deservedly so—in eternal oblivion.

# SELF-SURRENDER

## (PHIL. II)

It is perfectly delightful to contemplate the moral triumphs of Christianity—the victories which it gains over self and the world, and the marvellous way in which such victories are obtained. The law said, "Thou shalt do this; and thou shalt not do that." But Christianity speaks a totally different language. In it, we see life bestowed as a free gift—life flowing down from a risen and glorified Christ. This is something entirely beyond the range of the law. The language of the law was, "The man that doeth these things shall live in them." Long life in the land was all the law proposed to the man who could keep it. Eternal life in a risen Christ was something utterly unknown and unthought of under the legal system.

But Christianity not only gives eternal life; it gives also an object with which that life can be occupied—a centre round which the affections of that life can circulate—a model on which that life can be formed. Thus it gains its mighty moral triumphs. Thus it gains its conquests over a selfish nature and a selfish world. It gives divine life and a divine centre; and as the life moves round that centre we are taken out of self.

This is the secret of self-surrender. It cannot be reached in any other way. The unconverted man finds his centre in self; and, hence, to tell him not to be selfish is to tell him not to be at all. This holds good even in the matter of mere religiousness. A man will attend to his religion in order, as he thinks, to promote his eternal interest: but this is quite a different thing from finding an object and a centre outside himself. Christianity alone can supply these. The gospel of the grace of God is the only thing that can effectually meet man's need and deliver him from the selfishness which belongs to him. The unrenewed man lives for himself. He has no higher object. The life which he possesses is alienated from

16

the life of God. He is away from God. He moves round another centre altogether, and until he is born again, until he is renewed, regenerated, born of the word and Spirit of God, it cannot be otherwise. *Self* is his object, his centre, in all things. He may be moral, amiable, religious, benevolent, but until he is converted, he has not done with hmself, as to the ground of his being, or as to the centre round which that being revolves.

The foregoing train of thought naturally introduces us to the striking and beautiful illustration of our theme afforded in Philippians ii. In it we have a series of examples of self-surrender, commencing with a divinely perfect One, the Lord Himself.

But, ere we proceed to gaze upon this exquisite picture, it may be well to enquire what it was that rendered it needful to present such a picture before the Philippian saints. The attentive reader will, doubtless, observe, in the course of this most charming epistle, certain delicate touches from the inspired pen, leading to the conclusion that the keen and vigilant eye of the apostle detected a certain root of evil in the bosom of the beloved and cherished assembly gathered at Philippi. To this he addresses himself, not with a sledge-hammer or a long whip, but with a refinement and delicacy far more powerful than either the one or the other. The mightiest moral results are reached by those delicate touches from the hand of God the Holy Ghost.

But what was the root to which we have referred? It was not a splitting into sects and parties, as at Corinth. It was not a return to the law and ritualism, as at Galatia. It was not a hankering after philosophy and the rudiments of the world, as at Colosse. What was it then? It was a root of envy and strife. The sprouting of this root is seen very distinctly in the collision between those two sisters, "Euodias and Syntyche" (chap. iv. 2), but it is glanced at in earlier portions of the epistle, and a divine remedy supplied.

It is a great point with a medical man not only to understand what is wrong with his patient, but also to understand the true remedy. Some physicians are clever in discovering the root of the disease; but they do not so well know what remedy to apply. Others, again, are skilled in the knowledge of medicine, the powers of various drugs; but they do not know how to apply them to individual cases. The Divine Physician knows both the disease and its remedy. He knows exactly what is the matter with us, and He knows what will do us good. He sees the root of the matter, and He applies a radical cure. He does not treat cases superficially. He is perfect in diagnosis. He does not guess at our disease from mere surface-symptoms. His keen eye penetrates, at once, to the very bottom of the case, and His skillful hand applies the true remedy.

Thus it is in the epistle to the Philippians. These saints held a very large place in the large heart of the apostle. He loved them much, and they loved him. Again and again he speaks, in grateful accents, of their fellowship with him in the gospel from the very first. But all this did not and could not shut his eyes to what was wrong among them. It is said that "Love is blind." In one sense, we look upon this saying as a libel upon love. If it were said that "Love is superior to faults," it would be nearer the truth. What should any one give for blind love? of what use would it be to be loved by one who only loved us because he was ignorant of our blots and blemishes? If it be meant that love *will not see* our blots, it is blessedly true (Numb. xxiii. 21); but no one would care for a love that was not at once aware of, and superior to, our failures and infirmities.

Paul loved the saints at Philippi, and rejoiced in their love to him, and tasted the fragrant fruit of that love again and again. But then he saw that it was one thing to love and be kind to a distant apostle, and quite another thing to agree among themselves. Doubtless, Euodias and Syntyche both contributed to send a present to Paul, though they were not pulling harmoniously together in the wear and tear of daily life and service. This is, alas! no uncommon case. Many sisters and brothers too are ready to contribute of their substance to help some distant servant of Christ, and yet they do not walk pleasantly together. How is this? There is a lack of self-surrender. This, we may rest assured, is the real secret of much of the "strife and vainglory" so painfully manifest in the very midst of the people of God. It is one thing to walk alone, and it is another thing to walk in company with our brethren, in the practical recognition of that great truth of the unity of the

18

body, and in the remembrance that "we are members one of another." Christians are not to regard themselves as mere individuals, as isolated atoms, as independent persons. This cannot be, seeing that scripture declares "There is one body," and we are members thereof. This is a divine truth—a grand fact—a positive reality. We are not to be like the hairs of an electrified broom, each standing out in lonely individuality. We are living members of a living body, each one having to do with other members, with whom we are connected by a bond which no power of earth or hell can sever. In a word, there is a relationship formed by the presence of the Holy Ghost, who not only dwells in each individual member, but is the power of the unity of the one body. It is the presence of God the Spirit, in the Church, that constitutes that Church, the one living body of the living head.

Now, it is when we are called to walk in the actual acknowledgement of this great truth that there is a demand for self-surrender. If we were merely solitary individuals, treading each in his own self-chosen path, carrying out his own peculiar thoughts, walking in the sparks of his own kindling, pursuing his own peculiar line of things, indulging his own will, then indeed a quantity of self might be retained. If "Euodias and Syntyche" could have walked alone, there would have been no collision—no strife. But they were called to walk together, and here was the demand for self-surrender.

And be it ever remembered, that Christians are not members of a club, of a sect, or of an association; they are members of a body, each connected with all, and all connected, by the fact of the indwelling of the Holy Ghost, with the risen and glorified Head in heaven.

This is an immense truth, and the practical carrying out of it will cost us not only all we have, but all we are. There is no place in all the universe where self will be so pulled to pieces, as in the assembly of God. And is it not well? Is it not a powerful proof of the divine ground on which that assembly is gathered? Are we not —should we not be—glad to have our hateful self thus pulled to pieces? Shall we—ought we to—run away from those who do it for us? Are we not glad—do we not often pray, to get rid of self? And shall we quarrel with those who are God's instruments in answer-

19

ing our prayers? True, they may do the work roughly and clumsily; but no matter for that. Whoever helps me to crush and sink self does me a kind turn, however awkwardly he may do it. One thing is certain, no man can ever rob us of that which, after all, is the only thing worth having, namely, Christ. This is a precious consolation. Let self go; we shall have the more of Christ. Euodias might lay the blame on Syntyche, and Syntyche on Euodias; the apostle does not raise the question of which was right or of which was wrong, but he beseeches both to be "of the same mind in the Lord."

Here lies the divine secret. It is self-surrender But this must be a real thing. There is no use in talking about sinking self, while, at the same time, self is fed and patted on the back. We sometimes pray with marvelous fervour to be enabled to trample self in the dust, and the very next moment, if any one seems to cross our path, self is like a porcupine with all its quills up. This will never do. God will have us real, and surely we can say, with all our weakness and folly, we want to be real—real in everything, and therefore real when we pray for the power of self-surrender. But, most assuredly, there is no place where there is a more urgent demand for this lovely grace than in the bosom of the assembly of God.

# Part II

We may range through the wide domain of inspiration and not find a more exquisite model of self-surrender than that which is presented to us in the opening lines of Philippians ii. It is, we may safely say, impossible for any one to breathe the holy atmosphere of such a scripture, and not be cured of the sore evils of envy and jealousy, strife and vain glory. Let us approach the marvellous picture, and, gazing intently upon it, seek to catch its inspiration.

"If there be therefore any consolation in Christ, if any comfort of love, if any fellowship of the Spirit, if any bowels and mercies, fulfil ye my joy, that ye be lkeminded, having the same love, being of one accord, of one mind. Let nothing be done through strife or vain glory; but in lowliness of mnd, let each esteem other better than themselves. Look not every man on his own things, but every man also on the things of others. Let this mind be in you which was also in Christ Jesus, who, being in the form of God, thought it not robbery to be equal with God; but made himself of no reputation, and took upon him the form of a servant, and was made in the likeness of men: and being found in fashion as a man, he humbled himself, and became obedient unto death, even the death of the cross." Ver. 1-8.

Here, then, is the divine remedy for envy and jealousy, strife and vain glory—for self-occupation, in short, in all its hideous forms. The inspired penman introduces to our hearts the self-emptied, humble, obedient Man, Christ Jesus. Here was One who possessed all power in heaven and earth. Divine majesty and glory belonged to Him. He was God over all, blessed for ever. By Him all things were made, and by Him they subsist. And yet He appeared in this world as a poor man—a servant—one who had not where to lay His head. The foxes and the fowls, the creatures of His formation, were better provided for than He, their Maker. They had a place to rest in. He had none. "He thought of others, cared for them, laboured for them, wept with them, ministered to them; but He never did a thing for Himself. We never find Him taking care to supply Himself with aught. His was a life of perfect self-surrender. He who was everything, made Himself nothing. He stood in perfect contrast with the first Adam, who being but a man, thought to make himself like God, and became the serpent's salve. The Lord Jesus, who was the Most High God, took the very lowest place amongst men. It is utterly impossible that any man can ever take so low a place as Jesus. The word is, "He made himself of no reputation." He went so low that no one could possibly put Him lower. "He became obedient unto death, even the death of the cross."

And, be it observed, that the cross is here viewed as the consummation of a life of obedience—the completion of a work of self-surrender. It is what we may call, to use a Levitical term, the burnt-offering aspect of the death of Christ, rather than the sin offering. True it is, most blessedly true, that the self-same act which consummated a life of obedience, did also put away sin; but in the passage now before us, sin-bearing is not so much the thought as self-surrender. Jesus gave up all. He laid aside His glory, and came

21

down into this poor world; and when He came, He eschewed all human pomp and grandeur, and became a poor man. His parents were poor. They were only able to procure the lowest grade of sacrifice which the law admitted for the poor; not a bullock, not a lamb, but a pair of turtle doves. (Compare Lev. xv. 29, Luke ii 24.) He Himself worked, and was known as a carpenter. Nor are we to miss the moral force of this fact, by saying that every Jew was brought up to some trade. Our Lord Jesus Christ did really take a low place. The very town where He was brought up was a proverb of reproach. He was called "The Nazarene." And it was asked, with a sneer of contempt, "Is not this the carpenter?" He was a root out of a dry ground. He had no form nor comeliness, no beauty in man's eye. He was the despised, neglected, self-emptied, meek, and lowly man, from first to last. He gave up all, even to life itself. In a word, His self-surrender was complete.

And, now, mark the result. "Wherefore God also hath highly exalted him, and given him a name which is above every name; that at the name of Jesus every knee should bow, of things in heaven, and things in earth, and things under the earth; and that every tongue should confess that Jesus Christ is Lord, to the glory of God the Father."

The blessed Lord Jesus took the very lowest place; but God has given Him the very highest. He made Himself nothing; but God has made Him everything. He said, "I am a worm and no man;" but God has set Him as Head over all. He went into the very dust of death; but God has placed Him on the throne of the Majesty in the heavens.

What does all this teach us? It teaches us that *the way to get up is to go down*. This is a grand lesson, and one which we very much need to learn. It would effectually deliver us from envy and jealousy, from strife and vain glory, from self-importance and self-occupation. God will assuredly exalt those who, in the spirit and mind of Christ, take the low place; and, on the other hand, He will, as assuredly, abase those who seek to be somebody.

Oh! to be nothing! This is true liberty—true happiness—true moral elevation. And then what intense power of attraction in one who makes nothing of himself! And, on the other hand, how repulsive is a pushing, forward, elbowing, self-exalting spirit! How utterly unworthy of one bearing the name of Him who made Himself of no reputation! May we not set it down as a fixed truth that ambition cannot possibly live in the presence of One who emptied Himself? No doubt. An ambitious Christian is a flagrant contradiction.

But there are other samples of self-surrender presented to us in this exquisite Philippians ii.; inferior no doubt to the divine model at which we have been gazing, for in this as in all things else, Jesus must have the pre-eminence. Still, though inferior and imperfect, they are deeply interesting and valuable to us. Look at Paul. See how deeply he had drunk into his Master's spirit of self-surrender. Hearken to the following accents from one who, naturally, would have allowed none to outstrip him in his career of ambition. "Yea," he says, "and if I be poured forth [as a drink offering] upon the sacrifice and service of your faith, I joy, and rejoice with you all." Verse 17.

This is uncommonly fine. Paul was ready to be nothing—to be spent—to be poured forth as a libation upon the Philippians' sacrifice. It mattered not to him who presented the sacrifice, or who performed the service, provided the thing was done. Does not this put some of us to the blush? How little do we know of this excellent spirit! How prone we are to attach importance to work if we ourselves have aught to do with it! How little able to joy and rejoice with others in their sacrifice and service! Our work, our preaching, our writings, have an interest in our view quite different from those of any one else. In a word, self, self, detestable self, creeps in even in that which seems to be the service of Christ. We are drawn to those who think well of us and of our work, and retire from those who think otherwise. All this needs to be judged. It is unlike Christ, and unworthy of those who bear His holy Name. Paul had so learnt Christ as to be able to rejoice in the work and service of others as well as in his own; and even where Christ was preached of contention, he could rejoice.

Then, again, look at Paul's son, Timothy. Hearken to the glowing testimony borne to him by the pen of inspiration. "But I trust in the Lord Jesus to send Timotheus shortly unto you, that I also may be of good comfort, when I know your state. For I have no man likeminded, who will naturally care for your state. For *all seek their own*, not the things which are Jesus Christ's. *But ye know the proof of him*, that, as a son with the father, he hath served with me in the gospel." Verse 19-22.

Here was self-surrender. Timothy *naturally* cared for the saints; and that, too, at a moment when *all* sought their own things. And yet, dear as Timothy was to Paul's heart—valuable as such a self-denying servant must have been to him in the work of the gospel, he was willing to part with him for the sake of the Church. Timothy, likewise, was willing to be separated from his invaluable friend and father in the faith, in order to ease his anxious mind in reference to the state of the Philippians. This was indeed giving "proof" of real devotedness and self-surrender. Timothy did not talk of these things; he practised them. He did not make a parade of his doings; but Paul, by the Holy Ghost, engraved them on a tablet from which they can never be erased. This was infinitely better. Let another praise thee, and not thyself. Timothy made nothing of himself, but Paul made a great deal of him. This is divine. The sure way to get up is to go down. Such is the law of the heavenly road. A man who makes much of himself saves others the trouble of doing so. There is no possible use in two persons doing the same thing. Self-importance is a noxious weed nowhere to be found in the entire range of the new creation. It is, alas! often found in the ways of those who profess to belong to that blessed and holy creation, but it is not of heavenly growth. It is of fallen nature—a weed that grows luxuriantly in the soil of this world. The men of this age think it laudable to push and make way for themselves. A bustling, self-important, pretentious style takes with the children of this generation. But our heavenly Master was the direct opposite of all this. He who made the worlds, stooped to wash a disciples feet (John xiii.); and if we are like Him, we shall do the same. There is nothing more foreign to the thoughts of God, the mind of heaven, the spirit of Jesus, than self-importance and self-occupation. And, on the other hand, there is nothing that savours so of God, of heaven, and of Jesus, as self-surrender.

Look, once more, reader, at our picture in Philippians ii. Examine, with special care, that figure which occupies a very prom-inent place. It is Epaphroditus. Who was he? Was he a great preacher—a very eloquent speaker—a pre-eminently gifted brother? We are not told. But this we are told—and told right powerfully and touchingly; he was one who exhibited a lovely spirit of self-surrender. This is better than all the gifts and eloquence, power and learning, that could possibly be concentrated in any single in-dividual. Epaphroditus was one of that illustrious class who seek to make nothing of themselves; and, as a consequence, the inspired apostle spares no pains to exalt him. Hear how he expatiates upon the actings of this singularly attractive personage. "Yet I supposed it necessary to send unto you Epaphroditus, my brother and com-panion in labour, and fellow soldier, but your messenger, and he that ministered to my wants."

What a cluster of dignities! What a brilliant array of titles! How little did this dear and unpretending servant of Christ imagine that he was to have such a monument erected to his memory! But the Lord will never suffer the fruits of self-sacrifice to wither, nor the name of the self-emptied to sink into oblivion. Hence it is that the name of one who, otherwise, might never have been heard of, shines on the page of inspiration, as the brother, companion, and fellow soldier of the great apostle of the Gentiles.

But what did this remarkable man do? Did he spend a princely fortune in the cause of Christ? We are not told; but we are told what is far better—he spent himself. This is the grand point for us to seize and ponder. It was not the surrender of his fortune, merely, but the surrender of himself. Let us hearken to the record concerning one of the true David's mighty men. "He longed after you all, and was full of heaviness." Why? Was it because he was sick? because of his pains, and aches, and privations? Nothing of the sort. Epaphroditus did not belong to the generation of whiners and complainers. He was thinking of others. "He was full of heaviness, because that ye had heard that he had been sick." How lovely! He was occupied about the Philippians and their sorrow about him. The only thing that affected him in his illness was the thought of how it would affect them. Perfectly exquisite! This honoured servant of Christ had brought himself to death's door to

25

serve others, and when there, in place of being occupied about himself and his ailments, he was thinking of the sorrow of others. "He was sick and nigh unto death: but God had mercy on him; and not on him only, but on me also, lest I should have sorrow upon sorrow."

Can aught be more morally beautiful than this? It is one of the rarest pictures ever presented to the human eye. There is Epaphroditus, nigh unto death for the sake of others; but he is full of sorrow about the Philippians; and the Philippians are full of sorrow about him; Paul is full of sorrow about both, and God comes and mingles Himself with the scene, and, in mercy to all, raises up the loved one from the bed of death.

And then mark the tender solicitude of the blessed apostle. It is like some tender mother sending her darling son away, and committing him, with fond earnestness, to the care of some friend. "I sent him therefore the more carefully, that, when ye see him again, ye may rejoice, and that I may be the less sorrowful. Receive him therefore in the Lord with all gladness; and hold such in reputation." Why? Was it because of his gifts, his rank, or his wealth? No; but because of his self-surrender. "Because for the work of Christ he was nigh unto death, *not regarding his life*, to supply your lack of service toward me." Oh! dear christian reader, let us think on these things. We have introduced you to a picture, and we leave you to gaze upon it. The grouping is divine. There is a moral line running through the entire scene, and linking the figures into one striking group. It is like the anointing of the true Aaron, and the oil flowing down to the skirts of his garments. We have the blessed Lord, perfect in His self-surrender, as in all beside; and then we have Paul, Timothy, and Epaphroditus, each, in his measure, exhibiting the rare and lovely grace of self-surrender.

# RESTORATION

## (JOHN XXI. 1-19)

A careful study of these verses will enable us to trace, in them, distinct kinds of restoration, namely, restoration of conscience, restoration of heart, and restoration of position.

I. The first of these, restoration of conscience, is of all-importance. It would be utterly impossible to over estimate the value of a sound, clear, uncondemning conscience. A Christian cannot get on if there is a single soil on his conscience. He must walk before God with a pure conscience—a conscience without stain or sting. Precious treasure! May my reader ever possess it.

It is very obvious that Peter possessed it in the touching scene, "at the sea of Tiberias." And yet he had fallen—shamefully, grievously fallen. He had denied his Lord with an oath; but he was restored. One look from Jesus had broken up the deep fountains of his heart, and drawn forth floods of bitter tears. And yet it was not his tears, but the love that drew them forth, which formed the ground of his thorough restoration of conscience. It was the changeless and everlasting love of the heart of Jesus—the divine efficacy of the blood of Jesus—and the all-prevailing power of the advocacy of Jesus that imparted to Peter's conscience the boldness and liberty so strikingly and beautifully exhibited on the memorable occasion before us.

The risen Saviour is seen, in these closing chapters of John's Gospel, watching over His poor, foolish, feeble, erring disciples—hovering about their path—presenting Himself, in various ways, before them—taking occasion, from their very necessities, to make Himself known, in perfect grace, to their hearts. Was there a tear to be dried, a difficulty to be solved, a fear to be hushed, a bereaved heart to be soothed, an unbelieving mind to be corrected? Jesus was present, in all the fulness and variety of His grace, to meet all these things. So also when, under the guidance of the ever forward

27

Peter, they had gone forth to spend a night in fruitless toil, Jesus had His eye upon them. He knew all about the darkness, and the toil, and the empty net, and there He was on the shore, to kindle a fire and prepare a dinner for them. Yes, the selfsame Jesus who had died on the cross to put away their sins, now stood on the shore to restore them from their wanderings, gather them round Himself, and minister to all their need. "Have ye any meat?" developed the fruitlessness of their night's toil. "Come and dine," was the touching expression of the tender, thoughtful, all-providing love of the risen Saviour.

But let us note, particularly, the evidences of a thoroughly restored conscience, as exhibited by Simon Peter. "Therefore that disciple whom Jesus loved, saith unto Peter, It is the Lord. Now when Simon Peter heard that it was the Lord, he girt his fisher's coat unto him, (for he was naked,) and did cast himself into the sea." He could not wait for the ships, or for his fellow-disciples, so eager was he to get to the feet of his risen Lord. In place of saying to John or to the others, "You know how shamefully I have fallen, and although I have, since then, seen the Lord, and heard Him speak peace to my soul, yet I think it more becoming in one that has so fallen to keep back, do you therefore go first and meet the blessed One, and I shall follow after," in place of aught in this style, he flings himself boldly into the sea, as much as to say, "I must be the very first to get to my risen Saviour; none has such a claim on Him as poor, stumbling, failing Peter."

Now, here was a perfectly restored conscience—a conscience without a single spot—a conscience basking in the sunlight of unchanging love. Peter's confidence in Christ was unclouded, and this, we may boldly affirm, was grateful to the heart of Jesus. Love likes to be trusted. Let us ever remember this. No one need imagine that he is honouring Jesus by standing afar off on the plea of unworthiness; and yet it is very hard for one who has fallen or backslidden, to recover his confidence in the love of Christ. Such an one can see clearly that a sinner is welcome to Jesus, no matter how great or manifold his sins may have been; but then he thinks the case of a backsliding or stumbling Christian is entirely different. Should these lines be scanned by one who has backslidden or fallen, we would press upon him, most earnestly, the importance of immediate return to Jesus. "Return, ye backsliding children, and I will heal your backslidings." What is the response to this pathetic appeal? "behold, we come unto thee; for thou art the Lord our God." "If thou wilt return, O Israel, saith the Lord, return unto me." (Jer. iii. 22; iv. 1.) The love of the heart of Jesus knows no change. We change; but He is "the same yesterday, to-day, and for ever;" and He delights to be trusted. The confidence of Peter's heart was a rich feast to the heart of Christ. No doubt, it is sad to fall, to err, to backslide; but it is sadder still, when we have done so, to distrust the love of Jesus, or His gracious readiness to take us to His bosom again.

Beloved reader, have you fallen? Have you erred? Have you backslidden? Have you lost the sweet sense of divine favour, the happy consciousness of acceptance with God? If so, what are you to do? Simply this, "Return." This is God's own special word to the backslider. Return, in self-judgment, and in the fullest confidence in the boundless, changeless love of the heart of Christ. Do not, we beseech you, keep away in the distance of your own unbelief. Do not measure the heart of Jesus by your own thoughts. Let Him tell you what is in His heart toward you. You have sinned, you have failed, you have turned aside, and now, it may be, you are afraid or ashamed to turn your eyes toward the One whom you have grieved and dishonoured. Satan, too, is suggesting the darkest thoughts, for he would fain keep you at a chilling distance from that precious Saviour who loves you with an everlasting love. But you have only to fix your gaze upon the blood, the advocacy, the heart of Jesus, to get a triumphant answer to all the enemies terrible suggestions, and to all the infidel reasonings of your own heart. Do not, therefore, go on another hour without seeking to get a thorough settlement of the question between your soul and Christ. Remember, "His is an unchanging love, free and faithful, strong as death." Remember also His own words, "Return, ye backsliding children"—"Return to me." And, finally, remember that Jesus loves to be trusted.

II. But the heart has to be restored as well as the conscience. Let this not be forgotten. It often happens in the history of souls, that though the conscience may be perfectly clear as to certain acts which we have done, yet the roots from whence those acts have sprung have not been reached. The acts appear on the surface of daily life, but the roots are hidden down deep in the heart, unknown, it may be, to ourselves and others, but thoroughly exposed to the eye of Him with whom we have to do.

Now, these roots must be reached, exposed and judged ere the heart is in a right condition in the sight of God. Look at Abraham. He started on his course with a certain root in his heart a root of unbelieving reserve, in reference to Sarah. This thing led him astray when he went down into Egypt, and although his conscience was restored, and he got back to his altar at Bethel, yet the root was not reached for years afterwards, in the affair of Abimelech, king of Gerar.

All this is deeply practical and most solemn. It finds its illustration in Peter as well as in Abraham. But only mark the exquisitely delicate way in which our blessed Lord proceeds to reach the roots in the heart of His dear and honoured servant. "So when they had dined." Not till then. There was no allusion to the past, nothing that might cause a chill to the heart, or bring a cloud over the spirit while a restored conscience was fasting in company with a love that knows no change. This is a fine moral trait. It characterizes the dealings of God with all His saints. The conscience is set at rest in the presence of infinite and everlasting love, ere there is the most distant illusion to the roots of things in the heart. When Simon Peter, in the full confidence of a restored conscience, flung himself at the feet of his risen Lord, he was called to listen to that gracious invitation, "Come and dine." But, "when they had dined," Jesus, as it were, takes Peter apart in order to let in upon his soul the light of truth, so that by it he might discern the root from whence all his failure had sprung. That root was self-confidence, which had led him to place himself in advance of his fellow-disciples, and say, "Though all should deny thee, yet will not I."

This root had to be exposed, and, therefore, "When they had dined, Jesus saith to Simon Peter, Simon, son of Jonas, lovest thou me more than these?" This was a pointed and pungent question, and it went right to the very bottom of Peter's heart. Three times Peter had denied his Lord, and three times his Lord now challenges the heart of Peter—*for the roots must be reached if any permanent good is to be done.* It will not do merely to have the conscience purged from the effects which have been produced in practical life, there must also be the moral judgment of that which produced them. This is not sufficiently understood and attended to, and hence it is that again and again the roots spring up and bring forth fruit, and scatter their seed a thousand-fold around us, thus cutting out for us the most bitter and sorrowful work, which might all be avoided if the roots of things were thoroughly judged and kept under.

Christian reader, our object in this paper is entirely practical. Let us, therefore, exhort one another to judge our roots, whatever they may be. Do we know our roots? Doubtless, it is hard, very hard, to know them. They are deep and manifold; pride, personal vanity, covetousness, irritability, ambition—these are some of the roots of character, the motive springs of action, over which a rigid censorship must ever be exercised. We must let nature know that the eye of self-judgment is continually upon it. We have to carry on the struggle without cessation. We may have to lament over occasional failure; but we must maintain the struggle, for struggle bespeaks *life.* May God the Holy Ghost strengthen us for the ceaseless conflict.

III. We shall close this paper with a brief reference to restoration as bearing upon the soul's position or path. The conscience being thoroughly purged, and the heart, with its varied roots, judged, there is moral preparedness for our proper path. The perfect love of Jesus had expelled all fear from Peter's conscience; and His threefold question had opened up the roots in Peter's heart, and now He says to him, "Verily, verily, I say unto thee, when thou wast young, thou girdest thyself, and walkedst whither thou wouldest: but when thou shalt be old, thou shalt stretch forth thy hand, and another shall gird thee, and carry thee whither thou wouldest not. This spake he, signifying by what death he should glorify God. And when he had spoken this, he saith unto him, follow me."

31

Here, then, we have, in two words, the path of the servant of Christ. "*Follow* me." The Lord had just given Peter the sweetest pledges of His love and confidence. He had, notwithstanding all past failure, entrusted him with the care of all that was dear to His loving heart in this world, even the lambs and sheep of His flock. He had said to him, "If you have affection for me, feed my lambs, shepherd my sheep," and now, in one brief but comprehensive utterance, He opens before him his proper path. "Follow me." This is enough. It includes all beside. If we want to follow Jesus, we must keep the eye continually upon Him; we must mark His footprints and tread therein. Yes, mark them and walk in them; and when tempted, like Peter, to "turn about" in order to see what this one or that one has to do, or how he does it, we may hear the correcting words, "What is that to thee? Follow thou me." This is to be our one grand and all-absorbing business, come what may. A thousand things may arise to distract and hinder. The devil will tempt us to look hither and thither, to look at this one and that one; to imagine we could do better here than there, or there than here; to be occupied with, and imitating the work of some fellow-servant. All this is met by those pointed words, "Follow me."

There is immense danger, in the present day, of following in the wake of others, of doing certain things because others do them, or doing things as others do them. All this has to be carefully guarded. It will be sure to come to nothing. What we really want is a broken will—the true spirit of a servant that waits on the Master to know His mind. Service does not consist in doing this or that, or running hither and thither; it is simply doing the Master's will, whatever that may be. "They serve who stand and wait." It is easier to be busy than to be quiet. When Peter was "young," he went whither he would; but when he got "old," he went whither he would not. What a contrast between the young, restless, ardent, energetic Peter, going whither he would, and the old, matured, subdued, experienced Peter going whither he would not. What a mercy to have the will broken! To be able to say from the heart, "What thou wilt—as thou wilt—where thou wilt—when thou wilt." "Not my will, but thine, O Lord, be done."

32

*"Follow me."* Precious words! May they be engraved on our hearts, beloved reader Then shall we be steady in our course, and effective in our service. We shall not be distracted or unhinged by the thoughts and opinions of men. It may happen that we shall get very few to understand us or sympathize with us—few to approve or appreciate our work. It matters not. The Master knows all about it. Let us only be sure of what He has told us to do, and do it. If a master tells one of his servants, distinctly, to go and do a certain thing, or occupy a certain post, it is his business to go and do that thing, or occupy that post, no matter what his fellow-servants may think. They may tell him that he ought to be somewhere else, or to do something else; a proper servant will heed them not; he knows his master's mind, and has to do his master's work.

Would it were more thus with all the Lord's servants! Would that we all knew more distinctly and carried out more decidedly, the Master's will respecting us. Peter had his path and John had his. James had his work, and Paul had his. So it was of old, the Gershonite had his work, and the Merarite had his; and if one had interfered with the other, the work could not have been done. The Tabernacle was carried forward or set up by each man doing his own proper work. Thus it is in this our day. God has varied workmen in His house and in His vineyard; He has quarrymen, stone-squarers, masons, and decorators. Are all quarrymen? Surely not; but each has his work to do, and the building is carried forward by each one doing his own appointed work. Should a quarry-man despise a decorator, or a decorator look down with contempt upon a quarryman? Assuredly not. The Master wants them both, and whenever the one would interfere with the other, as, alas! we so often do, the faithful correcting word falls on the ear, *"What is that to thee? Follow thou me."*

# DELIVERANCE

It is a fact obvious, of course, to all, that when a Christian dies and goes to heaven he is completely delivered from the power of sin. It is manifestly impossible that sin can have any power or authority over a dead man. But then it is not so readily seen or admitted that the believer, even now, is as thoroughly delivered from the power of sin as though he were dead and gone to heaven. Sin has no more dominion over a Christian than over a man who is actually dead and buried.

We speak of the power of sin; not of its presence. Let the reader carefully note this. There is as regards the question of sin this material difference between a Christian here and hereafter. Here he is delivered only from the power of sin; hreafter, he will be freed from its presence. In his present condition sin dwells in him; but it is not to reign. By-and-by, it will not even dwell. The reign of sin is over and gone. The reign of grace has begun. "Sin shall not have dominion over you; for ye are not under law, but under grace."

And, be it carefully observed, the apostle is not speaking, in Romans vi., of the forgiveness of sins. This he treats in chapter iii. Blessed be God, our sins are all forgiven—blotted out—eternally cancelled. But, in chapter vi., the theme is not forgiveness of sins, but complete deliverance from sin as a ruling power or principle.

How do we obtain this immense boon? By death. We have died to sin—died in the death of Christ. Is this true of every believer? Yes, of every believer beneath the canopy of heaven. Is it not a matter of attainment? By no means. It belongs to every child of God, every true believer. It is the common standing of all. Blessed, holy standing! All praise to Him who has earned it for us, and brought us into it. We live under the glorious reign of grace— "grace which reigns through righteousness, unto eternal life, by Jesus Christ our Lord."

This enfranchising truth is little understood by the Lord's

34

people. Very few, comparatively, get beyond the forgiveness of sins, if they have even got so far. They do not see their full deliverance from the power of sin. They feel its pressure, and arguing from their painful feeling instead of reckoning themselves to be what God tells them they are, they are plunged in doubt and fear as to their conversion. They are occupied with their own inward self-consciousness instead of with Christ. They are looking at their state in order to get peace and comfort, and hence they are, and must be, miserable. We shall never get peace if we seek it in our spiritual state or condition. The way to get peace is to believe that we died with Christ, were buried with Him, were raised with Him, are justified in Him, accepted in Him. In short that, "As he is so are we in this world." 1 John iv. 17.

This is the solid basis of peace. And not only so, but it is the only divine secret of a holy life. We are dead to sin. We are not called to make ourselves dead. We are so in Christ. A monk, an ascetic, or an ardent striver after sinless perfection, may try to put sin to death by various bodily exercises. What is the inevitable result? Misery. Yes, misery in proportion to the earnestness. How different is Christianity! We start with the blessed knowledge that we are dead to sin; and in the blessed faith of this, we "mortify" not the body, but its "deeds."

May the reader enter, by faith, into the power of this full "deliverance!"

# THE LAW AND THE GOSPEL

## (READ LUKE X. 25-35)

In our leading article for July, we called the attention of our readers to the deeply interesting and important subject of "grace and government;* and we have abundant reason to bless God for the way in which He has, already, used that paper.

We now desire to dwell for a little upon two grand questions which are suggested and answered in our Lord's interview with the lawyer, namely, What is written in the law? What is revealed in the gospel? These questions have only to be named to secure the attention and awaken the interest of every intelligent and thoughtful reader. It is surely most needful to understand the object, the nature, and range of the law; and in no way can these things be so clearly seen as when examined in contrast with the glorious gospel of God's free grace in Christ. Let us, then, in the first place, proceed to enquire,

### WHAT IS WRITTEN IN THE LAW?

This question may be very simply answered. The law reveals what man ought to do. This is what is written in the law. We often hear it said that "The law is the transcript of the mind of God." This definition is altogether defective. What idea should we have of God, were we to regard "the ten words" uttered on the top of Mount Sinai, mid thunderings and lightnings, blackness, darkness and tempest, as the transcript of His mind? How should we know God, if it be true that "the ministration of death and condemnation, written and engraven in stones," is the transcript of His mind? May we not, with great justice, inquire of the framers of the above most objectionable defintion, "Is there nothing in the mind of God, save death and condemnation? Is there nothing

---

*[see *Misc. Writings of C. H. M.*, vol. V.]

in the mind of God, save 'thou shalt,' and 'thou shalt not?' " If there be more than these, then it is a mistake to affirm that "The law is the transcript of the mind of God." If it be said that "The law declares the mind of God as to what man ought to do," we have no objection to offer, for that is what we hold the law to be. But, then, let the reader remember that the declaration of what man ought to do, and the revelation of what God is, are two totally different things. The former is the law; the latter is the gospel. Both, we need hardly say, are perfect—divinely perfect, but they stand in vivid contrast; the one is perfect to condemn, the other is perfect to save.

But let us see how this point is unfolded in the scripture before us. "And, behold, a certain lawyer stood up, and tempted him, saying, Master, what shall I do to inherit eternal life? He said unto him, what is written in the law? How readest thou? And he answering said, Thou shalt love the Lord thy God with all thy heart, and with all thy soul, and with all thy strength, and with all thy mind; and thy neighbor as thyself. And he said unto him, Thou hast answered right: this do, and thou shalt live."

Now, it in no wise interferes with the teaching of this passage to say that the lawyer stood up with the wicked intention of tempting Christ, or that he could flippantly and unfeelingly repeat what was written in the law. What we have to see is this, that the great law-question, "What must I do?" is here proposed and answered. If a man is to get life by keeping the commandments, he must keep them. There is no mystery about this. It is so plain that the question is, "How readest thou?" A man has only to read the twentieth chapter of Exodus in order to know his duty toward God and his duty toward his neighbour.

But, then, dear reader, the solemn inquiry is, "Have I done my duty? have I loved God with all my heart, and my neighbour as myself?" Alas! Alas! I have not; far—very far from it. I have proved, times without number, that I loved many things which are quite contrary to God; that I have indulged in lusts and pleasures which God condemns; that my will is most thoroughly opposed to God's will; that I hate the things which He loves, and love the things which He hates. In a word, then, it is perfectly manifest that I have not loved God with all my heart, yea, that I have not given Him a single affection of my heart. And as to my neighbour, have I loved him as myself? Have I, at all times, and under all circumstances, as sedulously sought to promote my neighbour's interests as though they were my own? Have I rejoiced as unfeignedly in his prosperity as in my own? I dare not answer in the affirmative. I have only to bow my head and confess that I have utterly and shamefully failed in my bounden duty, both toward God and toward my neighbour. I own it, most fully, to be my duty to love God, with all my heart, and my neighbour as myself; but I own, as fully, that I have done neither the one nor the other.

What, then, can the law do for me? Curse me and slay me, on the spot. Is there no mercy? Not in the law. There is no mercy at Mount Sinai. If a man stands before that fiery mount, the tremendous alternative is *duty* or *damnation*. There is no middle ground. "This do, and thou shalt live" is the solemn, conclusive, and emphatic language of the law. "The man that doeth these things shall live in them;" but, on the other hand, "cursed is *every one* (without a single exception), that *continueth* not in *all things* which are written in the book of the law *to do* them." (Gal. iii. 10.) "He that despised Moses' law *died without mercy* under two or three witnesses." (Heb. x. 28.) The law makes no provision for imperfect obedience however sincere. It makes no allowance for infirmity. Its one brief, pointed inquiry is, "Have you continued in all things?" If you say *no*; (and who can say otherwise?) it can only curse you. And why? Because it is perfect. Were it to pass over a single transgression, it would not be what it is, namely, a perfect law. Its very perfection insures the condemnation of the transgressor. "As many as are of works of law, (that is, as many as work on the principle, stand on the ground, occupy the platform, of works of law) are under the curse," and cannot possibly be anything else. This establishes the point unanswerably. The law can only prove to be a ministration of death and condemnation to the sinner simply because he is a sinner, and "the law is holy, and just, and good." It is no use for a man to say, "I am not looking to the law for life or justification, but merely as a rule, and for sanctification." As a rule for what? For the sanctification of what? If you say, "for my old nature," the answer is, so far from being "a rule of life," it is "a ministration of death;" and so far from sanctifying the flesh, it condemns it, root and branch. If, on the other hand, you say it is for the new nature, then is your mistake equally obvious, inasmuch as the apostle expressly declares that "the law is not made for a righteous man." I Tim. i. 9.

This is plain enough for any one who is content to take the holy scriptures as his guide. The law can neither be the ground of life nor the rule of life to a fallen creature; neither can it be the ground of righteousness nor the power of sanctification. "By deeds of law there shall no flesh be justified in his sight: for by the law is the knowledge of sin." (Rom. iii. 20.) This one passage is conclusive both as to justification and sanctification. No flesh can be justified in God's sight by the law; and as to sanctification, how can I ever become holy by means of that which only shows me my ungodliness? If I measure a short web by a true measure I must prove it short. A true measure cannot make a short web the proper length, it can only show what it is. Just so with the law and the sinner. Again, "The law worketh wrath." (Rom. iv. 15.) How is this? Just because it is pure and I am impure. The law and the sinner are perfect opposites—wholly irreconcilable. I must get a new nature, stand upon new ground, be in the new creation, ere I can delight in the law of God. "I delight in the law of God, after the inward man." (Rom. vii. 22.) But how do I get this "inward man," this new nature? How do I get into the new creation? Not by works of law of any shape or description, but by faith of Jesus Christ. I become united to Christ in the power of a new and endless life, upon which the law has no claim. I died in Christ, and hence the law has no further demand on me. If a man is in prison for murder, and dies there, the law is done with him, inasmuch as the life in which the crime was committed is gone. Thus it is with the sinner who believes in Jesus. God sees him to be dead. His old man is crucified. The sentence of the law has been put into execution upon him in the Person of Christ. Had it been executed upon himself, it would have been death eternal; but having been executed upon Christ, His death is of infinite, divine, and eternal efficacy; and, moreover, having the power of eternal life in Himself, He rose, as a Conqueror, from the tomb, after having met every claim, and—wonderful to declare! the believer, having died in Him, now lives in Him for ever. Christ is his life; Christ is his righteousness; Christ is his rule of life; Christ is his model; Christ is his hope; Christ is his all and in all. See carefully Rom. vi., vii. *passim.* Gal. ii. 20, 21; iii. iv., Eph. ii. 4-6; Col. ii. 10-15.

But we must not anticipate what properly belongs to the second grand division of our subject, to which we shall pass on, having first sought to meet a difficulty which may perhaps exercise our reader's mind. It is possible that some may feel disposed to inquire, "If the law cannot yield life, furnish righteousness, or promote santification, then for what end was it given?" The apostle anticipates and answers this question. "Wherefore then the law? it was added because of transgression, till the seed should come to whom the promise was made." (Gal. iii. 19.) So also, in Romans, we read, "Moreover, the law entered (or came in by the way, between the promise and the accomplishment) that the offence might abound." (Chap. v. 20.) These two passages declare in simplest terms the object of the law. It is not said, "the law entered in order that we might get life, righteousness, or sanctification by it;" quite the opposite, it was "because of transgression," and "that the offence might abound." Where is it said in scripture that the law was given that we might get life, righteousness, or sanctification by it? Nowhere. But it is expressly declared that "the law was added because of transgression," and that "it came in by the way that the offence might abound." It is not possible to conceive two objects more diverse. The legal system speaks of life, righteousness, and sanctification by law; the scripture, on the contrary, speaks of "offence," "transgression," and "wrath." And why? Because we are sinners, and the law is holy. It demands strength, and we are weak; it demands life in order to keep it, and we are dead; it demands perfection in all things, and we are perfect in nothing; it is holy, and just, and good, and we are unholy, unjust, and bad. Thus it stands between us and the law; and it matters not in the least, as regards the principle of the law, whether we are regenerate or unregenerate, believers or unbelievers, saints or

40

sinners. The law knows nothing of any such distinctions. It is addressed to man in the flesh, in his old-Adam condition, in his old-creation standing. It tells him what he ought to do for God, and, inasmuch as he has not done that, it curses him, and it cannot do any thing else. It shows him no mercy, but leaves him in the place of death and condemnation.

Thus much as to "what is written in the law." Let us now proceed to inquire, in the second place,

### WHAT IS IN THE GOSPEL?

This is unfolded with uncommon beauty and power, in the touching parable of "the good Samaritan." The lawyer, like all legalists, "willing to justify himself," sought to ascertain who was his neighbour; and, in reply, our blessed Lord draws a picture in which is most vividly presented the true condition of every sinner, be he lawyer or else. "A certain man went down from Jerusalem to Jericho, and fell among thieves, which stripped him of his raiment, and wounded him, and departed, leaving him half dead." What a picture of man's career and man's condition! "A certain man"—the writer or the reader of these lines, "went down." How true! Reader, is it not so? Has not thy course ever been a downward one? Hast thou ever, when left to thyself, taken a step upward—a step in the right direction? There is no use in generalizing, in making statements about mankind, the whole human race, Adam's posterity, and the like. What we want is to bring the matter home to ourselves, and say, each for himself, "I am the 'certain man' of this singularly beautiful parable; it is my own very figure that appears in the foreground of this masterly picture; my course has been a downward one; I have gone down from the innocency of childhood, to the folly of youth, and from the folly of youth to the matured wickedness of manhood, and here I am, 'stripped' of every shred in which I might wrap myself; 'wounded' in every region of my moral being; and having the painful consciousness that death has already begun its terrible work in me."

Such is the career, such the condition of every sinner—his career, downward—his condition, death. What is to be done? Can he keep the law? Alas! he is not able to move. Can the "priest" do aught for him? Alas! he has no sacrifice, and no ability to rise and get one. Can the "Levite" not help him? Alas! he is so polluted with his wounds and bruises that neither Levite nor priest could touch him. In a word, neither law nor ordinances can meet his case. He is utterly ruined. He has destroyed himself. The law has flung him overboard as a defiled, good-for-nothing, condemned thing. It is useless talking to him about the law, or asking him will he take it as a means of justification, a rule of life, or the power of sanctification. It has cursed, condemned, and set him aside altogether, and he has only to cry out from the profound and awful depths of his moral ruin, "O wretched man that I am! who shall deliver me from the body of this death?"

Now, it is when a man is really brought to this that he is in a position to see the moral grandeur of the gospel. It is when he has discovered his own guilt, misery, and ruin, and also his entire inability to meet the just and holy claims of the law, or profit, in any wise, by the appliances of the legal system in its most attractive forms, that he is prepared to appreciate the ample provisions of the grace of God. This is most strikingly illustrated in the scene before us. When the poor man had got down from Jerusalem to Jericho, from the city of God to the city of the curse; (Josh. vi. 26; I Kings xvi. 33, 34,) when he lay stripped, wounded, and half-dead; when both priest and Levite had turned from him and gone their way; it was just then that he was in a position to prove the grace of the good Samaritan who, assuredly, is none other than the blessed Lord Jesus Himself, who, blessed for ever be His balmy, precious name! here appears in the form of a Samaritan only to enhance the grace that breathes forth upon our souls in this lovely scene. "The Jews have no dealings with the Samaritans," and, hence, had the Jew in this parable had sufficient strength, he would not, we may safely aver, have suffered the stranger to touch him. But he was so far gone, so powerless, so under the power of death, that the gracious Samaritan had it all his own way. And oh! what a tender way it was!

"But a certain Samaritan, as he journeyed, *came where he was:* and when he saw him, *he had compassion, and went to him,* and bound up his wounds, pouring in oil and wine, and set him on his own beast, and brought him to an inn, and took care of him. And on the morrow when he departed, he took out two pence, and gave them to the host, and said unto him, Take care of him; and whatsoever thou spendest more, when I come again, I will repay thee."

Here, then, is what is revealed in the gospel. Man has ruined himself. He has gone down from God. He has fallen under the power of the enemy. He is the victim of Satan, the slave of sin, the subject of death. His case is hopeless, so far as he is concerned. But, blessed be God, the true Samaritan has come down into all the ruin. The Son of God left His Father's bosom, His eternal dwelling-place, came down into this world, to remedy our ruin, to bear our guilt, to endure the wrath of God in our stead. All this he did, beloved reader, as the expression of His own tender compassion and love. "He had compassion," and came to bind up our wounds, to pour "the wine and oil" of His own most precious grace into our souls, to heal, restore, and bless us, to put us into His own position, according to the power which had brought Him into ours, to make ample provision for all our need, until that bright and happy moment when we shall be ushered into His presence to go no more out for ever.

The page of inspiration does not present a more touching picture than that which the Master's pencil has drawn for us in "The good Samaritan." It is perfectly beautiful, and beautifully perfect. It is divine. Every expression is fraught with exquisite moral loveliness. "He came where he was"—not half-way, or nine-tenths of the way, but all the way. "And when he saw him," what then? Did he turn away in disgust at his appearance, and despair of his condition? Ah! no; "He had compassion on him." His tender heart yearned over him. He cared not what he was or who he was, Jew or Gentile, it mattered not; the streams of tender compassion came gushing up from the deep fountains of a heart that found its own delight in ministering to every form of human need. Now was this "compassion" a mere movement of sentimentality—an evanescent feeling uttering itself in empty words and then passing away. No; it was a real, living, acting thing, expressing itself in the most unmistakeable manner. "He went to him." For what? To meet his every need, and not to leave him until he had placed him in a position of security, rest, and blessing.

Nor was this all. Not only did this gracious stranger fully meet the wounded one's present need; but, ere leaving, he dropped these touching words, "Take care of him." How this must have melted the poor man's heart. Such disinterested kindness! And all from a stranger! Yea, from one with whom he would naturally have "no friendly dealings."

Finally, as if to complete the picture, he says, "when I come again." He awakens in the heart, by these last words, "the blessed hope" of seeing him again. What a lovely picture! And yet it is all a divine reality. It is the simple story of our blessed Jesus who, in His tender compassion, looked upon us in our low and utterly hopeless condition, left His eternal dwelling-place of light and love, took upon Him the likeness of sinful flesh, was made of a woman, made under the law, lived a spotless life, and fulfilled a perfect ministry down here for three and thirty years, and, finally, died on the cross as a perfect atonement for sin, in order that God might be just and the Justifier of any poor, ungodly, convicted sinner that simply trusts in Jesus.

Yes, dear reader, whoever you are, high or low, rich or poor, learned or ignorant, Jesus has done all this; and He is now at the right hand of the Majesty in the heavens. The One who was nailed to the cross for us, is now on the throne. Eternal Justice has wreathed His sacred brow with the chaplet of victory, and that, be it remembered on our behalf. Nor is this all. He has said, "I will come again." Precious words! Say, wouldst thou be glad to see Him? Dost thou know Him as the good Samaritan? Hast thou felt His loving hand binding up thy spiritual wounds? Hast thou known the healing virtues of His oil, and the restoring, invigorating, and cheering influence of His wine! Hast thou heard Him speak thrilling words, "Take care of him?" If so, then, surely, thou wilt be glad to see His face: thou wilt cherish in thine heart's tender affections the blessed hope of seeing Him as He is, and of being like Him and with Him for ever. The Lord grant it may be so with thee, beloved reader, and then thou wilt be able to appreciate the immense difference between the Law and the Gospel—between what we ought to do for God, and what God has done for us—between what we are to Him, and what He is to us—between "do and live," and "live and do"—between "the righteousness of the law," and "the righteousness of faith."

May the blessing of the Father, of the Son, and of the Holy Ghost, rest upon the reader of these lines, now, henceforth, and for evermore!

# DEAD TO THE LAW

"For I through law, am dead to law, that I might live to God."
—(Gal. ii. 19.) This is a weighty word, and much needed just now.
The spiritual apprehension of the truth here forth will preserve
the soul from two errors which are very rife in the professing
church, namely, legality, on the one hand, and licentiousness on
the other. Were we to compare these two evils—were we compelled to choose between them, we should, undoubtedly, prefer the
former. We should much rather see a man under the authority of
the law of Moses, than one living in lawlessness and self-indulgence.
Of course, we know that neither is right, and that Christianity gives
us something quite different; but we have much more respect for a
man who, seeing nothing beyond Moses, and regarding the law of
Moses as the only divine standard by which his conduct is to be
regulated, bows down, in a spirit of reverence to its authority—than
for one who seeks to get rid of that law only that he may please
himself. Thank God, the truth of the gospel gives us the divine
remedy for both cases. But how? Does it teach us that the law is
dead? Nay! What then? It teaches that the believer is dead. "I
through law am dead to law." And to what end? That I may please
myself? That I may seek my own profit and pleasure? By no means;
but "that I may live to God."

Here lies the grand and all-important truth—a truth lying at the
very base of the entire christian system, and without which we can
have no just sense of what Christianity is at all. So also, in Romans
vii. we read, "Wherefore, my brethren, ye also have become dead
to the law (not the law is dead) by the body of Christ, in order
that ye may be to another (not to yourselves, but) even to him
that was raised from the dead, that ye might bring forth fruit unto
God." (v. 4.) And again, "But now ye are delivered from the law,
being dead to that wherein ye were held, that ye might serve in

46

newness of spirit and not in oldness of letter." (v. 6.)* Mark, it is that we may serve, not that we may please ourselves. We have been delivered from the intolerable yoke of Moses, that we may wear the "easy yoke of Christ," and not that we may give a loose run to nature.

There is something perfectly shocking to a serious mind, in the thought of men appealing to certain principles of the gospel, in order to establish a plea for the indulgence of the flesh. They want to fling aside the authority of Moses, not that they may enjoy the authority of Christ, but merely to indulge self. But it is vain. It cannot be done with any shadow of truth, for it is never said in scripture that the law is dead or abrogated; but it is said, and urged repeatedly, that the believer is dead to the law, and dead to sin, in order that he may taste the sweetness of living unto God, of having his fruit unto holiness, and the end everlasting life.

We earnestly commend this weighty subject to the attention of the reader. He will find it fully unfolded in Romans iv. and v., Galatians iii. and iv. A right understanding of it will solve a thousand difficulties, and answer a thousand questions; and, not only so, but deliver the soul from a vast mass of error and confusion. May God give His own word power over the heart and conscience!

---

* The marginal reading of verse 6 is, doubtless, the correct one. The words are ἀποθανόντες ἐν ᾧ, not ἀποθανόντος οὗ. It is well to note this, as also the difference between the way in which the apostle uses the illustration, it is the husband that dies, but in the application, it is the believer, not the law. Not seeing this had led many into the error of teaching that the law is dead, whereas in I Timothy i. 8, the apostle expressly declares, not that the law is dead, but the very reverse; "We know that *the law is good*, if a man use it lawfully." And how is it to be used lawfully? "Knowing this, that *the law is not made for a righteous man, but for the lawless*," &c., &c. It is of the utmost importance that the reader should be clear as to this.

47

# GRACE AND HOLINESS

## (A REPLY TO A CORRESPONDENT)

Thank God we are under grace. But does this blessed fact weaken, in any way, the truth that "Holiness becometh God's house for ever"? Has it ceased to be true, that "God is greatly to be feared in the assembly of his saints; and to be had in reverence of all those who are about him?" Is the standard of holiness lower for the church of God now, than it was for Israel of old? Has it ceased to be true that "our God is a consuming fire?" It does not say "God out of Christ;" but "our God." What do we know of God out of Christ? Is evil to be tolerated because "we are not under law, but under grace?" Why were many of the Corinthians weak and sickly? Why did many of them die? Why were Ananias and Sapphira struck dead in a moment? Did that solemn judgment touch the truth that the church was under grace? Assuredly not. But neither did grace hinder the action of judgment. God can no more tolerate evil in His assembly now, than He could in the days of Achan.

You say, "We must not draw comparisons between God's dealings with His earthly people, and His dealings with His church." What mean the following words, in I Corinthians x.? "Moreover, brethren, I would not that ye should be ignorant, how that all our fathers were under the cloud, and all passed through the sea; and were all baptized unto Moses in the cloud and in the sea; and did all eat the same spiritual meat; and did all drink the same spiritual drink; for they drank of that spiritual Rock that followed them; and that Rock was Christ. But with many of them God was not pleased; for they were overthrown in the wilderness. Now these things were our examples, to the intent we should not lust after evil things, as they also lusted. . . . Now all these things happened unto them for examples; and they are written for our admonition, upon whom the ends of the world are come."

Is not this drawing a comparison between God's dealings with

48

His earthly people and His church now? Yes, verily; and well will it be for us all to ponder and be admonished by the comparison. It would be sad indeed if we were to draw a plea from the pure and precious grace in which we stand for lowering the standard of holiness. We are called to purge out the old leaven, on the blessed ground that "Christ our passover is sacrificed for us." Is not this "drawing a comparison?" The assembly at Corinth was commanded—woe be unto them if they had refused—to put away from among them the wicked person, to deliver him to Satan for the destruction of the flesh.

True, they were not called to stone him, or to burn him; and here we have a contrast rather than a comparison. But they had to put him out from among them, if they would have the divine presence in their midst. "Thy testimonies are very sure; holiness becometh thy house, O Lord, FOR EVER." Can you not praise him for the holiness as well as the grace? Can you not, as the standard of holiness rises before you, add your doxology, "Blessed be his name for ever and ever! Amen, and amen?" We trust you can. We are disposed to think that your remarks are the fruit of that one-sidedness to which we are all so prone, and which must ever prove a sad hindrance to our progress in the knowledge of divine truth.

We must never forget that, while we stand in grace, we are to walk in holiness; and, as regards the assembly, if we refuse to judge bad doctrine and bad morals, we are not on the ground of the assembly of God at all. People say we must not judge; God says we must. "Do not ye judge them that are *within?* But them that are without God judgeth. Therefore put away from among yourselves that wicked person." If the assembly at Corinth had refused to judge that wicked person, it would have forfeited all title to be regarded as the assembly of God; and all who feared the Lord would have had to leave it. It is a very solemn matter indeed to take the ground of the assembly of God. All who do so have to bear in mind that it is not at all a question of whom we can receive, or what we can tolerate, but what is worthy of God? We hear a great deal now-a-days about the *"broad"* and the *"narrow;"* we have just to be as broad and as narrow as the word of God.

49

# ISOLATION

It is one of our great difficulties at the present moment—indeed it has ever been a difficulty—to combine a narrow path with a wide heart. There is very much, on all sides, tending to produce isolation. We cannot deny it. Links of human friendship seem so fragile; so many things crop up to shake confidence; so many things which one cannot possibly sanction, that the path becomes more and more isolated.

All this is unquestionably true. But we must be very careful as to how we meet this condition of things. We have little idea how much depends on the spirit in which we carry ourselves in the midst of scenes and circumstances which, all must admit, are peculiarly trying.

For example, I may retire in upon myself, and become bitter, morose, severe, repulsive, withered up, having no heart for the Lord's people, for His service, for the holy and happy exercises of the assembly. I may become barren of good works, having no sympathy with the poor, the sick, the sorrowful: living in the narrow circle within which I have retired; thinking only of myself, my personal and family interests.

What, we may well inquire, can be more miserable than this? It is simply the most deplorable selfishness; but we do not see it, because we are blinded by our inordinate occupation with other people's failures.

Now it is a very easy matter to find out flaws, foibles, and faults in our brethren and friends. But the question is, How are we to meet these things? Is it by retiring in upon ourselves? Never; no, never. To do this is to render ourselves as miserable in ourselves as we are worthless, and worse than worthless, to others. There are few things more, pitiable than what we call "a disappointed man." He is always finding fault with others. He has never discovered the real root of the matter, or the true secret of dealing with it. He has retired, but it is in upon himself. He is isolated, but his isolation is utterly false. He is miserable; and he will make all who come under his influence—all who are weak and foolish enough to listen to him—as miserable as himself. He has completely broken down in his practical career; he has succumbed to the difficulties of his time, and proved himself wholly unequal to meet the stern realities of actual life. And then, instead of seeing and confessing this, he retires into his own narrow circle, and finds fault with everyone except himself.

How truly delightful and refreshing to turn from this dismal picture to the only perfect Man that ever trod this earth! His path was indeed an isolated one—none more so. He had no sympathy with the scene around Him. "The world knew him not." "He came unto his own [Israel], and his own received him not." "He looked for some to take pity, but there was none; and for comforters, but he found none." Even His own beloved disciples failed to sympathise with, or understand Him. They slept on the mount of transfiguration, in the presence of His glory; and they slept in the garden of Gethsemane, in the presence of His agony. They roused Him out of His sleep with their unbelieving fears, and were continually intruding upon Him with their ignorant questions and foolish notions.

How did He meet all this? In perfect grace, patience, and tenderness. He answered their questions; He corrected their notions; He hushed their fears; He solved their difficulties; He met their need; He made allowance for their infirmities; He gave them credit for devotedness in the moment of desertion; He looked at them through His own loving eyes, and loved them, notwithstanding all. "Having loved his own which were in the world, he loved them unto the end."

Christian reader, let us seek to drink into our blessed Master's spirit, and walk in His footsteps; and then our isolation will be of the right kind, and though our path may be narrow, the heart will be large.

# A WORKMAN'S MOTTO

*"Therefore, my beloved brethren, be ye stedfast, immoveable, always abounding in the work of the Lord, forasmuch as ye know that your labour is not in vain in the Lord."* 1 Corinthians xv. 58.

Here we have an uncommonly fine motto for the christian workman—and every Christian ought to be a workman. It presents a most valuable balance for the heart. We have immoveable stability linked with unceasing activity.

This is of the utmost possible importance. There are some of us such sticklers for what we call principle that we seem almost afraid to embark in any scheme of large-hearted christian activity. And, on the other hand, some of us are so bent on what we call service, that in order to reach desired ends, and realize palpable results, we do not hesitate to overstep the boundary line of sound principle.

Now, our motto supplies a divine antidote for both these evils. It furnishes a solid basis on which we are to stand with steadfast purpose and immoveable decision. We are not to be moved the breadth of a hair from the narrow path of divine truth, though tempted to do so by the most forcible argument of a plausible expediency. "To obey is better than sacrifice; and to hearken, than the fat of rams."

Noble words! may they be engraved, in characters deep and broad, on every workman's heart. They are absolutely invaluable; and particularly so in this our own day, when there is such willfulness in our mode of working, such erratic schemes of service, such self-pleasing, such a strong tendency to do that which is right in our own eyes, such a practical ignoring of the supreme authority of holy scripture.

It fills the thoughtful observer of the present condition of things with the very gravest apprehensions to mark the positive and deliberate throwing aside of the word of God, even by those who professedly admit it to be the word of God. We speak not now of the insolence of open and avowed infidelity; but of the heartless indifference of respectable orthodoxy. There are thousands, nay millions, who profess to believe that the Bible is the word of God, who, nevertheless, have not the smallest idea of submitting themselves absolutely to its authority. The human will is dominant. Human reason bears sway. Expediency commands the heart. The holy principles of divine revelation are swept away like autumn leaves, or the dust of the threshing-floor, before the vehement blast of popular opinion.

How immensely valuable and important, in view of all this, is the first part of our workman's motto! "Therefore, my beloved brethren, be ye *stedfast* and *immoveable*." The "therefore" throws the soul back upon the solid foundation laid in the previous part of the chapter in which the apostle unfolds the most sublime and precious truth that can possibly engage the Christian's heart—truth which lifts the soul completely above the dark and chilling mists of the old creation, and plants it on the solid rock of resurrection. It is on this rock we are exhorted to be stedfast and immovable. It is not an obstinate adherence to our own notions—to some favourite dogma or theory which we have adopted—or to any special school of doctrine, high or low. It is not aught of this kind; but a firm grasp and faithful confession of the whole truth of God of which a risen Christ is the everlasting centre.

But then we have to remember the other side of our motto. The christian workman has something more to do than to stand firmly on the ground of truth. He has to cultivate the lovely activities of grace. He is called to be "always *abounding* in the work of the Lord." The basis of sound principle must never be abandoned; but the work of the Lord must be diligently carried on. There are some who are so afraid of doing mischief that they do nothing; and others, who rather than not be doing something will do wrong. Our motto corrects both. It teaches us to set our faces as a flint, where truth is, in any wise, involved; while on the other hand, it leads us to go forth, in largeness of heart, and throw all our energies into the work of the Lord.

And let the christian reader specially note the expression, "*The work of the Lord*." We are not to imagine for a moment that all that which engages the energies of professing Christians is entitled to be designated "the work of the Lord." Alas! alas! far from it. We see a mass of things undertaken as service for the Lord with which a spiritual person could not possibly connect the holy name of Christ. We do not attempt to go into details; but we do desire to have the conscience exercised as to the work in which we embark. We deeply feel how needful it is in this day of willfulness, laxity, and wild latitudinarianism, to own the authority of Christ in all that we put our hands to in the way of work or service. Blessed be His name, He permits us to connect Him with the most trivial and commonplace activities of daily life. We can even eat and drink in His holy name, and to His glory. The sphere of service is wide enough, most surely; it is only limited by that weighty clause, "The work of the Lord." The christian workman must not engage in any work which does not range itself under that most holy and all-important head. He must, ere he enters upon any service, ask himself this great practical question, "Can this honestly be called 'the work of the Lord?' "

# AUTHORITY AND POWER

If ever there was a moment, in the history of the professing church, in which it behoved people to have divine authority for their path, and divine power to pursue it, this is the moment. There are so many conflicting opinions, so many jarring voices, so many opposing schools, so many contending parties, that we are in danger, at all points, of losing our balance and being carried we know not whither. We find the very best of men ranged on opposite sides of the same question—men who, so far as we can judge, seem to have a single eye to the glory of Christ, and to take the word of God as their sole authority in all things.

What, then, is a simple soul to do? How is one to get on, in the face of all this? Is there no peaceful haven in the which to anchor one's tiny barque, away from the wild tossing of the stormy ocean of human opinion? Yes, blessed be God there is; and the reader may know the deep blessedness of casting anchor there this very moment. It is the sweet privilege of the very simplest child of God, the merest babe in Christ, to have divine authority for his path and divine power to pursue it—authority for his position, and power to occupy it—authority for his work, and power to do it.

What is it! Where is it! The authority is found in *the divine word;* the power is found in *the divine presence.* Thus it is, blessed be God; and each and all may know it—ought to know it, for the stability of their path and the joy of their heart.

In contemplating the present condition of professing christians generally, one is struck with this very painful fact, that so few, so very few, are prepared to face scripture, on all points and in all matters, personal, domestic, commercial and ecclesiastical. If the question of the soul's salvation be settled—and alas! how rarely it is settled—then, verily, people consider themselves at liberty to break away from the sacred domain of scripture, and launch forth upon the wild watery waste of human opinion and human will, where each one may think for himself, and choose for himself, and act for himself.

Now, nothing is more certain than this, that, where it is merely a question of human opinion, human will, or human judgment, there is not a shadow of authority—not a particle of power. No human opinion has any authority over the conscience; nor can it impart any power to the soul. It may go for what it is worth; but it has neither authority nor power for me. I must have God's word and God's presence, else I cannot get on. If aught, no matter what, comes in between my conscience and the word of God, I know not where I am, what to do, or whither to turn. And if aught, no matter what, comes in between my heart and the presence of God, I am perfectly powerless. The word of my Lord is my only directory; His dwelling in me and with me, my only power. "Have not I commanded thee? Lo, I am with thee."

But, it may be the reader feels disposed to enquire, "Is it really true that the word of God contains ample guidance for all the details of life? Does it tell me, for instance, where I am to go on the Lord's day; and what I am to do from Monday morning till Saturday night? Does it direct me in my personal path; in my domestic relationships; in my commercial position; in my religious associations and opinions?"

Most assuredly. The word of God furnishes you thoroughly to all good works, and any work for which it does not furnish you is not good but bad. Hence, if you cannot find authority for where you go on Lord's day—no matter where it is—you must, at once, give up going. And if you cannot find authority for what you do on Monday, you must, at once, cease to do it. "To obey is better than sacrifice; and to hearken, than the fat of rams." Let us honestly face scripture. Let us bow down to its holy authority in all things. Let us humbly and reverently yield ourselves to its heavenly guidance. Let us give up every habit, every practice, every association, be it what it may, or be it sanctioned by whom it may, for which we have not the direct authority of God's word, and in which we cannot enjoy the sense of His presence—the life of His appreciating countenance.

This is a point of the very gravest moment. Indeed it would be impossible for human language to set forth with due force or in adequate terms, the vast importance of absolute and complete submission to the authority of scripture in all things—yes, we would say, and with emphasis—*all things*.

One of our greatest practical difficulties, in dealing with souls, arises from the fact that they do not seem to have any idea of submitting in all things to scripture. They will not face the word of God, or consent to be taught exclusively from its sacred pages. Creeds and confessions; religious formularies; the commandments, the doctrines, and the traditions of men—these things will be heard and yielded to. Our own will, our own judgment, our own views of things will be allowed to bear sway. Expediency, position, reputation, personal influence; usefulness; the opinion of friends; the thoughts and example of good and great men; the fear of grieving or giving offence to those whom we love and esteem, and with whom we may have been long associated in our religious life and service; the dread of being thought presumptuous; intense shrinking from the appearance of judging or condemning many at whose feet we would willingly sit—all these things operate and exert a most pernicious influence upon the soul, and hinder full surrender of ourselves to the paramount authority of God's word.

May the Lord graciously stir up our hearts in reference to this weighty subject! May He lead us, by His Holy Spirit, to see the true place and the real value and power of His word! May that word be set up in our souls as the one all-sufficient rule so that everything—no matter what—may be unhesitatingly and utterly rejected that is not based upon its authority. Then we may expect to make progress. Then shall our path be as the path of the just, like a shining light that shineth more and more unto the perfect day. May we never rest satisfied until, in reference to all our habits, all our ways, all our associations, our religious position and service, all we do and all we do not do; where we go and where we do not go, we can truly say we have the sanction of God's word and the light of His presence. Here, and here alone, lies the deep and precious secret of AUTHORITY AND POWER.

# OBEDIENCE AND DEPENDENCE

In our December issue we ventured to call the attention of our readers to the weighty fact, that our God has, in His infinite mercy, provided for His people in this dark and evil world both authority and power—the authority of His word and the power of His Spirit—for the path which they are called to tread, and the work they are called to do. We have ample guidance in the word, and we have the power of God to count upon for all the difficulties and demands of the scene through which we have to pass home to our eternal rest above. We have authority and power for all.

But we must remember, that if God has furnished us with authority, we must be obedient. And if He has provided the power, we must be dependent. Of what use is authority if we do not obey it? I may give my servant the plainest and fullest directions as to where he is to go, and what he is to do, and what he is to say; but if, instead of acting simply upon my directions, he begins to reason, and think, and draw conclusions, to use his own judgment, and act according to his own will, of what use are my directions? None whatever, except it be to show how entirely he has departed from them. Clearly, the business of a servant is to obey, not to reason—to act according to his master's directions, not according to his own will or judgment. If he only does exactly what his master tells him, he is not responsible for the consequences.

The one grand business of a servant is to obey. This is the moral perfection of a servant. Alas! how rare! There has been but one absolutely obedient and perfectly dependent servant, in the entire history of this world—the man Christ Jesus. His meat and His drink were to obey. He found His joy in obedience. "Sacrifice and offering thou didst not desire; *mine ears hast thou opened*: burnt-offering and sin-offering hast thou not required. Then said I, Lo, I come: in the volume of the book it is written of me, *I delight to do thy will, O my God*: yea, thy law is within my heart." Psalm xl.

Our blessed Lord Jesus found in the will of God His only

motive for action. There was nothing in Him that needed to be restrained by the authority of God. His will was perfect, and His every movement was of necessity—the very necessity of His perfect nature—in the current of the divine will. "Thy law is within my heart;" "I delight to do thy will;" "I came down from heaven, not to do mine own will, but the will of him that sent me."

Now, what could Satan do with such a Man as this? Absolutely nothing. He tried to withdraw Him from the path of obedience and the place of dependence; but in vain. "If thou be the Son of God, command these stones to be made bread." Surely God would give His Son bread. No doubt; but the perfect Man refuses to make bread for Himself. He had no command, no authority, and therefore no motive for action. "It is written, Man shall not live by bread alone, but by every word that proceedeth out of the mouth of the Lord." So throughout the entire temptation. Nothing could withdraw the blessed One from the path of simple obedience. "It is written," was His one unvarying answer. He would not, could not act without a motive, and His only motive was found in the will of God. "I delight to do thy will, O my God; yea, thy law is within my heart."

Such was the obedience of Jesus Christ—an obedience perfect, from first to last. And not only was He perfectly obedient, but perfectly dependent. Though God over all, blessed for ever, yet, having taken His place as a man in this world, He lived a life of perfect dependence on God. He could say, "I clothe the heavens with blackness, and I make sackcloth their covering. The Lord God hath given me the tongue of the learned, that I should know how to speak a word in season to him that is weary: he wakeneth morning by morning, he wakeneth mine ear to hear as the learned. The Lord God hath opened mine ear, and I was not rebellious, neither turned away back. I gave my back to the smiters, and my cheeks to them that plucked off the hair: I hid not my face from shame and spitting. For the Lord God will help me; therefore shall I not be confounded: therefore have I set my face like a flint, and I know that I shall not be ashamed." (Is. 1.) And again, "Preserve me, O God, for in thee do I put my trust." And again, "I was cast upon thee from the womb." He was wholly and continually cast upon God, from the manger of Bethlehem to the cross of Calvary; and when He had finished all, He surrendered His spirit into the Father's hand, and His flesh rested in hope. His obedience and dependence were divinely perfect throughout.

But we must now ask the reader to turn with us, for a few moments, to two examples of the very opposite of all this—two cases in the which, through lack of obedience and dependence, the most disastrous results followed.

Let us, in the first place, turn to the thirteenth chapter of the First Book of Kings. Doubtless, the case is familiar to us: but let us look at it in connection with our present theme.

"And, behold, there came a man of God out of Judah, *by the word of the Lord*, unto Bethel: and Jeroboam stood by the altar to burn incense. And he cried against the altar in the word of the Lord." Thus far all was right. He spoke by the word of God, and the power of God accompanied the testimony, and the spirit of the king was humbled and subdued for the moment.

But more than this. The man of God was enabled to refuse the king's invitation to come home with him and refresh himself, and receive a reward. "And the man of God said unto the king, If thou wilt give me half thine house, I will not go in with thee, neither will I eat bread nor drink water in this place. *For so it was charged me by the word of the Lord*, saying, Eat no bread, nor drink water, nor turn again by the same way that thou camest."

All this was lovely—perfectly delightful to dwell upon. The feet of the man of God stand firm in the bright and blessed path of obedience, and all is victory. The offers of the king are flung aside without a moment's hesitation. Half the royal house cannot tempt him off the narrow, holy, happy path of obedience. He rejects every overture, and turns to pursue the straight path opened before him by the word of the Lord. There is no reasoning, no questioning, no hesitation. The word of the Lord settles everything. He has but to obey, regardless of consequences. And so far he does, and all is well.

But mark the sequel. "Now there dwelt an old prophet in Bethel" —reader, beware of old prophets!—And this old prophet followed the man of God, and said unto him, "Come home with me, and eat bread." This was the devil in a new shape. What the word of a king had failed to do, the word of a prophet might accomplish. It was a wile of Satan, for which the man of God was evidently unprepared. The garb of a prophet deceived him, and threw him completely off his guard: we can at once perceive his altered tone. When replying to the king he speaks with vividness, force, and bold decision—"If thou wilt give me half thine house, I will not go in with thee." And then he adds, with equal force, his reason for refusing: "For so was it charged me by the word of the Lord."

But, in his reply to the prophet, there is manifest decline in the way of energy, boldness, and decision. He says, "I may not return with thee nor go in with thee." And in assigning the reason, instead of the forcible word "charged," we have the feeble word, "It was said to me."

In short, the whole tone is lower. The word of God was losing its true place and power in his soul. No change had passed over that word. "For ever, O Lord, thy word is settled in heaven", and had that word been hidden in the heart of the man of God, had it been dwelling richly in his soul, his answer to the prophet would have been as distinct and decided as his answer to the king. "By the words of thy lips, I have kept me from the paths of the destroyer." The spirit of obedience is the great moral safeguard against every scheme and every snare of the enemy. The enemy may shift his ground; he may change his tactics, he may vary his agency; but obedience to the plain and simple word of God preserves the soul from all his wicked schemes and crafty devices. The devil can do nothing with a man who is absolutely ruled by the word of God, and refuses to move the breadth of a hair without divine authority.

But note how the enemy urges his point with the man of God. "He said unto him, I am a prophet also as thou art: and an angel spake unto me by the word of the Lord, saying, Bring him back with thee into thine house."

Now, what should the man of God have said to this? If the word of his Lord had been abiding in him, he would at once have said, "If ten thousand prophets, and ten thousand angels, were to say, Bring him back, I should regard them all as liars and emissaries of the devil, sent forth to allure me from the holy, happy, path of obedience." This would have been a sublime reply. It would have the same heavenly ring about it as is exhibited in these glowing words of the apostle: "Though we, or an angel from heaven, preach any other gospel unto you than that which we have preached, let him be anathema."

But, alas! alas! the man of God stepped off the path of obedience; and the very man whom Satan had used to draw him off, became the mouthpiece of Jehovah to announce in his ears the terrible consequence. He lied when Satan used him. He spoke truth when God used him. The erring man of God was slain by a lion, because he disobeyed the word of the Lord. Yes; he stepped off the narrow path of obedience into the wide field of his own will, and there he was slain.

Reader, let us beware of old prophets, and angels of light! Let us, in the true spirit of obedience, keep close, very close, to the word of our God. We shall find the path of obedience both safe and pleasant, holy and happy.

And now, for a moment, ere we close, let us glance at the ninth chapter of Joshua, which records for our admonition the manner in which even Joshua himself was ensnared through lack of simple dependence upon God. We do not quote the passage, or enter into any detail. The reader can turn to the chapter, and ponder its contents.

Why was Israel beguiled by the craft of the Gibeonites? Because they leaned to their own understanding, and judged by the sight of their eyes, instead of waiting upon God for guidance and counsel. He know all about the Gibeonites. He was not deceived by their tattered rags and mouldly bread; and neither would they, had they only looked to Him.

But here they *failed*. They did not wait on God. He would have guided them. He would have told them who these crafty strangers were. He would have made all clear for them, had they simply waited on Him in the sense of their own ignorance and feebleness. But no; they would think for themselves, and judge for themselves, and reason from what they saw, and draw their own conclusions. All these things they would do; and hence the tattered garments

62

of the Gibeonites accomplished what the frowning bulwarks of Jericho had failed to do.

Now, we may be quite sure that Israel had no thought of making a league with any of the Canaanites. Nay, they were in terrible indignation when they discovered that they had done so. But they did it, and had to abide by it. It is easier to make a mistake than to rectify it, and so the Gibeonites remained as a striking memorial of the evil of not waiting on God for counsel and guidance.

May the Holy Spirit teach us, from all that has passed before us, the solemn importance of *"obedience and dependence."*

# STABILITY AND PEACE

## (Joshua i. 9)

*"Have not I commanded thee? Be strong and of a good courage; be not afraid, neither be thou dismayed; for the Lord thy God is with thee withersoever thou goest."*

Here lies the true secret of stability and peace, at all times, and under all circumstances. The authority of God for the ground we occupy, and His presence with us thereon—the word of the Lord, as the warrant for what we are doing, and the light of His countenance in the doing of it. There is no possibility of getting on without these two things. It will not do merely to be able to give chapter and verse, as we say, for a certain position which we have taken up; we must realize the Lord's own presence with us. And, on the other hand, it will not do to say we have the Lord's presence with us, unless we can give a divine warrant—a "Thus saith the Lord"—for what we are doing, and for the path we are treading.

Joshua could never have faced the difficulties of his day, without these two things; and, although we may not have to meet the same things that lay in his path, yet, we may rest assured of this, we shall never get on, in this our day, without the word of God as our authority, and His presence as our strength. Our lot is cast in a moment of special confusion. A multitude of conflicting voices fall on the ear. Men are taking sides. We see apparently the best and holiest, the most devoted and intelligent men ranged on opposite sides of the same question, and pursuing opposite ways, though professing to follow the same Lord. What are we to think? What are we to do? What do we want? We want to hear, deep down in our very inmost soul, these two weighty and imperishable sentences, "Have not I commanded thee?"—"Lo, I am with thee." These are grand realities, which the very feeblest and most unlettered saint may enjoy, and without which none can possibly make head against the tide of evil at present rising around us.

Never, perhaps, in the annals of Christianity, was there a moment which more imperatively demanded the most direct personal dealing of the soul with God and His truth. It will not do for any one to pin his faith to the sleeve of another. God is testing souls in a very remarkable manner. The sieve is doing its solemn work in the midst of the Church. No doubt, those who are enabled to go through the sifting and testing, with God, will reap a rich harvest of blessing; but we must go through it. It is being made manifest, just now, in a very special way, whose faith is standing merely in the wisdom of men, and whose in the power of God. All that is hollow is being exposed, and will be so more and more; but God will keep those whose hearts are true to the name of Jesus. "Thou wilt keep him in *perfect peace* whose mind is stayed on thee, because he trusteth in thee."

This is the soul's unfailing refuge, at all times. It was to this the apostle Paul directed the elders of Ephesus, at the close of his touching and pathetic address, in Acts xx. "And now, brethren, I commend you to GOD, and to the WORD of his grace." He does not commend them to any order of men; not even to apostles or their successors; to general councils or their decrees; to fathers or their traditions; to doctors or their dogmas. Ah! no; none of these would avail in the presence of the "grievous wolves" which were about to enter in among them, and amid the "perverse things" which some from among themselves would give utterance to. Nothing but God Himself and the word of His grace could stand, in an evil day, or enable a soul to stand.

There is something perfectly beautiful in the jealous care of the apostle Paul lest any should lean upon him, or upon anything save the living God Himself. Hearken to the following glowing passage, "For this cause also thank we God without ceasing, because, when ye received *the word of God* which ye heard of us, ye received it *not as the word of men*, but as it is in truth, *the word of God*, which effectually worketh also in you that believe." (1 Thess. ii. 13.) That devoted, single-hearted workman only sought to connect souls with God by means of His word. This is the object of all true ministry. Where the ministry is not true, not of God, it will connect souls with itself; and, in that case human influence will be brought to bear—weight of character—education—mental power —wealth—position—a thousand things, in short, which are all used to form a foundation for the soul's confidence and shut it out from God. Thus the faith of the soul is made to rest in the wisdom of men and not in the power of God.

Christian reader, we want you to ponder this matter deeply. Be assured it demands your serious attention. See that your soul is resting on the deep and solid foundation of God's word—that you have His direct and positive authority for where you are and what you are doing. And then see also that you have His presence with you. These two things will impart sweet peace to your spirit, and holy stability to your path, come what may. "Have not I commanded thee?"—"Lo, I am with thee." It is your happy privilege to know the reality of these things, just as fully and just as distinctly in your day, as did Joshua in his day, Jeremiah in his day, and the apostles in their day. The measure of apprehension may vary—the circumstances may differ; but the ground of principle is the same always. Do not, therefore, we entreat of you, be satisfied with anything less than God's authority and God's presence. Be not troubled or perplexed about the conflicting opinions of men. You must expect these. They are nothing new. But remember that, far above all the din and confusion, the strife and controversy, the opposition of sects and parties—far above all these things, in the clear light of the divine presence, in the calmness of the inner sanctuary, faith can hear with distinctness those precious, soul-sustaining accents, "Have not I commanded thee?"—"Lo, I am with thee."

These things can never fail, they are imperishable. See that you possess them, just now. Be able, in the calm dignity of a faith that rests only in the power and on the authority of God, to give a reason for the path that you tread, the work you do, the niche you fill. This is not highmindedness or haughtiness, dogmatism or pride, self-confidence or vainglory. It is the very reverse. It is self-abnegation and confidence in God. "With the lowly is wisdom." Precious truth! May we all remember it! It is the lowly mind that really possesses heavenly wisdom. It is not the learned, the astute, the long-headed, or clear-headed among men that can thread their way through the labyrinths of the present moment; no, it is the lowly, the simple, the self-distrusting, the childlike, the unpretending. These are they who will have wisdom to guide them, in darkest times—these are they who will possess peace in their souls and stability in their ways. May God's Spirit lead us into these things!

# OBEDIENCE: WHAT IS IT? AND ARE WE YIELDING IT?

It is of the very last possible importance for the Christian to have a clear apprehension of the true character of christian obedience. It is, of course, perfectly evident that I must be a Christian before ever I can yield christian obedience. A child can understand this. I must be in a position in order to discharge the duties which belong to it. I must be in a relationship ere I can know, feel, or display the affections which flow out of it.

If we keep this simple principle in our minds, it will prevent our attaching a legal idea to the word obedience. There is not, and cannot be, a single trace of legality in the obedience to which we are called as Christians, seeing that, ere we can take a step in that most blessed path, we must have divine life. And how do we get this life? "Not by works of righteousness," surely; not by legal efforts of any kind whatsoever, but by the free gift of God—all praise and thanks to His holy name! "The gift of God is eternal life, through Jesus Christ our Lord." And how is this life communicated? How are we quickened, or born again? By the word and Spirit of God, and in no other way. We are by nature "dead in trespasses and sins." There is not in any son or daughter of Adam a single pulsation of divine life. Take the very fairest specimen of mere nature—take the most refined, cultivated, moral, and amiable person in the very highest circle of social life; take the most religious and devout person in mere nature, and there is not so much as one spark of divine or spiritual life.

This, no doubt, is very humbling to the human heart, but it is the plain truth of holy scripture, which must be constantly maintained and faithfully set forth. We are by nature alienated from God, enemies in our minds by wicked works, and hence we have neither the will nor the power to obey. There must be a new life, a new nature, before a single step can be taken in the blessed pathway of obedience; and this new life is communicated to us by the free grace of God, through the operation of the Spirit, who quickens us by the word.

A passage or two of holy scripture will set this matter clearly before the mind of the reader. In John iii. we read, "Except a man be born of water and of the Spirit, he cannot enter the kingdom of God." Here we have the word presented under the figure of water, as we read in Ephesians v. of "the washing of water by the word." Again, in James i. we read, "Of his own will begat he us, by the word of truth." It is not possible to conceive anything more entirely independent of human effort than the new birth as here set forth. It is wholly of God, of His own will, and by His own power. What has a man to do with his natural birth? Surely nothing. What, then, can he have to do with his spiritual birth? It is of God exclusively, from first to last. All praise to Him that it is so!

Take one more uncommonly fine passage on this great subject. In I Peter i. 23, we read, "Being born again, not of corruptible seed, but of incorruptible, by the word of God, which liveth and abideth for ever. For all flesh is as grass, and all the glory of man as the flower of grass. The grass withereth, and the flower thereof falleth away. But the word of the Lord endureth for ever. And this is the word which by the gospel is preached unto you."

Nothing can be more precious than this. When the glad tidings of salvation fall with power upon the heart, that is the birth moment. The word is the seed of divine life, deposited in the soul by the Holy Ghost. Thus we are born again. We are renewed in the very deepest springs of our moral being. We are introduced into the blessed relationship of sons, as we read in Galatians iv. "When the fulness of the time was come, God sent forth his Son"—marvellous grace!—"made of a woman, made under the law, to redeem them that were under the law, that we might receive the adoption of sons. And because ye are sons, God hath sent forth the Spirit of His Son into your hearts, crying, Abba, Father. Wherefore thou art no more a servant, but a son; and if a son, then an heir of God through Christ."

Here, then, we have the true ground of obedience clearly and fully set before us. It is eternal life possessed, and eternal relationship enjoyed. There can be no legality here. We are no more servants on legal ground, but sons, on the blessed and elevated ground of divine love.

But we must remember that we are called to obedience. "Lord, what wilt thou have me to do?" is the very first breathing of a new-born soul. It was the question which emanated from the broken and penitent heart of Saul of Tarsus, when smitten to the ground by the manifested glory of the Son of God. Up to that moment, he had lived in rebellion against that blessed One; but now he was called to yield himself, body, soul, and spirit, to a life of unqualified obedience. Was there aught of the legal element in this? Not a trace, from beginning to end. "The love of Christ," he says, "constraineth us; because we thus judge, that if one died for all, then were all dead. And that he died for all, that they which live should not henceforth live unto themselves, but unto him which died for them, and rose again." 2 Corinthians v.

Here, beloved christian reader, lies the grand motive-spring of all christian obedience. Life is the ground; love the spring. "If ye love me, keep my commandments." And again, "He that hath my commandments, and keepeth them, he it is that loveth me; and he that loveth me shall be loved of my Father, and I will love him, and will manifest myself to him." How precious! Who can adequately set forth the blessedness of this manifestation of Christ to the obedient heart? Should we not earnestly long to know more of it? Can we expect it if we are living in the habitual neglect of His holy commandments? It is "he that hath my commandments, and keepeth them, he it is that loveth me." Have we His commandments? And are we keeping them? How utterly worthless is mere lip profession! It is like the son in the parable, who said, "I go, sir, and went not." It is empty, hollow, contemptible mockery. What father would care for loud profession of affection on the part of a son who cared not to carry out his wishes? Could such a son expect to enjoy much of his father's company or confidence? Surely not; indeed it is more than questionable if he could value either the one or the other. He might be ready enough to accept all that the father's hand could bestow to meet his personal wants; but there is a very wide difference indeed between receiving gifts

70

from a father's hand, and enjoying fellowship with that father's heart.

It is this latter we should ever seek, and it is the precious fruit of loving obedience to our Father's words. "If a man love me, he will keep my words; and my Father will love him, and we will come unto him, and make our abode with him. He that loveth me not, keepeth not my sayings." Can aught, this side of heaven, be more precious than to have the Father and the Son coming to us, and making their mansion with us? Do we know what it means? Do we enjoy it? Is it common to all? By no means! It is known only to those who know, and have, and keep the words of Jesus. He speaks of "his commandments" and "his words." What is the difference? The former set forth our holy duty; the latter are the expression of His holy will. If I give my child a commandment, it is his duty to obey, and if he loves me, he will delight to obey. But supposing he has heard me saying, "I like so-and-so," and that he does that thing, without being directly commanded to do it, he gives me a much more touching proof of his love, and of his affectionate interest in all my wishes; and this, we may rest assured, is most grateful to a loving father's heart, and he will respond to this loving obedience by making the obedient child his companion, and the depositary of this thoughts.

But there is more than this. In John xv. we read, "If ye abide in me, and my words abide in you, ye shall ask what ye will, and it shall be done unto you. Herein is my Father glorified, that ye bear much fruit; so shall ye be my disciples. As the Father hath loved me, so have I loved you."—Amazing truth!—"Continue [or abide] ye in my love." How is this to be done? "If ye keep my commandments, ye shall continue [or abide] in my love; even as I have kept my Father's commandments, and abide in his love."

Here we learn the wondrous truth that we are called to the very same kind of obedience as that which our adorable Lord and Saviour rendered to the Father, when He walked as a man on this earth. We are brought into full fellowship with Himself, both in the love wherewith we are loved, and the obedience which we are privileged to render. This is most blessedly confirmed by the Spirit in the First Epistle of Peter, where Christians are spoken of as

71

"Elect according to the foreknowledge of God the Father, through sanctification of the Spirit, unto obedience, and sprinkling of the blood of Jesus Christ." Chapter i. 2.

Let the reader carefully note this. We are elected of the Father, and sanctified by the Spirit to obey as Jesus obeyed. Such is the plain teaching of the passage. That blessed One found His meat and drink in doing the Father's will. His only motive for acting was the Father's will. "I delight to do thy will, O my God." There was no opposing element in Him, as there is, alas! in us. But, blessed be His name! He has linked us with Himself, and called us into blessed fellowship, both in the Father's love to Him, and in His obedience to the Father.

Marvellous privilege! Would that we appreciated it more! Oh, that we rendered a more loving obedience to all His precious commandments and sayings, that so He might manifest Himself to us, and make His abode with us. Blessed Lord, do make us more obedient in all things!

# PREACHING CHRIST: WHAT IS IT?

"Philip went down to Samaria, and preached Christ unto them."
(Acts viii.) This brief and simple statement embodies in it a grand
characteristic feature of Christianity—a feature which distinguishes
it from every system of religion that now exists, or that ever was
propounded in this world. Christianity is not a set of abstractions
—a number of dogmas—a system of doctrines. It is, pre-eminently,
a religion of living facts—of divine realities—a religion which finds
its centre in a divine Person, the Man Christ Jesus. He is the
foundation of all christian doctrine. From His divine and glorious
Person all truth radiates. He is the living fountain whence all the
streams issue forth in fulness, power, and blessing. "In him was
life, and the life was the light of men." Apart from Him all is
death and darkness. There is not one atom of life, not one ray of
light, in all this world, save what emanates from Him. A man may
possess all the learning of the schools; he may bask in the most
brilliant light that science can pour upon his understanding and
his pathway; he may garnish his name with all the honours which
his fellow mortals can heap upon him; but if there is the breadth
of a hair between him and Jesus—if he is not in Christ and Christ
in him—if he has not believed on the Name of the only begotten
Son of God, he is involved in death and darkness. Christ is "the
true light which lighteneth every man that cometh into the
world;" and hence no man can, in a divine sense, be termed an
enlightened man, save "a man in Christ."

It is well to be clear as to this. It is needful to press it, in this
day of man's pride and pretension. Men are boasting of their light
and intelligence—of the progress of civilization—of the research
and discovery of the age in which our lot is cast—of the arts and
sciences and what has been wrought and produced by their means.
We do not want to touch these things. We are quite willing to
let them stand for what they are really worth; but we are arrested
by these words which fell from the Master's lips, "I am the light

of the world; he that followeth me shall not walk in darkness, but shall have the light of life." Here it is, "He that followeth me." Life and light are only to be had in Jesus. If a man is not following Jesus, he is plunged in death and darkness, even though he were possessed of the most commanding genius, and enriched with all the stores of science and knowledge.

Doubtless, we shall be deemed narrow-minded, in thus writing. We shall, by very many, be regarded as men of very contracted views indeed—men of one idea, and even that one idea presented in a one-sided way. Well, be it so. We are men of one idea; and we heartily desire we were more so. But what is that one idea? Christ. He is God's grand idea, blessed be His Name, for evermore. Christ is the sum and substance of all that is in the mind of God. He is the central object in heaven—the grand fact of eternity—the object of God's affection—of angels' homage—of saints worship—of devils' dread—the alpha and the omega of the divine counsels—the keystone of the arch of revelation—the central sun of God's universe.

All this being so, we need not marvel at Satan's constant effort to keep souls from coming to Christ, and to draw them away from Him, after they have come to Him. He hates Christ, and will use anything and everything to hinder the heart in getting hold of Him. He will use cares or pleasures, poverty or riches, sickness or health, vice or morality, profanity or religion; in short, he cares not what it is, provided he can keep Jesus out of the heart.

On the other hand, the constant object of the Holy Ghost is to present Christ Himself to the soul. It is not something about Christ, doctrines respecting Him, or principles connected with Him merely; but His own very self, in living power and freshness. We cannot read a page of the New Testament without noticing this. The whole book, from the opening lines of Matthew, to the close of the Revelation, is simply a record of facts, as some one has truly said, respecting Jesus. It is not our purpose, just now, to follow out this record; to do so would be interesting beyond expression; but it would lead us away from our immediate thesis to which we must now, in the name of the Lord, and in dependence upon His Spirit, address ourselves. May it be unfolded and applied in the power of the Holy Ghost!

In studying scripture in connexion with our subject, we shall find the Lord Jesus Christ presented in three ways, namely, as a *test*; as a *victim*; and as a *model*. Each of these points contains in itself a volume of truth, and when we view them in their connection, they open to our souls a wide field of christian knowledge and experience. Let us, then, in the first place, consider what is meant when we speak of

### CHRIST AS A TEST

In contemplating the life of the Lord Jesus, as a man, we have the perfect exhibition of what a man ought to be. We see in Him the two grand creature perfections, namely, obedience and dependence. Though God over all, the Almighty Creator and Sustainer of the wide universe—though He could say, "I clothe the heavens with blackness, and I make sackcloth their covering." Yet so thoroughly and absolutely did He take the place of a man on this earth, that He could say, "the Lord God hath given me the tongue of the learned, that I should know how to speak a word in season to him that is weary: he wakeneth morning by morning, He wakeneth mine ear to hear as the learned. The Lord hath opened mine ear, and I was not rebellious, neither turned away back." (Is. 1.4-5.) He never moved one step without divine authority. When the devil tempted Him to work a miracle, in order to satisfy His hunger, His reply was, "*It is written*, Man shall not live by bread alone, but by every word that proceedeth out of the mouth of the Lord." He would readily work a miracle to feed others, but not to feed Himself. Again, when tempted to cast Himself from the pinnacle of the temple, He replied, "*It is written*, Thou shalt not tempt the Lord thy God." He had no command from God to cast Himself down, and He could not act without it; to do so would be a tempting of Providence. So also, when tempted with the offer of all the kingdoms of this world, on condition of doing homage to Satan, His reply was, "*It is written*, Thou shalt worship the Lord thy God, and him only shalt thou serve."

In a word, the Man Christ Jesus, was perfectly obedient. Nothing could tempt Him to diverge the breadth of a hair from the narrow path of obedience. He was the obedient Man from first to last. It was quite the same to Him where He served, or what He did. He would act by the authority of the divine word. He would take bread from God; He would come to His temple when sent of God, and He would wait for God's time to receive the kingdoms of this world. His obedience was absolute and uninterrupted, from the manger to the cross, and in this He was well pleasing to God. It was creature perfection; and nothing in any wise different from this could be agreeable to God. If perfect obedience is grateful to God, then disobedience must be hateful. The life of Jesus, in this one feature of it, was a continual feast to the heart of God. His perfect obedience was continually sending up a cloud of the most fragrant incense to the throne of God.

Now, this is what a man ought to be. We have here a perfect test of man's condition; and when we look at ourselves in the light of this one ray of Christ's glory, we must see our entire departure from the true and only proper place of the creature. The light that shines from the character and ways of Jesus reveals, as nothing else could reveal, the moral darkness of our natural state. We are not obedient; we are willful; we do our own pleasure; we have cast off the authority of God; His word does not govern us. "The carnal mind is enmity against God; it is not subject to the law of God; neither indeed can be." (Rom. viii.)

It may be asked, "Did not the law make manifest the wilfulness and enmity of our hearts?" No doubt; but who can fail to see difference between a law demanding obedience, and the Son of the God, as Man, exhibiting obedience? Well then, in so far as the life and ways of the blessed Lord Jesus Christ transcend in glory the entire legal system, and in so far as the Person of Christ transcends in glory and dignity the person of Moses, just so far does Christ, as a test of man's condition, exceed, in moral power, the law of Moses; and the same holds good of every test that was ever applied, and every other standard that was ever set up. The Man Christ Jesus, viewed in the one point of perfect obedience, is an absolutely perfect test by which our natural state can be tried and made manifest.

But take another ray of Christ's moral glory. He was as absolutely *dependent* upon God, as He was *obedient* to Him. He could say, "preserve me, O God, for in thee do I put my trust." (Ps. xvi.) And again, "I was cast upon thee from the womb." (Ps. xxii.) He never, for one moment, abandoned the attitude of entire dependence upon the living God. It is befitting the creature to be dependent upon God for everything. This the blessed Jesus ever was. He breathed the very atmosphere of dependence, all the way through from Bethlehem to Calvary. He was the only man that ever lived a life of uninterrupted dependence upon God, from first to last. Others have depended partially, He did it perfectly. Others have occasionally, or, it may be, mainly looked to God; He never looked anywhere else. He found *all* His springs; not some of them, or most of them, in God.

This, too, was most grateful to God. To have a man, on this earth, whose heart was never, for one single moment of time, out of the attitude of dependence, was ineffably precious to the Father, and hence, again and again, heaven opened, and the testimony came forth, "This is my beloved Son, in whom I am well pleased."

But, if this feature in the perfect life of the Man, Christ Jesus, was infinitely agreeable to the mind of God, it also furnishes an infinitely powerful test of the natural state of man. We can here see, as we can see nowhere else, our apostacy from the creature's only proper place—the place of dependence. True, the inspired historian informs us, in Genesis iii. that the first Adam fell from his original place of obedience and dependence. True, also, the law of Moses makes manifest that Adam's descendants are, every one of them, in a condition of revolt and independence; but who can fail to see with what superior power all this is brought out by the life and ways of Jesus, in this world? In Him we see a man perfectly obedient and perfectly dependent, and that, too, in the midst of a scene of disobedience and independence, and in the face of every temptation to abandon the position which He occupied.

Thus, the life of Jesus, in this one particular point of perfect dependence, tests man's condition, and proves his entire departure from God. Man, in his natural state, ever seeks to be independent of God. We need not go into any detailed proof of this. This one ray of light, emanating from the glory of Christ, and shining into man's heart, lays bare every chamber thereof, and proves beyond all question—proves, in a way that nought else could prove, man's departure from God, proves the haughty independence which marks our natural condition. The more intense the light which you bring to bear upon an object, the more perfectly you can see what it is. There is a vast difference between looking at a picture in the dim morning twilight, and examining it in broad daylight. Thus it is, exactly, in reference to our real state by nature. We may view it in the light of the law, in the light of conscience, in the light of the loftiest standard of morality known amongst men; and, so viewing it, we may see that it is not what it ought to be; but it is only when we view it in the full blaze of the moral glory of Christ that we can see it as it really is. It is one thing to say, "We have done those things which we ought not to have done, and left undone those things which we ought to have done;" and it is another thing altogether to see ourselves in that perfect light which makes everything manifest. It is one thing to look at our ways in the light of law, conscience, or morality, and another thing to look at our nature, in the light of that all-powerful test, namely, the life of the Man Christ Jesus.

But we must proceed, and shall merely refer to one more feature in the character of Christ, and that is His perfect self-emptiness. He never once sought His own interest, in anything. His was a life of constant self-sacrifice. "The Son of Man has come to serve and to give." These two words "serve" and "give" formed the motto of His life, and were written, in letters of blood, upon His cross. In His marvelous life, and in His mysterious death, He was the Servant and the Giver. He was ever ready to answer every form of human need. We see Him, at Sychar's lonely well, opening the fountain of living water to a poor thirsty soul. We see Him, at the pool of Bethesda, imparting strength to a poor impotent cripple. We see Him, at the gate of Nain, drying the widow's tears, and giving back to her bosom her only son.

All this and much more we see; but we never see Him looking

after His own interests. No, never! We cannot too deeply ponder this fact in the life of Jesus; nor can we too jealously scrutinize ourselves in the light which this wondrous fact emits. If in the light of His perfect obedience, we can detect our terrible wilfulness; if in the light of His absolute dependence, we can discern our pride and haughty independence; then surely, in the light of His self-emptiness and self-sacrifice, we may discover our gross selfishness, in its ten thousand forms, and as we discover it, we must loathe and abhor ourselves. Jesus never thought of Himself, in anything he ever said or did. He found meat and His drink in doing the will of God, and in meeting the need of man.

What a test is here! How it proves us! How it makes manifest what is in us, by nature! How it sheds its bright light over man's nature and man's world, and rebukes both the one and the other! For what, after all, is the great root-principle of nature and of this world? Self. "Men will praise thee when thou doest well to thyself." (Ps. xlix.) Self-interest is really the governing principle in the life of every unrenewed man, woman, and child, in this world. No doubt, nature may clothe itself in very amiable and attractive forms—it may assume a very generous and benevolent aspect—it can scatter as well as hoard; but of this we may rest assured, that the unregenerate man is wholly incapable of rising above self as an object; and in no way could this be made so thoroughly manifest—in no way could it be developed with such force and clearness—in no way could its vileness and hideousness be so fully detected and judged, as in the light of that perfect test presented in the disinterested, self-sacrificing life of our blessed Lord Jesus Christ. It is when that penetrating light shines upon us that we see ourselves in all our true native depravity and personal vileness.

The Lord Jesus came into this world, and lived a perfect life—perfect in thought, perfect in word, perfect in action; He perfectly glorified God, and not only so, but He perfectly tested man. He shewed what God is, and He shewed also what man ought to be—shewed it not merely in His doctrine, but in His walk. Man was never so tested before, and, hence, the Lord Jesus could say, "If I had not come and spoken unto them, they had not had sin; but now they have no cloke for their sin. He that hateth me, hateth my Father also. If I had not done among them the works which none other man did, they had not had sin; but now have they both seen and hated both me and my Father." John xv. 22-24.

Again, He says, "I judge no man; and yet if I judge, my judgment is true." (John viii. 15-16.) The object of His mission was not judgment but salvation, yet the effect of His life was judgment upon everyone with whom He came in contact. It was impossible for anyone to stand in the light of Christ's moral glory, and not be judged in the very centre and source of His being. When Peter saw himself in that light, he exclaimed, "Depart from me for I am a sinful man, O Lord." Luke v.

Such was the certain result of a man's seeing himself in the presence of Christ. Not all the thunderings and lightnings of Mount Sinai—not all the denunciations of the legal system—not all the voices of the prophets could produce such an effect upon a sinner as one single ray of the moral glory of Christ darting into his soul. I may look at the law and feel I have not kept it, and own I deserve its curse; conscience may terrify me and tell me I deserve hell-fire because of my sins. All this is true: but oh! the very moment I see myself in the light of what Christ is, my whole moral being is laid bare—every root, every fibre, every motive spring, every element, all the sources of thought, feeling, desire, affection, and imagination are exposed to view, and I abhor myself. It cannot possibly be otherwise. The whole book of God proves it. The history of all God's people illustrates it. To adduce cases would fill a volume. True conviction is produced in the soul when the Holy Ghost lets in upon it the light of the glory of Christ. Law is a reality, conscience is a reality, and the Spirit of God may and does make use of the former to act on the latter; but it is only when I see myself in the light of what Christ is, that I get a just view of myself, and then I am led to exclaim, with Job, "I have heard of thee by the hearing of the ear; but now mine eye seeth thee, therefore I abhor myself."

Reader, have you ever seen yourself in this way? Have you ever really tested yourself by the perfect standard of the life of Christ? It may be you have been looking at your fellow man and comparing yourself with that imperfect standard, and trying yourself by that imperfect test. This will never do. Christ is the true standard —the perfect test—the divine touchstone. God cannot have anything different from Christ. You must be like Him—conformed to His image, ere you can find your place in the presence of God. Do you ask, "How can this ever be?" By knowing Christ as the Victim, and by being formed after Him as the Model. But these points must be unfolded, if the Lord will, in our next.

# PART II

It is most needful, ere we proceed with the subject which has been engaging our attention, that the whole world, as such, and each human heart, in particular, should be seen and judged in the light of the moral glory of Christ—that divine and perfect test by which every one and everything must be tried. Christ is God's standard for all; and the more fully and faithfully the world and self are measured thereby, the better. The grand question for the whole world, and for each human heart, is this, "How has Christ been treated?—what have we done with Him?" God sent His only begotten Son into the world, as the expression of His love to sinners. He said, "It may be they will reverence my Son, when they see him." Did they do so? Alas! no. "They said, This is the heir; come let us kill him." It was thus the world treated Christ.

And, be it observed, it was not the world, in its dark pagan form, that so treated the blessed One. No; it was the world of the religious Jew, and of the polished and cultivated Greek. It was not into the dark places of the earth, as men speak, that Jesus came; but into the very midst of His own highly favoured people "who were Israelites; to whom pertained the adoption, and the glory, and the covenants, and the giving of the law, and the service of God, and the promises." It was to them He came, in meekness, lowliness, and love. It was among them He lived and laboured, and "went about doing good, and healing all that were oppressed of the devil, for God was with him." How did they treat Him? This is the question; let us ponder it deeply, and ponder, too, the answer. They preferred a murderer to the holy, spotless, loving Jesus. The world—the heart, got its choice. Jesus and Barabbas

81

were set before it; and the question was put, "Which will you have?" What was the answer—the deliberate, determined, answer? "Not this man, but Barabbas. Now Barabbas was a robber."

Tremendous fact!—a fact little weighed, little understood, little entered into—a fact which stamps the character of this present world, and tests and makes manifest the state of every unrepentant, unconverted heart beneath the canopy of heaven. If I want a true view of the world—of nature—of the human heart—of myself, whither shall I turn? To police reports? To the calendars of our Grand Juries? To the various statistics of the social and moral condition of our cities and towns? Nay; all these, it is true, may set before us facts which fill the soul with horror, and make the blood run cold. But let it be distinctly seen, and deeply felt, that all the facts that were ever recorded of crime, in its blackest and most fearful forms, are not to be compared with that one fact, the rejection and crucifixion of the Lord of glory. This crime stands out in bold black relief from the background of man's entire history, and fixes the true condition of the world, of man, of nature, of self.

Now, it is this we are anxious to urge upon the heart of the reader, ere we proceed to the second division of our subject. We do want him to seize this great, this potent fact. We have, again and again, referred to it, in the pages of "Things New and Old;" but it cannot possibly be too much enforced. It is the only way in which to get a right sense of what the world is, and of what the human heart is. Men may speak of the vast improvement which has taken place in the world, and of the dignity of human nature; but ah! the heart turns back to that hour in the which the world, when called to make a choice between the Lord of glory and a murderer, deliberately selected the latter and nailed the former to a tree, between two malefactors. This crime of crimes remains, so far as the world is concerned, uncancelled, unforgiven. It stands recorded, in dark and awful characters, on the eternal page. And not only is this so, as regards the world as a whole, but it also holds good, in reference to the unrepentant, unconverted reader of these lines. The solemn question still remains to be answered—answered by the world—answered by the individual sinner, namely, "What have you done with the Son of God? What has become of Him? How have you treated Him?" Of what use is it to point to the progress of the human race? to the march of civilization? to the advance of the arts and sciences? to railroads and telegraphs? to Armstrong guns and iron clad ships? to the ten thousand forms in which human genius has tasked itself in order to minister to human lust, luxury and self-indulgence! All these things might be far outweighed by the misery, the moral degradation, the squalid poverty, the ignorance and vice in which more than nine-tenths of the human race are, at this moment, involved.

But it is not thus we meet the question at all. We do not attempt to put barbarism against civilization, poverty against luxury, grossness against refinement, ignorance against intelligence; by no means. We have but the one test, the one standard, the one gauge, and that is the cross to which Jesus was nailed by the representatives of this world's religion, its science, its politics, and its civilization.

It is here we take our stand and ask this question, Has the world ever yet repented of this act? Nay; for had it done so, the kingdoms of this world would have become the kingdoms of our Lord and of His Christ. It is here we take our stand, and ask the reader, Have you repented of this act? He may say, "I never did it. It was done by wicked Jews and wicked Romans eighteen hundred and thirty three years ago. How could I be counted guilty of a crime which was committed so many centuries before I was born?"

We reply, It was the act of the world, and you are either, at this moment, part and parcel of that world which stands before God under the guilt of the murder of His Son, or you have, as a repentant and converted soul, found refuge and shelter in the pardoning love of God. There is no middle ground, and the more clearly you see this the better, for in no way can you have a just sense of the condition of this world, or of your own heart, save in the light which is cast thereon by the life and death of Christ, as a test. We cannot stop short of this mark, if we would form a true estimate of the character of the world, the nature of man, the condition of the unconverted soul. In so far as the world is concerned, there can be no real improvement in its condition, no radical change in its state, until the sword of divine judgment has settled the question of its treatment of the Son of God; and, in so far as the individual sinner is concerned, the divine testimony is, "Repent and be converted, that your sins may be blotted out."

But this leads us, in the second place, to contemplate

## CHRIST AS A VICTIM

This is a much more pleasing subject to dwell upon, though, surely, the other must never be omitted, in preaching Christ. It is too much lost sight of in our preaching. We do not sufficiently press home upon the conscience of the sinner, Christ both in life and death, as a test of nature's true condition, and a proof of its irremediable ruin. The law may be used, and rightly so, no doubt, to do its testing work in the conscience, and yet, through the blindness and folly of our hearts, we may attempt to take up that very law in order to work out a righteousness for ourselves—that law by which, when rightly viewed, is the knowledge of sin. But it is impossible for any one to have his eyes opened to see the death of Christ as the terrible exhibition of the enmity of the heart against God, and not be convinced of this that he is utterly and hopelessly ruined and undone. This is true repentance. It is the moral judgment, not merely of my *acts*, but of my *nature*, in the light of the cross as the only perfect test of what that nature really is.

All this is very fully brought out, in the preaching of Peter, in the earlier chapters of the Acts of the Apostles. Look, for example, at the second chapter, where we find the Holy Ghost presenting Christ both as a test and as a victim. "Ye men of Israel, hear these words: Jesus of Nazareth, a man approved of God among you, by miracles and wonders and signs, which God did, by him, in the midst of you, as ye yourselves also know. Him, being delivered by the determinate counsel and foreknowledge of God, ye have taken, and by wicked hands have crucified and slain; whom God hath raised up, having loosed the pains of death; because it was not possible that he should be holden of it. . . . Therefore let all the house of Israel know assuredly, that God hath made that same Jesus, whom ye have crucified, both Lord and Christ."

84

Here we have solemn and pungent dealing with conscience as to the way in which they had treated the Lord's Anointed. It was not merely that they had broken the law; that was true; nor yet that they had merely rejected all the inferior messengers, the minor witnesses that had been sent to them; that was equally true, but that was not all; they had actually crucified and slain "a man approved of God," and that Man none other than the Son of God Himself. This was the naked and startling fact which the inspired preacher urges home, with solemn emphasis, upon the consciences of his hearers.

And, mark the result! "Now, when they heard this, they were pricked in their hearts, and said unto Peter and to the rest of the apostles, Men and brethren, what shall we do?" No marvel, surely, that they were pierced to the very heart. Their eyes were open, and what did they discover? Why, that they were actually at issue with God Himself—the God of Abraham, Isaac, and Jacob. And about what were they at issue? About the law? Nay. About the prophets? Nay. About the rites and ceremonies the statutes and institutions of the Mosaic economy? Nay. All this was true, and bad enough. But there was something far beyond all this. Their guilt had reached its culminating point in the rejection and crucifixion of Jesus of Nazareth. "The God of Abraham, and of Issac, and of Jacob, the God of our fathers, hath glorified his Son Jesus, whom ye delivered up, and denied him in the presence of Pilate, when he was determined to let him go. But ye denied the Holy One and the Just, and desired a murderer to be granted unto you; and killed the prince of life, whom God hath raised from the dead; whereof we are witnesses."

This truly was and is the climax of man's guilt, and when brought home, in the mighty energy of the Holy Ghost, to any heart in all this world, it must produce true repentance, and evoke from the depths of the soul the earnest inquiry, "Men and brethren, what shall I do?" "Sirs, what must I do to be saved?" It is not merely that we have failed in keeping the law, in doing our duty to God, and our duty to our neighbour, in living as we ought; all this alas! is but too true. But oh! we have been guilty of the dreadful sin of crucifying the Son of God. Such is the measure of human

85

guilt, and such was the truth pressed home by Peter on the consciences of the men of his time.

And what then? When the sharp edge of this powerful testimony had penetrated the hearts of the hearers—when the arrow from the quiver of the Almighty had pierced the soul, and drawn forth the bitter penitential cry, "What shall we do?" What was the answer? What had the preacher to say? "Repent and be baptized, every one of you in the name of Jesus Christ, for the remission of sins, and ye shall receive the gift of the Holy Ghost." So also in the third chapter, he says, "And now, brethren, I wot that through ignorance ye did it, as did also your rulers. But those things which God before had shewed by the mouth of all his prophets, that Christ should suffer, he hath so fulfilled. Repent ye therefore, and be converted, that your sins may be blotted out, when the times of refreshing shall come from the presence of the Lord."

Here, then, we have the two things, very distinctly, presented, namely, Christ as a test and Christ as a victim—the cross as the exhibition of man's guilt, and the cross as the exhibition of the love of God. "Ye killed the Prince of life." Here was the arrow for the conscience. "But those things which God before had shewed that Christ should suffer, he hath so fulfilled." Here was the healing balm. It was the determinate counsel of God that Christ should suffer, and, while it was perfectly true that man had displayed his hatred of God in nailing Jesus to the cross, yet no sooner is any soul made sensible of this, and thus brought to divine conviction, than the Holy Ghost holds up to view that very cross as the foundation of the counsels of redeeming love, and the ground of the full remission of sins to every true believer.

Thus it was, in that most touching scene between Joseph and his brethren, as recorded in Genesis xliv. and xlv. The guilty brethren are made to pass through deep and painful exercises of heart, until, at length, they stand in the presence of their injured brother, with the arrow of conviction piercing their inmost soul. Then, but not until then, these soothing accents fall upon their ears, "Now, therefore, be not grieved, nor angry with yourselves, that ye sold me hither; for God did send me before you to preserve life. . . . So now it was not you that sent me hither, but God."

Exquisite, matchless grace! The moment they entered the place of confession, Joseph was in the place of forgiveness. This was divine. "He spake roughly to them," when they were thoughtless as to their sin; but no sooner did they give utterance to these words, "We are verily guilty concerning our brother," than they were met by the sweet response of grace, "It was not you, but God."

Thus it is, beloved reader, in every case. The very instant the sinner takes the place of contrition, God takes the place of full and free forgiveness; and, most assuredly, when God forgives, the sinner is forgiven. "I said, I will confess my transgressions unto the Lord, and thou forgavest the iniquity of my sin." Psalm xxxii.

And would we have it otherwise? Surely not. An hard heart, an unbroken spirit, an unreached conscience, could not understand, or make a right use of such words as, "Be not grieved; it was not you, but God." How could it? How could an impenitent heart appreciate accents which are only designed to soothe and tranquillize a broken and contrite spirit? Impossible. To tell a hard hearted impenitent sinner not to be grieved, would be fatally false treatment. Joseph could not possibly have said to his brethren, "Be not grieved with yourselves" until they had said and felt "We are verily guilty."

Such is the order, and it is well to remember it. 'I will confess, and thou forgavest." The moment the sinner takes his true place in the presence of God, there is not one syllable said to him about his sins except it be to tell him that they are all forgiven and all forgotten. "Their sins and iniquities will I remember no more." God not only forgives but forgets. The convicted sinner stands and gazes upon the cross, and sees himself in the light of the glory of Christ, as the divine and perfect test, and cries out, "What shall I do?" How is he answered? By the unfolding of Christ, as a victim, slain by the determinate counsel and foreknowledge of God, to put away sin by the sacrifice of Himself.

And who can define the feelings of a soul that has been convicted of desiring a murderer and crucifying the Son of God, when he learns that that very crucified One is the channel of pardon and life to him—that the blood which was shed puts away for ever the guilt of shedding it? What language can adequately set forth the emotion of one who has seen his guilt, not merely in the light of the ten commandments, but as shewn out in the cross of a world-rejected Jesus; and yet knows and believes that his guilt is all and for ever put away? Who could attempt to embody in language the feelings of Joseph's brethren when they felt his tears of affection dropping upon them? What a scene! Tears of contrition and tears of affection mingled! Precious mixture! The mind of God alone can duly estimate its value and sweetness.

But here let us just guard against misunderstanding. Let no one suppose, for a moment, that tears of contrition are the procuring cause of pardon, or the meritorious ground of peace. Far—far away be the thought from the reader's mind! All the tears of contrition that ever gushed forth from the fountains of broken hearts, from the days of Joseph's brethren to the days of the third of Acts, and from these latter to the present moment, could not form the just foundation of a sinner's acceptance and peace with God, or wash away a single stain from the human conscience. The blood of the divine Victim, and that alone, in prospect from the fall of man to Calvary, and in retrospect, from Calvary till this moment— nought save that precious blood—that atoning death—that peerless sacrifice could justify a holy God in forgiving one sin. But, blessed be God, so perfectly has that sacrifice vindicated and glorified His Name, that the very moment any sinner sees his true state—his guilt—his rebellion—his enmity—his base ingratitude—his hatred of God and of His Christ; the very moment he takes the place of true contrition in the divine presence—the place of one utterly broken down, without plea of palliation—that moment, infinite grace meets him with those healing, soothing, tranquillizing words, "Be not grieved"—"your sins and iniquities will I remember no more"—"Go in peace."

Some might suppose that we attach undue importance to the measure of contrition, or that we mean to teach that every one must feel the same character or degree of conviction as was produced by Peter's powerful appeal in the second of Acts. Nothing is further from our thoughts. We believe there must and there will be conviction and contrition; and further we believe that the cross

88

is the only adequate measure of human guilt—that it is only in the light of that cross that any one can have a just sense of the vileness, sinfulness, and loathsomeness of his nature. But all may not see this. Many there are who never think of the cross as a test and proof of their guilt, but merely as the blessed ground of their pardon. They are bowed down under a sense of their manifold sins and shortcomings, and they look to the cross of Christ as the alone ground of pardon; and, most surely they are right. But there is something deeper than this. There is a deeper view of sin—a deeper sense of what human nature, in its fallen state, really is—a deeper conviction of the utterly godless and christless condition of the heart. And where is this to be reached? At the cross, and there alone. It will never do to look back at the men of the first century, and say what terrible sinners they were to crucify the living embodiment of all that was holy and good, gracious and pure. No; what is needed is to bring the cross forward into this our own nineteenth century and measure nature, the world, and self thereby.

This, be assured of it, reader, is the true way to judge the question. There is no real change. "Crucify him! Crucify him!" is as positively the cry of the world of the nineteenth century as it was of the world of the first. The cross was, then, and is, now, the only true measure of human guilt; and when any one, man, woman, or child is brought to see this, he has a far deeper sense of his condition than ever he can have by looking at his sins and shortcomings in the light of conscience, or of the ten commandments.

And to what, let us enquire, will all this lead the soul? What will be the effect of seeing *self* in the light which the cross, as a test, throws upon it? The deepest self-abhorrence. Yes, and this holds good in the case of the most refined moralist, and amiable pietist that ever lived, just as much as in the case of the grossest and vilest sinner. It is no longer a question of grades and shades of character, to be settled by the graduated scale of human conscience or the moral sense. Oh! no; the cross is seen as the only perfect standard. Nature, the world, the heart, self, is measured by that standard, and its true condition reached and judged.

We are intensely anxious that the reader should thoroughly enter into this point. If we mistake not, he will find it to be of immense moral power in forming his convictions, both as to his own heart, and as to the real character of the world through which he is passing—its moral foundations—its framework—its features—its principles—its spirit—its aim—its end. We want him to take the cross as the perfect measure of himself and all around him. Let him not listen to the suggestions of Satan to the thoughts that spring up in his own heart, to the vapourings of philosophy and science, falsely so-called, to the infidel vauntings of this pre-eminently infidel age. Let him listen to the voice of holy scripture, which is the voice of the living God. Let him use the test which scripture furnishes, and that is a crucified Christ, and let him try all that, and see where that will lead him. One thing is certain, it will lead him down, in his own self-consciousness, into those profound depths where nought can avail him save Christ as the divine Victim who bore the judgment of God against *sin*, and opened heaven to the sinner.

# PART III

Having, in our numbers for March and April, sought to present Christ as a *test*, and Christ as a *victim*, we shall now, in dependence upon divine guidance and teaching, proceed to consider Him as

### THE MODEL

to which the Holy Ghost seeks to conform every true believer. This will give great completeness to our subject, and open up a wide field of thought to the christian reader. God has predestinated His people to be conformed to the image of His Son, that He might be the firstborn among many brethren. (Rom. viii.) But how, it may be asked, can we ever be formed after such a model? How can we ever think of being conformed to such an image? The answer to these enquiries will unfold, still more fully, the blessedness and infinite value of the truth which has already passed before us. If the reader has followed the line of thought we have been pursuing—if he has experimentally entered into it, or if it has entered into him, in the power of the Spirit of God—if, in a word, he has made his own of it, he will see, and feel, and own, that in himself, by nature, there is not a single atom of good, not one point on which he can rest his hopes for eternity. He will see that, so far as he is concerned, he is a total wreck; and, moreover, that the divine purpose, as revealed in the gospel, is not to reconstruct this moral wreck, but to erect an entirely new thing. Of this new thing, the cross of Christ is the foundation.

The reader cannot ponder this too deeply. Christianity is not the old nature made better, but the new nature implanted. "Except a man be born again, he cannot see the kingdom of God." (John iii.) "If any man be in Christ, he is a new creation; old things are passed away; behold, all things are become new. And all things are of God who hath reconciled us to himself by Jesus Christ, and hath given to us the ministry of reconciliation." 2 Cor. v.

The effect of the mission of Christ to this world was to prove, as nothing else could have proved, man's totally irremediable ruin. When man rejected and crucified the Son of God, his case was proved to be hopeless. It is of the deepest importance to be thoroughly clear as to this. It solves a thousand difficultes, and clears the prospect of many a dark and heavy cloud. So long as a man is possessed with the idea that he must improve his nature, by any process whatever, so long he must be a total stranger to the fundamental truth of Christianity.

There is, alas! a fearful amount of darkness and error abroad, in the professing Church, as to this simple truth of the gospel. Man's total ruin is denied or reasoned away, in one way or another; and the very truths of Christianity as well as the institutions of the Mosaic economy, are made use of to improve fallen nature and fit it for the presence of God. Thus the true nature of sin is not felt; the claims of holiness are not understood; the free, full, and sovereign grace of God is set aside; and the sacrificial death of Christ is thrown overboard.

The sense of all this makes us long for more earnestness, power, and faithfulness in setting forth those old foundation truths which are constantly affirmed and maintained in the New Testament. We believe it to be the solemn duty of every writer and every speaker, of all authors, editors, preachers, and teachers to make a firm stand against the strong current of opposition to the simplest truths of divine revelation, so painfully and alarmingly apparent in every direction. There is an urgent demand for faithfulness in maintaining the standard of pure truth, not in a spirit of controversy, but in meekness, earnestness, and simplicity. We want to have Christ preached as a test of all that is in man—in nature—in the world. We want Christ preached as a victim, bearing all that was due to our sins; and we want Him preached as a model on which we are to be formed, in all things.

This is Christianity. It is not fallen nature trying to work out righteousness by keeping the law of Moses. Neither is it fallen nature striving to imitate Christ. No; it is the complete setting aside of fallen nature, as an utterly good-for-nothing thing, and the reception of a crucified and risen Christ, as the foundation of all of our hopes for time and eternity. How could the unrenewed sinner get righteousness by keeping the law, by the which is the knowledge of sin? How could he ever set about such a work as "The imitation of Christ?" Utterly impossible. "He must be born again." He must get new life in Christ, ere he can exhibit Christ. This cannot be too strongly insisted upon. For an unconverted man to think of imitating the example, or walk in the footsteps of Jesus, is the most hopeless thing in the world. Ah! no; the only effect of looking at the blessed example of Jesus is to put us in the dust in self-abasement and true contrition; and when from this place we lift our eyes to the cross of Calvary to which Jesus was nailed, as our surety, our sin-bearer, our substitute, we see pardon and peace flowing down to us through His most precious sacrifice; then, but not until then, we can calmly and happily sit down to study Him as our model.

Thus, if I look at the life of Jesus, apart from His atoning death—if I measure myself by that perfect standard—if I think of working myself into conformity to such an image, it must plunge me in utter despair. But when I behold that perfect, spotless, holy One bearing my sins in His own body on the tree—when I see Him laying in His death and resurrection the everlasting foundation of life, and peace, and glory for me, then, with a peaceful conscience, and liberated heart, I can look back over the whole of that marvellous life and see therein how I am to walk, for "He has left us an example, that we should follow his steps." Thus, while Christ, as a *test*, shews me my guilt; Christ, as a *victim*, cancels that guilt; and Christ, as a *model*, shines before the vision of my soul, as the standard at which I am to aim continually. In a word, Christ is my life, and Christ is my model; and the Holy Ghost, who has taken up His abode in me, on the ground of accomplished redemption, works in me for the purpose of conforming me to the image of Christ. True, I must ever feel and own how infinitely short I come of that lofty standard; still, Christ is my life, though the manifestation of that life is sadly hindered by the infirmities and corruptions of my old nature. The life is the same, as the apostle John says, "Which thing *is* true in him and in you, because the darkness is past, and the true light now shineth." (I John ii. 8.) We can never be satisfied with aught less than this, namely, "Christ, our life—Christ, our model." "For me to live is Christ." It was Christ reproduced, in the daily life of Paul, by the power of the Holy Ghost.

This is true Christianity. It is not flesh turned religious and leading a pious life. It is not unrenewed, fallen, ruined *nature* trying to recover itself, by rites and ceremonies, prayers, alms, and vigils. It is not the old man turning from "wicked works" to "dead works" —exchanging the gin palace, the theatre, the gaming table, and the race course, for the cloister, the pew, the meeting house, or the lecture hall. No reader; it is "Christ in you, the hope of glory;" and Christ reproduced in your daily life, by the powerful ministry of God the Holy Ghost.

Be not deceived! It is of no possible use for fallen nature to clothe itself in forms of piety. It may do so—it may betake itself to the attractive appliances of ritualism—to sacred music—pious pictures—sculpture—architecture—dim religious light—it may scatter, in princely profusion, the fruits of a large-hearted benevolence —it may visit the sick, feed the hungry, clothe the naked, shed on all around the sunshine of a genial philanthropy—it may read the Bible and go through every form of religious routine—it may even attempt a specious and hollow imitation of Christ—schoolmen may discipline it, quietists may subdue it, mystics may enwrap it in their cloudy reveries, and lead it into quiet contemplation, with nothing to contemplate—in short, all that religion, morality, and philosophy can do for it and with it, may be done, and all in vain, inasmuch as it still remains true that, "That which is born of the flesh is flesh"—"It cannot see or enter the kingdom of God"—ye must be born again."

Here lies the deep and solid, the divine and eternal foundation of Christianity. There must be the life of Christ in the soul—the link with "the Second Man, the last Adam." The first man has been condemned and set aside. The Second Man came and stood beside the first, He proved him and tested him, and shewed out, most fully, that there was not a single ingredient in his nature, his character, or his condition which could be made available in that new creation, that heavenly kingdom which was about to be introduced—that not a single stone or timber in the old building could be worked into the new—that "in the flesh dwelleth no good thing"—and, finally, that the ground must be thoroughly cleared of all the rubbish of ruined humanity, and the foundation laid in the death of the Second Man, who, in resurrection, has become, as the last Adam, the Head of the new creation. Apart from Him there is, and can be, no life. "He that hath the Son hath life; he that hath not the Son of God hath not life." I John v. 12.

Such is the conclusive language of Holy Scripture, and this language must hold good, in spite of all the reasonings of those who boast themselves in their liberal and enlightened views—the compass of their intellectual powers—and the breadth of their theology. It matters but little indeed what men may think or say; we have only to hearken to the word of our God which must stand for ever, and that word declares, "Ye must be born again." Men cannot alter this. There is a kingdom which can never be moved, and, in order to see or enter this heavenly kingdom, we must be born again. Man has been tried in every way, and proved wanting, and now, "Once, in the end of the ages, hath Christ appeared to put away sin by the sacrifice of himself." Heb. ix. 26.

This is the only ground of life and peace, and when the soul is firmly settled thereon, it can find its delight in studying Christ as its model. It is done with all its own poor efforts to obtain life, pardon, and the favour of God; it flings aside its "deadly doings;" it has found life in Jesus, and now its grand business is to study Him, to mark His footsteps and walk therein—to do as He did, to aim always at being like Him; to seek, in everything, to be conformed to Him. The great question for the Christian, on all occasions, is not, "What harm is there in this or that?" but, "Is this like Christ?" He is our divine pattern. Are husbands exhorted to love their wives? It is "As Christ loved the church." What a model! Who can ever come up to it? No one; but we are still to keep it before us; and thus we shall enter into the truth of those lines of our own poet,

> "The more thy glories strike mine eyes,
>   The humbler I shall lie,
> Thus while I sink, my joys shall rise
>   Immeasurably high."

The christian reader will, at once, perceive what a wide field of practical truth is opened up by this closing point in our subject. What an unspeakable privilege to be able, day by day, to sit down and study life and ways of our Great Exemplar—to see what He was—to mark His words, His spirit, His style—to trace Him in all the details of His marvellous path—to note how "He went about doing good"—how it was His meat and His drink to do the will of God, and to minister to the need of man. And then to think that He loves us, that He died for us, that He is our life, that He has given us of His Spirit to be the spring of power in our souls, for the subjugation of all that is of the old root of self, and the producing, in our daily life, the expression of Christ.

What mortal tongue can unfold the preciousness of all this? It is not living by rules and regulations—it is not in pursuing a dead round of duties—it is not in subscribing to certain dogmas of religious belief—no; it is union with Christ and the manifestation of Christ. This, we repeat, and reiterate, and would impress upon the reader, this and nothing less, nothing different, is true, genuine, living Christianity. Let him see that he possesses it, for if not, he is dead in trespasses and sins; he is far from God, and far from the kingdom of God. But if, on the otherhand, he has been led to believe on the name of the only begotten Son of God; if as a consciously ruined and guilty sinner he has fled for refuge to the blood of the cross, then, in very deed, Christ is his life, and it should be his one unvarying object, day by day, to study his model, to fix his eye on the headline and aim at coming as near to that as possible. This is the true secret of all practical godliness and sanctification. It is this which alone constitutes a living Christianity, and it stands in vivid contrast with what is commonly called "a religious life," which, alas! very often resolves itself into a mere dead routine, a rigid adherence to lifeless forms, a barren ritualism, which, so far from exhibiting aught of the freshness and reality of the new man in Christ, is positively a distortion of nature itself. Christianity brings a living Christ into the heart, and into the life. It diffuses, thus, a divine influence all around. It enters into all the relations and associations of human life. It teaches us how to act as husbands, as fathers, as masters, as children, as servants. It teaches us not by dry rules and regulations, but by setting before us, in the Person of Christ, a perfect model of what we ought to be. It presents to our view the very One who, as a test, left us without a single plea, and, as a victim, left us without a single stain, and who now, as our model, is to be the subject of our admiring study, and the standard at which we are ever and only to aim. It does not matter where we are or what we are, provided Christ be dwelling in the heart, and exhibited in the daily life. If we have Him in the heart and before the eye, it will regulate everything; and if we have not Him, we have nothing.

We shall here close our paper; not, surely, because our theme is exhausted, but because it is inexhaustible, and further because we believe that the Spirit of God alone can open the subject and apply it, in living power and freshness to the soul of the reader, and thus lead him into a higher type of Christianity than is ordinarily exhibited, in this day of widely extended and worldly profession. May the Lord stir up all our hearts, to seek greater nearness to Himself, and more faithful conformity to Him, in all our ways! May we be enabled to say, with a little more truth and sincerity,

"Our citizenship is in heaven; from whence also we look for the Saviour, the Lord Jesus Christ; who shall change the body of our humiliation, that it may be fashioned like unto his body of glory, according to the working whereby he is able even to subdue all things unto himself."

# JONATHAN

## (I Samuel xviii. 1-4)

"And it came to pass, when he had made an end of speaking unto Saul, that the soul of Jonathan was knit with the soul of David: and Jonathan loved him as his own soul. . . . Then Jonathan and David made a covenant, because he loved him as his own soul. And Jonathan stripped himself of the robe that was upon him, and gave it to David, and his garments, even to his sword, and to his bow, and to his girdle."

What an exquisite picture we have here! A picture of love stripping itself to clothe its object. There is a vast difference between Saul and Jonathan in this scene. Saul took David home with him in order to magnify himself by keeping such an one about his person and in his house. But Jonathan stripped himself to clothe David. This was love in one of its charming activities. Jonathan, in common with the many thousands of Israel, had watched, with breathless interest, the scene in the valley of Elah. He had seen David go forth, single handed, to meet the terrible foe whose height, demeanour, and words had struck terror into the hearts of the people. He had seen that haughty giant laid low by the hand of faith. He participated with all in the splendid victory.

But there was more than this. It was not merely the victory but the victor that filled the heart of Jonathan—not merely the work done, but the one who had done it. Jonathan did not rest satisfied with saying, "Thank God, the giant is dead, and we are delivered, and may return to our homes and enjoy ourselves." Ah! no; he felt his heart drawn and knit to the person of the conqueror. It was not that he valued the victory less, but he valued the victor more, and hence he found his joy in stripping himself of his robes and his armour in order to put them upon the object of his affection.

Christian reader, there is a lesson here for us; and not only a lesson but a rebuke. How prone are we to be occupied with redemption rather than the Redeemer—with salvation rather than with the Saviour! No doubt we should rejoice in our salvation; but should we rest here? Should we not, like Jonathan, seek to strip ourselves in order to magnify the Person of Him who went down into the dust of death for us? Assuredly we should, and all the more because He does not exact aught of us. David did not ask Jonathan for his robe or his sword. Had he done so, it would have robbed the scene of all its charms. But no; it was a purely voluntary act. Jonathan forgot himself and thought only of David. Thus it should be with us and the true David. Love delights to strip itself for its object. "The love of Christ constraineth us." And again. "But what things were gain to me, those I counted loss for Christ. Yea, doubtless, and I count all things but loss, for the excellency of the knowledge of Christ Jesus my Lord: for whom I have suffered the loss of all things, and do count them but dung that I may win Christ." Phil. iii. 7, 8.

Oh! for more of this spirit! May our hearts be drawn out and knit, more and more, to Christ, in this day of hollow profession, and empty, religious formality! May we be so filled with the Holy Ghost, that with purpose of heart we may cleave unto our Lord and Saviour Jesus Christ!

# THE ALABASTER BOX

## (Matthew xxvi. 6-13.)

It is very needful to bear in mind, in this day of busy doing and restless activity, that God looks at everything from one standpoint, measures everything by one rule, tries everything by one touchstone, and that touchstone, that rule, that standpoint is Christ. He values things just so far as they stand connected with the Son of His love, and no farther. Whatever is done to Christ, whatever is done for Him, is precious to God. All beside is valueless. A large amount of work may be done, and a great deal of praise drawn forth thereby, from human lips; but when God comes to examine it, He will simply look for one thing, and that is, the measure in which it stands connected with Christ. His great question will be, Has it been done in, and to, the Name of Jesus? If it has, it will stand approved, and be rewarded; if not, it will be rejected and burnt up.

It does not matter in the least what men's thoughts may be about any particular piece of work. They may laud a person to the skies, for something he is doing; they may parade his name in the public journals of the day; they may make him the subject of discourse in their drawing room circle; he may have a great name as a preacher, a teacher, a writer, a philanthropist, a moral reformer; but, if he cannot connect his work with the name of Jesus—if it is not done to Him and to his glory—if it is not the fruit of the constraining love of Christ, it will all be blown away like the chaff of the summer threshing floor, and sunk into eternal oblivion.

On the contrary, a man may pursue a quiet, humble, lowly path of service, unknown and unnoticed. His name may never be heard, his work may never be thought of; but what has been done, has been done in simple love to Christ. He has wrought, in obscurity, with his eye on his Master. The smile of his Lord has been quite enough for him. He has never thought, for one moment, of seeking man's approval; he has never sought to catch his smile or shun his frown; he has pursued the even tenor of his way, simply looking to Christ, and acting for Him. His work will stand. It will be remembered and rewarded, though he did not do it for remembrance or reward, but from simple love to Jesus. It is work of the right stamp—genuine coin which will abide the fire of the day of the Lord.

The thought of all this is very solemn, yet very consolatory—solemn for those who are working, in any measure, under the eye of their fellows—consolatory for all those who are working beneath the eye of their Lord. It is an unspeakable mercy to be delivered from the time-serving, menpleasing, spirit of the present day; and to be enabled to walk, ever and only, before the Lord—to have "all our works begun, continued, and ended in Him."

Let us look, for a few moments, at the lovely and most touching illustration of this, presented to us in "the house of Simon, the leper," and recorded in Matthew xxvi. "Now when Jesus was in Bethany, in the house of Simon the leper, there came unto him a woman having an alabaster box of very precious ointment, and poured it on his head, as he sat at meat."

Now, if we enquire as to this woman's object, as she bent her steps to Simon's house, what was it? was it to display the exquisite perfume of her ointment, or the material and form of her alabaster box? Was it to obtain the praise of men for her act? Was it to get a name for extraordinary devotedness to Christ, in the midst of a little knot of personal friends of the Saviour? No, reader, it was none of these things. How do we know? Because, the Most High God, the Creator of all things, who knows the deepest secrets of all hearts, and the true motive spring of every action—He was there in the person of Jesus of Nazareth—He, the God of knowledge, by whom actions are weighed, was present; and He weighed her action, in the balances of the sanctuary, and affixed to it the seal of His approval. He sent it forth as genuine coin of the realm. He would not, He could not, have done this, if there had been any alloy, any admixture of base metal, any false motive, any under current. His holy and all-penetrating eye went right down into the very depths of this woman's soul. He knew, not only what she had done, but, how and why she had done it; and He declared, "She hath wrought a *good work* upon me."

In a word, then, Christ Himself was the immediate object of this woman's soul; and it was this which gave value to her act, and sent the odour of her ointment straight up to the throne of God. Little did she know or think that untold millions would read the record of her deep-toned personal devotedness. Little did she imagine that her act would be stereotyped, by the Master's hand, on the very pages of eternity, and never be obliterated. She thought not of this. She sought not, nor dreamed of such marvellous notoriety; had she done so, it would have robbed her act of all its charms, and deprived her sacrifice of all its fragrance.

But the blessed Lord to whom the act was done, took care that it should not be forgotten. He not only vindicated it, at the moment, but handed it down into the future. This was quite enough for the heart of this woman. Having the approval of her Lord, she could well afford to bear the "indignation" even of "the disciples," and to hear her act pronounced "waste." It was sufficient for her that His heart had been refreshed. All the rest might go for what it was worth. She had never thought of securing man's praise, or of avoiding his scorn. Her one undivided object, from first to last, was Christ. From the moment she laid her hand upon that alabaster box, until she broke it, and poured its contents upon His sacred Person, it was of Himself alone she thought. She had a kind of intuitive perception of what would be suitable and grateful to her Lord, in the solemn circumstances in which He was placed at the moment, and, with exquisite tact, she did that thing. She had never thought of what the ointment might fetch; or, if she had, she felt that He was worth ten thousand times as much. As to "the poor," they had their place, no doubt, and their claims also; but she felt that Jesus was more to her than all the poor in the world.

In short, the woman's heart was filled with Christ, and it was this that gave character to her action. Others might pronounce it "waste;" but we may rest assured that nothing is wasted which is spent for Christ. So the woman judged: and she was right. To put honour upon Him, at the very moment when earth and hell were rising up against Him, was the very highest act of service that man or angel could perform. He was going to be offered up. The shadows were lengthening, the gloom was deepening, the darkness thickening. The cross—with all its horrors—was at hand; and this woman anticipated it all, and came, beforehand, to anoint the body of her adorable Lord.

And mark the result. See how immediately the blessed Lord enters upon her defence, and shields her from the indignation and scorn of those who ought to have known better. "When Jesus understood it, he said unto them, Why trouble ye the woman? for she hath wrought a good work upon me. For ye have the poor always with you; but me ye have not always. For in that she hath poured this ointment on my body, she did it for my burial. Verily, I say unto you, Wheresoever this gospel shall be preached in the whole world, there shall also this, that this woman hath done, be told for a memorial of her."

Here was a glorious vindication, in the presence of which all human indignation, scorn, and misunderstanding must pass away, like the vapour of the morning before the beams of the rising sun. "Why trouble ye the woman? for she hath wrought a good work upon me." It was this that stamped the act—"a good work upon me." This marked it off from all beside. Everything must be valued according to its connection with Christ. A man may traverse the wide wide world, in order to carry out the noble objects of philanthropy; he may scatter, with a princely hand, the fruits of a large-hearted benevolence; he may give all his goods to feed the poor; he may go to the utmost possible length, in the wide range of religiousness and morality, and yet he may never have done one single thing of which Christ can say, "It is a good work upon me."

Reader, whoever you are, or however you are engaged, ponder this. See that you keep your eye directly upon the Master, in all you do. Make Jesus the immediate object of every little act of service, no matter what. Seek so to do your every work as that He may be able to say, "It is a good work upon me." Do not be occupied with the thoughts of men as to your path or as to your work. Do not mind their indignation or their misunderstanding, but pour your alabaster box of ointment upon the person of your

Lord. See that your every act of service is the fruit of your heart's appreciation of Him; and be assured He will appreciate your work and vindicate you before assembled myriads. Thus it was with the woman of whom we have been reading. She took her alabaster box, and made her way to the house of Simon the leper, with one object in her heart, namely, Jesus and what was before Him. She was absorbed in Him. She thought of none beside, but poured her precious ointment on His head. And note the blessed issue. Her act has come down to us, in the gospel record, coupled with His blessed Name. No one can read the gospel without reading also the memorial of her personal devotedness. Empires have risen, flourished, and passed away into the region of silence and oblivion. Monuments have been erected to commemorate human genius, greatness, and philanthropy—and these monuments have crumbled into dust; but the act of this woman still lives, and shall live for ever. The hand of the Master has erected a monument to her, which shall never, no never, perish. May we have grace to imitate her; and, in this day, when there is so much of human effort in the way of philanthropy, may our works, whatever they are, be the fruit of our heart's appreciation of an absent, rejected, crucified Lord!

# PART II

There is nothing which so thoroughly tests the heart as the doctrine of the cross—the path of the rejected, crucified Jesus of Nazareth. This probes man's heart to its deepest depths. If it be merely a question of religiousness, man can go an amazing length; but religiousness is not Christ. We need not travel farther than the opening lines of our chapter (Matt. xxvi.) in order to see a striking proof of this. Look, for a moment, at the palace of the high priest and what do you see? A special meeting of the heads and leaders of the people. "Then assembled together the chief priests, and the scribes, and the elders of the people, unto the palace of the high priest, who was called Caiaphas."

Here, asuredly, you have religion, and that, too, in a very imposing form. We must remember that these priests, scribes, and elders were looked up to, by the professed people of God, as the great depositaries of sacred learning, as the sole authority in all matters of religion, and as holding office under God, in that system which had been set up of God in the days of Moses. The assembly in the palace of Caiaphas was not composed of the pagan priests and augurs of Greece and Rome, but of the professed leaders and guides of the Jewish nation. And what were they doing in their solemn conclave? They were "consulting that they might take Jesus by subtlety, and kill him."

Reader, ponder this. Here were religious men, and men of learning, men of weight, no doubt, and influence among the people; and yet these men hated Jesus, and they were met in council, in order to plot His death—to take Him craftily and kill Him. Now those men could have talked to you about God and His worship—about Moses and the law—about the Sabbath and all the great ordinances and solemnities of the Jewish religion. But they hated Christ. Remember this most solemn fact. Men may be very religious; they may be the religious guides and teachers of others, and yet hate the Christ of God. This is one grand lesson to be learnt in the palace of Caiaphas the high priest. Religiousness is not Christ; on the contrary, the most zealous religionists have often been the most bitter and vehement haters of that blessed One.

But, it may be said, "Times are changed. Religion is now so intimately associated with the Name of Jesus, that to be a religious man is, of necessity, to be a lover of Jesus. You could not, now, find aught answering to the palace of Caiaphas." Is this really so? We cannot believe it, for a moment. The Name of Jesus is as thoroughly hated in Christendom, now, as it was in the palace of Caiaphas. And those who seek to follow Jesus will be hated too. We need not go far to prove this. Jesus is still a rejected one, in this world. Where, let us ask, will you hear His Name? Where is He a welcome theme? Speak of Him where you will, in the drawing-rooms of the wealthy and the fashionable, in the railway carriage, in the saloon of a steam-boat, in the coffee-room, or the dining-hall, in short, in any of the resorts of men, and you will, in almost every case, be told that such a theme is out of place. You may speak of anything else, politics, money, business, pleasure, nonsense. These things are always in place, everywhere; Jesus is never in place anywhere. We have seen in our streets, times without number, the public thoroughfares interrupted by German bands, balad-singers, and puppet-shows, and they have never been molested, reproved, or told to move on; but let a man stand, in such places, to speak of Jesus, and he will be insulted, or told to move on and not stop a thoroughfare. In plain language, there is room everywhere, in this world, for the devil, but no room for the Christ of God. The world's motto as to Christ is, "Oh! breathe not his Name."

But, thank God, if we see around us much that answers to the palace of the high priest, we can also see, here and there, that which corresponds with the house of Simon the leper. There are, blessed be God, those who love the Name of Jesus, and who count Him worthy of the alabaster box. There are those who are not ashamed of His precious cross—those who find their absorbing object in Him and who count it their chief joy and highest honour to spend and be spent for Him, in any little way. It is not with them a question of work, of religious machinery, of running hither and thither, of doing this or that: No; it is Christ, it is being near Him, and being occupied with Him; it is sitting at His feet, and pouring the precious ointment of the heart's true devotion upon Him.

Reader, be thou well assured that this is the true secret of power both in service and testimony. A just appreciation of a crucified Christ is the living spring of all that is acceptable to God, whether in the life and conduct of an individual Christian, or in all that goes on in our public assemblies. Genuine attachment to Christ and occupation with Him must characterize us personally and congregationally, else our life and history will prove of little worth in the judgment of heaven, however it may be in the judgment of earth. We know of nothing which imparts such moral power to the individual walk and character as intense devotion to the Person of Christ. It is not merely being a man of great faith, a man of prayer, a deeply taught student of Scripture or a scholar, a gifted preacher or a powerful writer. No; it is being a lover of Christ.

And so, as to the assembly; what is the true secret of power? Is it gift, eloquence, fine music, or an imposing ceremonial? No; it is the enjoyment of a present Christ. Where He is, all is light, life, and power. Where He is not, all is darkness, death, and desolation. An assembly where Jesus is not, is a sepulchre, though there be all the fascination of oratory, all the resistless attraction of fine music, and all the influence of an impressive ritual. All these things may exist in perfection, and yet the devoted lover of Jesus may have to cry out, "Alas! they have taken away my Lord, and I know not where have laid Him." But, on the other hand, where the presence of Jesus is realized—where His voice is heard, and his very touch felt by the soul, there is power and blessing, though, to man's view, all may seem the most thorough weakness.

Let Christians remember these things; let them ponder them; let them see to it that they realize the Lord's presence in their public assemblies; and if they cannot say, with full confidence, of their meetings that the Lord is there, let them humble themselves and wait upon Him, for there must be a cause. He has said, "Where two or three are gathered together in my name there am I in the midst." But let us never forget that, in order to reach the divine result, there must be the divine condition.

# RESPONSIBILITY AND POWER

The question of man's responsibility seems to perplex many minds. They find it difficult, if not impossible, to reconcile it with the fact of his total want of power. If, it is argued, man is perfectly powerless, how can he be responsible? If he cannot of himself repent or believe the gospel, how can he be responsible? And then, again, if he is not responsible to believe the gospel, on what ground can he be judged for rejecting it?

Thus the mind reasons and argues; and, alas! theology does not help it to a solution of the difficulty, but, on the contrary, increases the mist and confusion. For, on the one hand, a certain school of divinity teaches, and rightly so, man's utter powerlessness —that he will not, and cannot, come if left to himself—that it is only by the mighty power of the Holy Spirit that any one ever does come—that, were it not for free, sovereign grace, not a single soul would ever be saved—that, if left to ourselves, we should only go wrong, and never do right.

From all this it infers that man is not responsible. Its teaching is right, but its inference is wrong. Another school of divinity teaches—and rightly so—that man is responsible—that he will be punished with everlasting destruction for rejecting the gospel— that God commands all men everywhere to repent—that He beseeches sinners, all men, the world, to be reconciled to Him—that He will have all men to be saved, and to come to the knowledge of the truth.

From all this it infers that man has power to repent and believe. Its teaching is right; its inference, wrong. Hence it follows that neither human reasonings, nor the teachings of mere theology— high or low—can ever settle the question of responsibility and power. The word of God alone can do this, and it does it in a very simple and conclusive manner. It teaches, proves, and illustrates, from the opening of Genesis to the close of Revelation, man's utter powerlessness for good, his ceaseless proneness to evil.

It declares, in Genesis vi., that every imagination of the thoughts of man's heart is only and continually evil. It declares, in Jeremiah xvii., that the heart is deceitful above all things, and desperately wicked. It teaches us, in Romans iii., that there is none righteous, no, not one; there is none that understandeth, there is none that seeketh after God. They are all gone out of the way, they are together become unprofitable; there is none that doeth good, no, not one.

Further, not only does scripture teach the doctrine of man's utter and hopeless ruin, his incorrigible evil, his perfect powerlessness as to good, and his invariable proneness to evil; but it furnishes us with an array of evidence, perfectly unanswerable, in the shape of facts and illustrations drawn from man's actual history, to prove the doctrine. It shews us man in the garden, believing the devil, disobeying God, and driven out. It shews him, when thus driven out, going on in wickedness until God had to send the deluge. Then, in the restored earth, man gets drunk and degrades himself. Man is tried without law, and proves himself a lawless rebel. He is tried under law, he becomes a wilful transgressor. Prophets are sent, he stones them; the Baptist is sent, he beheads him; the Son is sent, he crucifies Him; the Holy Ghost is sent, he resists Him.

Thus, in every volume, as it were, of man's history—the history of the human race—in every section, every page, every paragraph, every line, we read his total ruin, his utter alienation from God. We are taught in the most distinct manner possible, that, if left to himself, he never could, and never would—though most surely he should—turn to God, and do works meet for repentance. And, in perfect keeping with all this, we learn from our Lord's parable of the great super, in Luke xiv. that not so much as a single merely invited guest will be found at the table. All who sit down there are "brought," or "compelled." Not one ever would come, if left to himself. Grace, free grace, must force them in; and so it does, blessed for ever be the God of all grace!

But, on the other hand, side by side with all this, and taught with equal force and clearness, stands the solemn and weighty truth of man's responsibility. In creation, under the law, and in the gospel, man is addressed as a responsible being, for such he undoubtedly is. And further, his responsibility is, in every case, measured by his advantages. Thus, in the opening of the Epistle to the Romans, the Gentile is viewed as without law, but responsible to listen to the testimony of creation, which he has not done. The Jew is viewed as under law, and responsible to keep it, which he has not done. Then, in chapter xi., Christendom is viewed, as responsible to continue in the goodness of God, which it has not done. And in 2 Thessalonians i. we read that those who obey not the gospel of our Lord Jesus Christ shall be punished with everlasting destruction. And, finally, in Hebrews ii., the apostle urges home this most solemn question, "How shall we escape if we neglect so great salvation?"

Now, the Gentile will not be judged on the same ground as the Jew; nor the Jew on the same ground as the nominal Christian. Each will be dealt with on his own distinct ground, and according to his light and privilege. There will be the few stripes and the many stripes, as in Luke xii. It will be "more tolerable" for some than for others, as in Matthew xi. The Judge of all the earth will do right; but man is responsible, and his responsibility is measured by the light and advantage afforded him. All are not huddled together promiscuously, as though they were all on one common ground. On the contrary, there is the nicest discrimination, and no one will ever be condemned for slighting and refusing advantages which were not within his reach. But surely, the very fact that there will be a judgment at all, proves, even were there no other proof, that man is responsible.

And by whom, let us ask, is the very highest type of responsibility incurred? By the rejecter or the neglecter of the gospel of the grace of God. The gospel brings out all the fulness of the grace of God. All His resources are there displayed. The love of God; the precious work and glorious Person of the Son; the testimony of the Holy Ghost. Moreover, God is seen in the gospel, in the marvellous ministry of reconciliation, actually beseeching sinners to be reconciled to Him.* Nothing can exceed this. It is the very highest and

---

* Some would teach us that the expression, "We pray, in Christ's stead, be ye reconciled to God," refers to Christians who are exhorted to be reconciled to the dealings of God. What a mistake! What a complete overlooking of the

110

fullest display of the grace, mercy, and love of God; and therefore all who reject or neglect it incur the most solemn responsibility, and bring down upon themselves the very heaviest judgment of God. Those who refuse the testimony of creation are guilty. Those who break the law are guiltier still; but those who refuse God's proffered grace are the guiltiest of all.

Will any still object, and say they cannot reconcile the two things, man's powerlessness and man's responsibility? Let them bear in mind that it is none of our business to reconcile them. God has done that for us by placing them side by side, in His own eternal word. It is ours to submit and believe, not to reason. If we listen to the conclusions and deductions of our own minds, or to the dogmas of conflicting schools of divinity, we shall be ever in a muddle and a jumble, perplexed and confused. But if we simply bow to scripture we shall know the truth. Men may reason and rebel; but the question is whether is man to judge God, or God to judge man? Is God sovereign, or is He not? If man is to sit in judgment on God, then God is no longer God. "O man, who art thou that repliest against God?"

This is the great question. Can we answer it? The plain fact is, this difficulty as to the question of power and responsibility is all a complete mistake, arising from ignorance of our own true condition, and our want of absolute submission to God. Every soul in a right moral condition will freely own his responsibility, his guilt, his utter powerlessness, his exposure to the just judgment of God, and that were it not for the sovereign grace of God, in Christ, he should inevitably be damned. Any one who does not own this, from the very depths of his soul, is ignorant of himself, and virtually sitting in judgment upon God. Thus it stands, if we are to be taught by scripture.

---

plain sense and actual terms of the passage! God was in Christ, not reconciling believers to His dealings, but reconciling the world unto Himself. And now the word of reconciliation is committed to Christ's ambassadors, who are to beseech sinners to be reconciled unto God. The force and beauty of this most lovely passage are sacrificed, in order to support a certain school of doctrine which cannot face the full teaching of holy scripture. How much better to abandon every school and every system of theology, and come like a little child to the boundless and bottomless ocean of divine inspiration.

Take a case. A certain man owes me a hundred pounds; but he is unprincipled and extravagant, and he has rendered himself quite unable to pay me. And not only is he unable, but unwilling. He has no desire to pay, no desire to have anything to do with me. If he sees me coming along the street, he skulks away down the first opening, to avoid me. Is he responsible? And am I justified in taking legal proceedings against him? Does his total inability to pay do away with his responsibility?

Further, I send my servant to him with a kind message; he insults him. I send another; he knocks him down. I send my son to beg of him to come to me, and to own himself my debtor, to confess, and take his proper place, and that I will not only forgive him his debt, but take him into partnership with myself. He insults my son in every possible way, heaps all sorts of indignity upon him, and, finally, murders him.

All this is but a very feeble illustration of the actual condition of things between God and the sinner; and yet some will reason and argue about the injustice of holding man responsible. It is all a fatal mistake, and such it will yet be found to be, in every case. There is not a soul in hell that has any difficulty in the matter. And, most surely, there is no difficulty felt by any in heaven. All who find themselves in hell will own that they receive the due reward of their deeds; and all who find themselves in heaven will own themselves "debtors to mercy alone." The former will have to thank themselves; the latter will have to thank God. Such we conceive to be the only true solution of the question of "responsibility and power."

# PRIVILEGE AND RESPONSIBILITY

(READ DEUT. xx. 1-9)

Privilege and responsibility! Yes, this is the divine order; and how important it is, in dealing with the things of God, to place them in the order in which he places them, and leave them there! The human mind is ever prone to displace things; and hence it is that we so frequently find the responsibilities, which attach to the people of God, pressed upon those who are yet in their sins. This is a great mistake. I must be in a position before I can fulfil the responsibilities attaching thereto. I must be in a relationship before I can know the affections which belong to it. If I am not a father, how can I know or exhibit the affections of a father's heart? Impossible. I may descant upon them, and attempt to describe them; but, in order to *feel* them, I must be a father.

Thus it is in the things of God. I must be in a position before I can enter into the responsibilities which belong to it. I must be in a relationship before I can understand the affections which flow out of it. Man has been tested in every possible way. He has been tried in creation. He has been tried under divine government. He has been tried under law. He has been tried with ordinances. He has been tried by the ministry of the prophets. He has been tried by the ministry of righteousness, in the person of John the Baptist. He has been tried by the ministry of grace, in the person of Christ. He has been tried by the mnistry of the Holy Ghost. What has been the result? Total failure! An unbroken chain of testimony from Paradise to Pentecost has only tended to make manifest man's utter failure in every possible way. In every position of responsibility, in which man has been set, he has broken down. Not so much as a single exception can be adduced.

So much for man's responsibility. He has proved himself unfaithful in every thing. He has not a single inch of ground to stand upon. He has destroyed himself, but in God is his help. Grace has

113

come in, in the Person of Christ, and perfectly met man's desperate case. The cross is the divine remedy for all the ruin, and by that cross the believer is introduced into a place of divine and everlasting privilege. Christ has met all the need, answered all the demands, discharged all the responsibilities, and, having done so by his death upon the cross, He has become, in resurrection, the basis of all the believer's privileges. We have all in Christ, and we get Him, not because we have fulfilled our responsibilities, but because God loved us even when we had failed in every thing. We find ourselves, unconditionally, in a place of unspeakable privilege. We did not work ourselves into it; we did not weep ourselves into it; we did not pray ourselves into it; we did not fast ourselves into it. We were taken up from the depth of our ruin, from that deep, deep pit into which we had fallen, in consequence of having failed in all our responsibilities; we have been set down, by God's free grace, in a position of unspeakable blessedness and privilege, of which nothing can ever deprive us. Not all the powers of hell and earth combined; not all the malice of Satan and his emissaries; not all the power of sin, death, and the grave, arrayed in their most terrific form, can ever rob the believer in Jesus of that place of privilege in which, through grace, he stands.

My reader cannot be too simple in his apprehension of this. We do not reach our place of privilege as the result of faithfulness in the place of responsibility. Quite the reverse. We have failed in every thing. "All have sinned and come short of the glory of God." We deserved death; but we have received life. We deserved hell; but we have received heaven. We deserved eternal wrath; but we have received eternal favour. Grace has entered the scene, and it "reigns through righteousness, unto eternal life, by Jesus Christ our Lord."

Hence, then, in the economy of grace, privilege becomes the basis of responsibility, and this is beautifully illustrated in the passage of scripture which stands at the head of this paper. I shall quote it for my reader, lest he should not have his Bible at hand. "When thou goest out to battle against thine enemies, and seest horses, and chariots, and a people more than thou, be not afraid of them: for the Lord thy God is with thee, which brought thee up out of

114

the land of Egypt. And it shall be, when ye are come nigh unto the battle that the priest shall approach, and speak unto the people, and shall say unto them, Hear, O Israel; ye approach this day unto battle against your enemies; let not your hearts faint; fear not, and do not tremble, neither be ye terrified because of them; for the Lord your God is he that goeth with you, to fight for you against your enemies, to save you."

Here we have Israel's privileges distinctly set forth. "The Lord thy God is with thee," and that moreover, in the very character in which He had brought them up out of the land of Egypt. He was with them in the power of that sovereign grace which had delivered them from the iron grasp of Pharoah, and the iron bondage of Egypt, which had conducted them through the sea, and led them across "the great and terrible wilderness." This made victory sure. No enemy could possibly stand before Jehovah acting in unqualified grace on behalf of His people.

And let my reader note carefully, that there is not a single condition proposed by the priest in the above quotation. He states, in the most absolute way, the relationship and consequent privilege of the Israel of God. He does not say, "The Lord thy God will be with you, if you do so and so." This would not be the proper language of one who stood before the people of God as the exponent of those privileges which grace had conferred upon them. Grace proposes no conditions, raises no barriers, makes no stipulations. Its language is, "The Lord thy God is with thee . . . he goeth with you . . . to fight for you . . . to save you." When Jehovah fights for His people they are sure of victory. "If God be for us, who can be against us?" Grant me but this, that God is with me, and I argue full victory over every spiritual foe.

Thus much as to the question of privilege: let us now turn, for a moment, to the question of responsibility.

"And the officers shall speak unto the people, saying, What man is there that hath built a new house, and hath not dedicated it? let him go and return to his house lest he die in the battle, and another man dedicate it. And what man is he that hath planted a vineyard, and hath not yet eaten of it? let him also go and return to his house, lest he die in the battle, and another man eat of it.

And what man is there that hath betrothed a wife, and hath not taken her? let him go and return unto his house, lest he die in the battle, and another man take her. And the officers shall speak further unto the people, and they shall say, What man is there that is fearful and fainthearted? let him go and return unto his house, lest his brethren's heart faint as well as his heart."

There is uncommon moral beauty in the order in which the priest and the officer are introduced in this passage. The former is the exponent of Israel's privileges; the latter, of Israel's responsibilities. But how interesting it is to see that, before the officers were permitted to address the assembly on the grand question of responsibility, the priest had established them in the knowledge of their precious privilege. Imagine the case reversed. Suppose the officer's voice had first been heard, and what would have been the result? Fear, depression, and discouragement. To press responsibility before I know my position—to call for affections ere I am in the relationship, is to place an intolerable yoke upon the neck—an insufferable burden upon the shoulder. This is not God's way. If you search from Genesis to Revelation, you will find, without so much as a single exception, that the divine order is privilege and responsibility. Set me upon the rock of privilege, and I am in a position to understand and fulfil my responsibility; but talk to me of responsibility while yet in the pit of ruin, the mire of legality, or the slough of despond, and you rob me of all hope of ever rising into that hallowed sphere, upon which the sunlight of divine favour pours itself in living lustre, and where alone responsibilities can be discharged to the glory of the name of Jesus.

Some there are who talk to us of "gospel conditions." Who ever heard of a gospel fenced with conditions? We can understand law-conditions; but a gospel with conditions is "a different gospel, which is not another." (Gal. i. 6, 7.) Conditions to be fulfilled by the creature pertain not to the gospel, but to the law. Man has been tried under all possible conditions. And what has been the issue? Failure! Yes, failure only—failure continually. Man is a ruin —a wreck—a bankrupt. Of what use can it ever be to place such an one under conditions, even though you should call them by the anomalous title of "gospel conditions?" None whatever. Man,

116

under any kind of conditions, can only prove unfaithful. He has been weighed in the balance and found wanting. He has been condemned, root and branch. "They that are in the flesh cannot please God." It does not say, "they that are in *the body*." No: but "they that are in *the flesh*." But the believer is not in the flesh, though in the body. He is not looked at in his old creation standing—in his old Adamic condition, in which he has been tried and condemned. Christ has come down and died under the full weight of his guilt. He has taken the sinner's place, with all its liabilities, and by His death settled every thing. He lay in the grave after having answered every claim and silenced every enemy. Justice, law, sin, death, wrath, judgement, Satan, every thing, and every one. There lay the divine Surety in the silent tomb; and God entered the scene, raised Him from the dead, set Him at His own right hand in the heavens, sent down the Holy Ghost to testify to a risen and exalted Saviour, and to unite to Him, as thus risen and exalted, all who believe in His name.

Here, then, we get on to new ground altogether. We can now listen to the officer as he tells out in our hearing the claims of Christ upon all those who are united to Him. The priest has spoken to us, and told us of the imperishable ground which we occupy, the indestructible relationship in which we stand, and now we are in a position to listen to the one who stands before us as the exponent of our high and holy responsibilities. Had "the officer" come first, we should have fled from his presence, discouraged and dismayed by the weight and solemnity of his words, and giving utterance to the despairing inquiry, "Who then can be saved?" But, inasmuch as "the priest"—the minister of grace—the exponent of privilege, has set us upon our feet in the new creation, and strengthened our hearts by unfolding the unconditional grace in which we stand, we can listen to the "commandments" of the officer, and find them "not grievous," because they come to us from off the mercy-seat.

And what does the officer say to us? Just this: "No man that *warreth entangleth* himself with the affairs of this life." This is the sum and substance of the officer's message. He demands, on the part of God's warriors, a disentangled heart. It is not a question of

117

salvation, of being a child of God, of being a true Israelite; it is simply a question of ability to wage an effectual warfare; and, clearly, a man cannot fight well if his heart is entangled with "a house," "a vineyard," or "a wife."

Nor was it a question of *having* such things. By no means. Thousands of those, who went forth to tread the battle-field, and gather the spoils of victory, had houses, and lands, and domestic ties. The officers had no quarrel with the possessors of these things; the only point was, not to be *entangled* with them. The apostle does not say, "No man that warreth engages in the affairs of this life." Had he said this, we should all have to live in idleness and isolation, whereas he distinctly teaches us, elsewhere, that, "If any man will not work, neither shall he eat." The grand point is to keep the heart disentangled. God's warriors must have free hearts, and the only way to be free is to cast all our care upon Him who careth for us. I can stand in the battle-field with a free heart when I have placed my house, my vineyard, and my wife, in the divine keeping.

But, further, God's warriors must have courageous hearts as well as free hearts. "The fearful and the faint-hearted" can never stand in the battle, or wear the laurel of victory. Our hearts must be disentangled from the world, and bold by reason of our artless confidence in God; and, be it well remembered, that these things are not "gospel *conditions*," but gospel *results*—a deeply-important distinction. What a mistake to speak of gospel conditions! It is simply the old leaven of legality presented in a new and strange form, and dubbed with a name which, in itself, involves a contradiction. If those precious clusters which are the result of union with the living Vine, be set forth as the necessary conditions of that union, what must become of the sinner? Where shall we get them if not in Christ? And how do we become united to Christ? Is it by conditions? Nay; but by faith.

May the Holy Ghost instruct my reader as to the divine order of "PRIVILEGE AND RESPONSIBILITY!"

# EXHORTATION

There are few things less understood than the real nature of exhortation. We are apt to attach an idea of legal effort to that word which is quite foreign to it. Divine exhortation, always assumes that a certain relationship exists, that a certain standing is enjoyed, that certain privileges are apprehended. The Spirit never exhorts save on a divine basis. For example. "I beseech you, therefore, brethren, *by the mercies of God*." (Rom. xii. I.) Here we have a fine instance of divine exhortation. "The mercies of God" are first put before us, in all their fulness, brightness, and preciousness, ere we are called to hear the voice of exhortation.

Again, "Grieve not the Holy Spirit of God *whereby ye are sealed* unto the day of redemption." (Eph. iv. 30.) Here we are exhorted on the settled ground of our being "sealed." He does not say, "Grieve not the Spirit, lest ye be eternally lost." Such would not be in keeping with the true character of divine exhortation. We "are sealed," not so long as we behave ourselves, but "until the day of redemption." It is absolutely done, and this is the powerful reason why we are not to grieve the Holy Spirit. If that which is the eternal seal of God, set upon us until the day of redemption, be the *Holy* Spirit, how careful should we be not to grieve Him.

Again, "Since ye then are risen with Christ, seek those things which are above." (Col. iii. 1.) As those who are risen, what should we seek but "things above?" We do not seek these things in order to be risen, but because we are. In other words, the solid basis of our standing is laid down, by the Spirit of grace, before ever the voice of exhortation falls on the ear. This is divine. Aught else would be mere legality. To call upon a man to set his affections upon things above, before he knows, upon divine authority, that he is "risen with Christ," is to begin at the wrong end, and to lose your labour. It is only when I believe that precious emancipating truth that when Christ died, I died; when He was buried, I was buried; when He rose, I rose; it is only when this grand reality takes possession of my soul that I can lend an open ear, and an understanding heart to exhortation's heavenly voice.

It is well for my reader to understand this thoroughly. There is no need whatever for a multitude of words. Let him simply take his New Testament, and beginning with the epistle to the Romans, trace, throughout, the exhortations of the Spirit of God; and he will find, without a single exception, that they are as completely divested of the legal element as are the promises which glitter like gems on the page of inspiration. This subject is not fully understood. Exhortation in the hands of man is widely different from what it is in the hands of the Holy Ghost. How often do we hear men exhorting us to a certain line of action *in order that we may* reach certain privileges. The way of the Spirit is the reverse of this. He sets before us our *standing* in Christ, in the first place, and then He unfolds the *walk*. He first speaks of privilege—free, unconditional, inalienable privilege, and then He sets forth the holy responsibility connected therewith. He first presents the settled and unalterable relationship in which free grace has set us, and then dwells upon the affections belonging thereto.

There is nothing so hateful to the Spirit of God as legality, that hateful system which casts us as *doers* back upon *self*, instead of casting us as lost *sinners* over upon Christ. Man would fain *do* something; but he must be brought to the end of himself, and to the end of all beside, and then as a lost sinner, find his rest in Christ—a full, precious, all-sufficient Christ. In this way alone can he ever expect solid peace and true happiness; and only then will he ever be able to yield an intelligent response to the Spirit's "word of exhortation."

# THE TWO LINKS

There are two very important links in Christianity which we should seek to understand, namely, first, the link of everlasting life; and, secondly, the link of personal communion. These links, being perfectly distinct, should never be confounded; and, being intimately connected, should never be separate. The former is the ground of our security; the later, the secret spring of our enjoyment and the source of all our fruitfulness. That can never be broken; this may be snapped by a thousand things.

Seeing, then, that these links are of such immense importance, let us reverently and prayerfully enter upon the examination of them in the divine light of inspiration.

And, first, then, as to the precious link of everlasting life, we cannot possibly do better than quote a few plain passages of scripture setting forth whence it comes, what it is, when, and how, it is formed.

But, first of all, it must be distinctly borne in mind that man, in his natural state, knows nothing of this link, "That which is born of the flesh is flesh." There may be much that is truly amiable, great nobility of character, great generosity, strict integrity; but there is no eternal life. The first link is unknown. It matters not how you cultivate and elevate nature, you cannot, by any possibility, form the grand link of everlasting life. You may make it moral, learned, religious, but so long as it is mere nature, there is no eternal life. You may select all the very finest moral virtues, and concentrate them in one individual, and that individual may never have felt so much as a single pulsation of everlasting life. It is not that these virtues and qualities are not good and desirable in themselves; no one in his senses would question that. Whatever is morally good in nature is to be estimated at its proper value. No one would think, for a moment, of placing a sober, industrious, amiable, well-principled man on a level with a drunken, idle, cross-grained spendthrift. Looked at from a social and moral point of view, there is, obviously, a wide and very material difference. But, be it clearly understood, and well-remembered, that we can never by the finest virtues and noblest qualities of the old creation purchase a place in the new; we can never by all the excellencies of the first Adam, even if concentrated in one individual, establish a title to membership in the Second. The two are totally distinct—the old and the new—the first and the Second. "That which is born of the flesh is flesh; and that which is born of the Spirit is spirit." "Therefore, if any man be in Christ he is a new creation; old things are passed away; behold all things are become new."

Nothing can be more explicit, nothing more conclusive, than the last quoted passage from the fifth chapter of Second Corinthians. "*Old things*," of what kind soever they be, "are passed away." They are not recognized as having any existence in the new creation, wherein, "*all things* are of God." The old foundation has been completely removed, and new foundations laid in redemption. Nor is there so much as a single particle of the old material worked up into the new. "All things are become new"—"All things are of God." The old creation "bottles" have been flung aside, and redemption bottles set in their stead. The old creation "garment" has been cast away, and the new, the spotless robe of redemption, substituted. In this fair robe man's hand never wove a thread, nor set a stitch. How do we know? How can we speak with such confidence and authority? For the best of all reasons, because the divinely authoritative, and therefore absolutley conclusive voice of holy scripture declares that, in the new creation, "*All things* are of God." The Lord be praised that it is so! It is this that makes all so secure—that places all so entirely beyond the reach of the enemy's power. He cannot touch anything or anyone in the new creation. Death is the limit of Satan's domain. The grave forms the boundary of his dominion. But the new creation begins at the other side of death—it opens upon our enraptured gaze at heaven's side of that tomb where the Prince of Life lay buried—it pours the brilliant beams of its glories around us in the midst of a scene where death can never enter, where sin and sorrow are unknown, where the hiss of the serpent can never be heard, nor his hateful trail be seen. "All things are of God."

Now, it would remove a host of difficulties and perplexities, and simplify matters amazingly, if this point of the new creation were clearly understood. If we look around on what is called the religious world, or the professing church, what do we see? A large amount of effort to improve man, in his Adamic, his natural, or old creation condition. Philanthropy, science, philosophy, religion, are all brought into play; every species of moral leverage is brought to bear, for the purpose of raising man in the scale of existence. What do men mean when they talk, as they often do, of "elevating the masses?" How far can they go in their operations? To what point can they elevate them? Can they raise them into the new creation? Clearly not, seeing that in that creation all things are of God.

But, further, who, or what, are these "masses" that are sought to be elevated? Are they born of the flesh, or born of the Spirit? Of the flesh confessedly and assuredly. Well, then, "That which is born of the flesh is flesh." You may elevate it as high as you please. You may apply the most powerful lever, and raise it to the very loftiest point attainable. Educate, cultivate, sublimate it as you will. Let science, philosophy, religion (socalled), and philanthropy bring all their resources to bear; and what has been done? You cannot make it spirit—you cannot bring it into the new creation—you cannot form the first grand link of everlasting life. You have done absolutely nothing towards man's best, his spiritual, his eternal interests. You have left him still in his old Adamic state, his old creation circumstances; you have left him in his liabilities, his responsibilities, his sins, his guilt; you have left hm exposed to the righteous wrath of a sin-hating God. He may be more cultivated in his guilt, but he is guilty all the while. Cultivation cannot remove guilt; education cannot blot out sins; civilization cannot remove from man's horizon the dark and heavy clouds of death and judgment.

Let us not be misunderstood. We do not want to make little of education or civilization, true philanthropy or true philosophy. We say, distinctly, let them go for what they are really worth, let them be estimated at their true value. We are ready to allow as large a margin as may be demanded, in which to insert all the possible advantages of education, in all its branches; and having done so, we return with accumulated force to our grand thesis, namely, that in "elevating the masses," you are elevating that which has no existence before God, no place in the new creation; and we repeat it, with emphasis, and urge it with energy, that until you get the soul into the new creation, you have done absolutely nothing for it, with respect to eternity, to heaven, and to God. True, you may smooth man's way through this world; you may remove some of the roughnesses from the highway of human life; you may dandle the flesh in the delusive lap of luxury and ease; all this you may do, and much more; you may wreath man's brow with every species of laurel that ever was won in the various arenas in which men have carried on the competitive struggle for fame; you may adorn his name with all the titles that ever were bestowed by mortal upon his fellow mortal, and after all this, you may leave him in his sins, and exposed to death and eternal damnation. If the first grand link be not formed, the soul is like a vessel broken from her moorings, and driven over the watery waste, without either rudder or compass.

Now, we most earnestly desire to press this point upon the attention of the reader. We deeply feel its immense practical importance. We believe there is hardly any truth to which the devil offers fierce and constant opposition than the truth of the new creation. He knows well its mighty moral influence, its power to lift the soul up out of present things, to produce deadness to the world, and practical and habitual elevation above the things of time and sense. Hence his efforts to keep people ever engaged in the hopeless work of trying to elevate nature and improve the world. He has no objection to morality, to religion as such, in all its forms. He will even use Christianity itself as a means of improving the old nature. Indeed his masterpiece is to tack on the Christian religion as a "new piece" upon the "old garment" of fallen nature. You may do what you like, provided you leave man in the old creation; for Satan knows full well that so long as you leave him there, you have left him in his clutches. All in the old creation is in the grasp of Satan, and within the full range of his guns. All in the new creation is beyond him. "He that is born of God keepeth himself and that wicked one toucheth him not." It is not said that the believer keepeth himself and that wicked one toucheth him not. The believer is a complex being, having two natures—the old and the new, the flesh and the Spirit, and if he does not watch, "that wicked one" will speedily touch him, upset him, and cut out plenty of sorrowful work for him. But the divine nature, the new creation, cannot be touched, and so long as we walk in the energy of the divine nature, and breathe the atmosphere of the new creation, we are perfectly safe from all the assaults of the enemy.

And, now, let us proceed to enquire how it is we get into the new creation—how we become possessed of the divine nature—how this link of everlasting life is formed. A quotation or two from the word will suffice to open this point to us. "God so loved the world, that he gave his only begotten Son, that whosoever *believeth in him* should not perish, but have everlasting life." Mark these words, reader, observe the connection, "Believeth in him"—"Have everlasting life." This is the link—simple faith. Thus it is we pass from the old creation, with all its belongings, into the new creation with all its belongings. This is the precious secret of the new birth—faith wrought in the soul by the grace of God the Holy Ghost—faith that takes God at His word, that sets to its seal that God is true—faith that links the soul with a risen Christ, the Head and beginning of the New Creation.

Take another quotation, "Verily, verily, I say unto you, he that heareth my words, and believeth on him that sent me, hath everlasting life, and shall not come into judgment; but is passed from death unto life." Here is the link again. "Believeth on me"—"*Hath everlasting life.*" Nothing can be more simple. By natural birth we enter the precincts of the old creation, and become heirs of all that appertained to the first Adam. By spiritual birth, we enter the precincts of the new creation, and become the heirs of all that appertains to the Second Adam. And if it be asked, what is the secret of this great mystery of the spiritual birth? the answer is, "Faith." "He that believeth on me." Hence, if the reader is one who believes in Jesus, according to the language of the above passages, he is in the new creation—he is a possessor of the divine nature—he is linked on to Christ, by a link which is perfectly indissoluble. Such an one can never perish. No power of earth or hell, men or devils can ever snap that link of everlasting life which connects all Christ's members with their risen Head in glory, and with one another.

And let the reader note particularly that, in reference to the link of eternal life, and its formation, we must take God's thoughts in place of our own; we must be governed exclusively by the word of God, and not by our own vain reasonings, foolish imaginings, and ever changing feelings. Moreover, we must be careful not to confound the two links which, though intimately connected, are perfectly distinct. We must not displace them, but leave them in their divine order. The first does not depend upon the second; but the second flows out of the first. The second is as much a link as the first; but it is second, and not first. All the power and malice of Satan cannot snap the first link; the weight of a feather may snap the second. The first link endureth for ever; the second may be broken in a moment. The first link owes its permanency to the work of Christ *for* us, which was finished on the cross, and to the word of God *to* us, which is settled for ever in heaven; the second link depends upon the action of the Holy Ghost *in* us, which may be, and alas! is, interfered with by a thousand things, in the course of a single day. The former is based upon Christ's victory *for* us; the latter is based upon the Spirit's victories *in* us.

Now, it is our firm conviction that thousands get shaken as to the reality and perpetuity of the first link of everlasting life, by reason of failure in the maintenance of the second link of personal communion. Something occurs to snap the latter, and they begin at once to question the existence of the former. This is a mistake; but it only serves to show the immense importance of holy vigilance in our daily walk so that the link of personal communion may not be broken by sin, in thought, word, or deed; or, if it should be broken, of having it instantly restored by self-judgment and confession, founded upon the death and advocacy of Christ. It is an undeniable fact, confirmed by the sad experience of thousands of true saints of God, that when the second link is snapped, it is next to impossible to realize the first. And this, though so vitally important to us, is, in reality, but a secondary thing; for, surely,

126

the suspension of our communion is a small thing when compared with the dishonour done to the cause of Christ, and the grief offered to the Holy Ghost by that which occasioned the suspension.

May the Spirit of God work in us mightily to produce watchfulness, prayerfulness, seriousness, and earnestness; that nothing may occur to interrupt our communion, but that the two links may be understood and enjoyed in their due place and order, to the glory of God by us, the stability of our peace in Him, and the integrity and purity of our walk before Him!

# PART III

In order to unfold, somewhat more fully, the subject of "The two links," we should like to call our reader's attention, for a few moments, to a very important passage in the fifth chapter of the First Epistle to the Corinthians. "For even Christ our passover is slain for us; therefore let us keep the feast." In this brief quotation, we have a wide range of truth presented. We have, first, a great fact stated, "Christ our passover is slain;" and, secondly, an earnest appeal, "Let us keep the feast." In the former, we have the ground of our security, in the latter, the true secret of personal holiness.

Now, here again, we have the two links, in their proper distinctness, and yet in their proper order. We have a sacrifice and a feast, two things quite distinct, but yet intimately connected. The sacrifice is complete; but the feast is to be celebrated. Such is the divine order. The completeness of the sacrifice secures the believer's title, and the celebration of the feast involves the whole of the believer's practical life.

We must be careful not to confound these things. The feast of unleavened bread was founded upon the death of the paschal lamb, and it typified that practical holiness which is to characterize the whole of a Christian's life down here. "Christ is slain." This secures everything as to title. "When I see the blood, I will pass over you." God, as a Judge, was fully met and satisfied by the blood of the lamb. The destroying angel passed through the land of Egypt, at the midnight hour, with the sword of judgment in his hand, and the only means of escape was the sprinkled blood. This was divinely sufficient. God had declared, "When I see the blood, I will pass over." Israel's salvation rested on God's estimate of the blood, of the lamb. This is a most precious truth for the soul to dwell upon. Man's salvation rests upon God's satisfaction. The Lord be praised! "Christ our passover is slain for us." Mark these words, "*is slain*"—and that, "*for us.*" This settles everything as to the great and all-important question of salvation from judgment and wrath. Thus the precious link of salvation is formed—a link which can never be broken. The link of eternal life, and the link of eternal salvation, is one and the same. The Lord Jesus Christ—the living Saviour—the risen Head, maintains, and ever will maintain, this link in unbroken integrity, as He says, "Because I live, ye shall live also." "If, when we were enemies, we were reconciled to God by the death of his Son, much more, being reconciled, we shall be saved by his life." "He ever liveth to make intercession for us."

And, now, a word or two as to the exhortation of the apostle, "Therefore let us keep the feast." Christ keeps us, and we are to keep the feast. He was slain to spread a feast for us, and that feast is a life of personal holiness—practical separation from all evil. Israel's feast was composed of three things, namely, a roasted lamb, bitter herbs, and unleavened bread. Precious ingredients! setting forth, in typical language, first, Christ as having endured the wrath of God for us; secondly, those deep, spiritual exercises of heart which flow from our contemplating the cross; and, thirdly, personal holiness, or practical separation from evil. Such was the feast of God's redeemed; and such is our feast now. Oh! that we may have grace to celebrate it according to its due order! May our loins be girt, our feet shod, and our pilgrim staff in hand.

And be it remembered, it is not a feast celebrated in order to reach a sacrifice; but a sacrifice slain to provide a feast. We must not reverse this order. We are very prone to reverse it, because we are apt to regard God as an *exactor*, instead of a *giver*—to make duty the basis of salvation, instead of making salvation the basis of duty. An Israelite did not put away leaven in order to be saved from the sword of the destroyer, but because he was saved. In other words, there was first the blood-stained lintel, and then, the unleavened bread. These things must not be confounded, neither

128

must they be separated. We are not saved from wrath by unleavened bread, but by a blood-stained lintel; but we can only enjoy the latter as we are diligently and jealousy maintaining the former. The two links are ever to stand in their divine order, and in their inseparable connection. Christ Himself infallibly maintains the one; and we, by the grace of His Spirit, are to maintain the other. May He enable us so to do!

# FOUR POINTS OF KNOWLEDGE

(READ DEUT. VIII. 1-9)

In these verses we have four valuable points of knowledge connected with our walk through the wilderness: namely, 1. the knowledge of ourselves; 2. the knowledge of God; 3. the knowledge of our relationship; and, 4. the knowledge of our hope.

1. And, first, as to the knowledge of self, we read, "Thou shalt remember all the way which the Lord thy God led thee these forty years in the wilderness, to humble thee, and to prove thee, to know what was in thine heart." Here is a wondrous point of knowledge. Who can utter it? Who can penetrate the depths of a human heart? Who can tell its windings and labyrinths? The details of a wilderness life tend to bring out a vast deal of the evil that is in us. At our first starting upon our christian career, we are apt to be so occupied with the present joy of deliverance that we know but very little of the real character of nature. It is as we get on, from stage to stage of our desert course, that we become acquainted with self.

II. But, then, we are not to suppose that, as we grow in self-knowledge, our joy must decline. Quite the opposite. This would be to make our joy depend upon *ignorance of self*, whereas it really depends upon *the knowledge of God*. In point of fact, as the believer advances in the knowledge of himself, his joy becomes deeper and more solid, inasmuch as he is led more thoroughly out of, and away from, himself, to find his sole object in Christ. He learns that nature's total ruin is not merely a true doctrine of the christian faith, but a deep reality in his own experience. He also learns that divine grace is a reality, that salvation is a reality—a deep, personal reality; that sin is a reality; the cross, a reality; the advocacy of Christ, a reality. In a word, he learns the depth, the fulness, the power, the application of God's gracious resources. "He humbled thee, and suffered thee to hunger," not that you might be driven to despair, but that He might "feed thee with manna, which thou knewest not, neither did thy fathers know, that He might make thee to know that man doth not live by bread only, but by every word that proceedeth out of the mouth of the Lord doth man live. Thy raiment waxed not old upon thee, neither did thy foot swell, these forty years."

Touching and beautiful appeal! "Forty years" of interrupted evidence of what was in the heart of God toward His redeemed people. "Six hundred thousand footmen" clothed, fed, kept and cared for, during "forty years," in "a vast howling wilderness!" What a noble and soul-satisfying display of the fulness of divine resources! How is it possible that, with the history of Israel's desert wanderings lying open before us, we could ever harbour a single doubt or fear? Oh! that our hearts may be more completely emptied of self, for this is true humility; and more completely filled with Christ, for this is true happiness and true holiness. "For the Lord thy God hath blessed thee in all the works of thy hand; *he knoweth thy walking through this great wilderness*: these forty years the Lord thy God hath been with thee, THOU HAST LACKED NOTHING." (Deut. ii. 7.)

III. All that we have been dwelling upon flows out of another thing, and that is, the relationship in which we stand. "*Thou shalt also consider in thine heart, that as a man chasteneth his son, so the Lord thy God chasteneth thee*." This accounts for all. The hunger and the food; the thirst and the water; the trackless desert and the guiding pillar; the toil and the refreshment; the sickness and the healing—all tell of the same thing, a Father's hand, a Father's heart. It is well to remember this, "lest we be weary and faint in our minds." (Heb. xii.) An earthly father will have to take down the rod of discipline, as well as to imprint the kiss of affection—to administer the rebuke as well as express his approval; to chasten as well as minister supplies. Thus it is with our heavenly Father. All His dealings flow out of that marvellous relationship in which He stands towards us. He is a "Holy Father." All is summed up in this. Our Father is the "Holy One;" and "the Holy One" is our Father. To walk with, lean on, and imitate Him "as dear children," must secure everything in the way of genuine happiness, real strength, and true holiness. When we walk with Him, we are happy; when we lean on Him, we are strong; and when we imitate Him, we are practically holy and gracious.

IV. Finally, in the midst of all the exercises, the trials, the conflicts, and even the mercies and privileges of the wilderness, we must keep the eye steadily fixed on that which lies before us. The joys of the kingdom are to fill our hearts, and to give vigour and buoyancy to our steps, as we pass across the desert. The green fields and vine-clad hills of the heavenly Canaan, the pearly gates and golden streets of the New Jerusalem are to fill the vision of our souls. We are called to cherish the hope of glory—a hope which will never make ashamed. When the sand of the desert tries us, let the thought of Canaan cheer us. Let us dwell upon the "inheritance incorruptible, undefiled, and that fadeth not away, reserved in heaven for us." (I Peter i. 4.) "For the Lord thy God bringeth thee into a good land, a land of brooks of water, of fountains and depths, that spring out of valleys and hills; a land of wheat, and barley, and vines, and fig-trees, and pomegranates; a land of oil olive and honey; a land wherein thou shalt eat bread without scarceness, thou shalt not lack anything in it; a land whose stones are iron, and out of whose hills thou mayest dig brass." Bright and blessed prospect! May we dwell upon it, and upon Him who will be the eternal source of all its brightness and blessedness!

> "To Canaan's sacred bound
>   We haste with songs of joy,
> Where peace and liberty are found,
>   And sweets that never cloy;
>     Hallelujah!
>   We are on our way to God!
>
> "How sweet the prospect is!
>   It cheers the pilgrim's breast;
> We're journeying through the wilderness,
>   But soon we'll gain our rest.
>     Hallelujah!
>   We are on our way to God!"

# "IF THE LORD TARRY"

My Beloved Friend,

Since our last conversation, I have been thinking a good deal of the subject which was then before us; and the more I think of it, the more disposed I am to doubt the moral fitness of the use so frequently made of the sentence which stands at the head of my letter. I have never been able to adopt the phrase, either in writing or speaking. In fact, it is not according to scripture, though it seems, of late years, to have become a favourite expression with many christian people who, I feel assured, desire to speak and act as in the divine presence, and according to the direct teaching of holy scripture.

I trust I need not assure you, my friend, that in raising an objection to this special form of speech, I would not, for a moment, even seem to weaken in any heart, the sense of the nearness of the Lord's coming—that most blessed hope which ought, each day, to become brighter and brighter in the vision of our souls. Far be the thought! That hope abides, in all its moral power, and, in no wise, depends on the using or not using any set form of words.

But then supposing I say, "If the Lord tarry, I mean to go to London next week," I make my going to London dependent upon the Lord's tarrying, whereas, He may tarry, and yet it may not be His will that I should go at all; and hence I ought to place all my movements, all my actions, all my plans, under the commanding influence of my Lord's will.

Is not this in direct accordance with scripture? What does the inspired apostle James say on the point? "Go to now, ye that say, To-day or to-morrow we will go into such a city, and continue there a year, and buy and sell, and get gain; whereas, ye know not what shall be on the morrow. For what is your life? It is even a vapour, that appeareth for a little time, and then vanisheth away. For that ye ought to say, *If the Lord will*, we shall live, and do this or that." James iv.

133

Here, the Spirit of God furnishes us with the proper form of words to be used in all our acts and ways; and surely we cannot find anything better than what He graciously deigns to give. "If the Lord will" includes everything which is to regulate our movements, whether the Lord is pleased to tarry or not.

But in writing this I have no thought, I assure you, of judging any one in his use of any particular phrase. I am merely giving you my reasons for not adopting the formulary in question. And I may just add, in conclusion, that whether we say, "If the Lord tarry," or "If the Lord will," we should ever seek, most earnestly, to be in the present power of the words we use, and thus avoid everything bordering, in the most remote degree, upon mere empty phraseology or religious cant. May the Lord make us *very real*, in all our words and ways!

Ever, my beloved friend,
Most affectionately yours,
C. H. M.

# GOD PREACHING PEACE

*"The word which God sent unto the children of Israel, preaching peace by Jesus Christ: he is Lord of all."* Acts x. 36.

One of the most momentous questions which can be put to a human being is this, "Have you peace with God?" It is a question of the deepest solemnity, and it claims a direct and immediate answer from every heart. There is no reason why any truly anxious soul should continue for one hour, yea, for one moment, without settled peace with God. Christ has made peace by the blood of His cross. God is preaching peace by Jesus Christ; and here we have the solid foundation of the believer's peace—Christ's finished work received on the authority of God's word by the power of the Holy Ghost.

This is the divine basis of peace; and the more simply we build thereon, the more solid our peace will be. The reason why so many are in a state of miserable uncertainty is because they do not rest, in artless faith, on God's foundation. They are occupied with themselves, instead of building exclusively on Christ. They are looking to experience, in place of to a risen Saviour. Frames, feelings, and attainments engage them instead of Christ. They are vainly hoping to find some sort of improvement in themselves, and not finding it, to their satisfaction—for what honest soul ever does?—they are filled with gloomy doubts; the heart is oppressed with anxious fear; the spirit overcast with heavy clouds. They have no divine certainty; and they are trying to find comfort in the exercises of a religious life, and inasmuch as imperfection attaches to their very best and most pious exercises, they are ever kept in a condition of spiritual darkness and bondage. Neither in our inward frames and experiences, nor in our outward exercises—of what kind soever these may be—have we the true ground of our peace in the divine presence. God did not send to the children of Israel, nor does He now send to us Gentiles, preaching peace by spiritual experiences or by religious exercises, but simply by Jesus Christ.

135

The reader cannot be too simple in laying hold of this great truth. He may rest assured that it is God's gracious desire that his soul should find peace. If not, why should God send, preaching—proclaiming—announcing peace. If God sends us a message of peace, He surely means that we should have it. He has provided it for us, by the precious atoning death of His Son, and He declares it unto us by His Spirit, in the holy scriptures. Thus it is all of God, from first to last; and hence it is called the peace of God. It comes forth from His heart. It bears the impress of His hand; and it is to the praise of His own eternal Name. We have nothing to do but to receive, with all thankfulness, this precious peace, and let it flow, like an even river, through our souls.

And here we would turn directly to the reader and press home upon his soul this grand question, "Hast thou peace with God?" Do not, we beseech thee, put it aside. It is a question of eternal importance—a question, in comparison with which all mere earthly questions dwindle into utter insignificance.

But it may be that some one whose eye scans these lines feels really anxious about this grand question, and would give worlds, if he possessed them, for a full, clear, and satisfactory answer. Such an one may feel disposed to ask, "What is the ground of this peace, and how may I have it for myself?" Two deeply important questions, most surely; and questions which we shall seek, by the grace of God, to answer.

And first, as to the real ground of the soul's peace; if the reader will turn to the last verse of Romans iv. he will find it set forth in two brief but weighty sentences. In this passage the inspired apostle, in speaking of our Lord Jesus Christ, declares that "He was delivered for our offences, and raised again for our justification."

Here, we have the solid and imperishable foundation of the sinner's peace—the divine ground on which God can preach peace. Jesus Christ was delivered for our offences. Let this be carefully noted. Let us mark particularly who was delivered; who delivered Him; and for what He was delivered. All these are essential to our enjoyment of peace.

Who, then, was delivered? The Holy One, the spotless One, the Lamb, the Christ, the Son of God, that blessed One who lay in

136

the bosom of the Father from all eternity, the object of the Father's supreme delight from everlasting, the Eternal Son. This blessed One, who lay in the bosom, from before all worlds, lay in the womb of the virgin, in the manger of Bethlehem, was baptized in Jordan, was tempted in the wilderness, was transfigured on the Mount, was bowed down in the garden, was nailed to a tree, buried in the grave, raised from the dead, and is now seated on the throne of the Majesty in the heavens.

This is He who was "delivered." He stood with our offences. He represented us on the cross. He stood in our stead, and received from the hand of Eternal Justice all that we deserved. There was a regular transfer of all our guilt, all our offences, all our iniquities, all our transgressions to Him who knew no sin, who had no more to do with sin than we had to do with righteousness. He died in our stead. The One whose whole human life was a sweet odour ever ascending to the throne of God, was delivered up to death, charged with all our offences.

But who delivered Him? This is a cardinal question. Who delivered Jesus up to the death of the cross? Isaiah liii. and 2 Corinthians v. furnish the answer: "It pleased Jehovah to bruise him." Such is the language of the inspired prophet. And now hear the apostle: "God hath made him (Christ) to be sin for us." God has done it. It will not do to say that "we lay our sins on Jesus." We want much more than this. If it were merely a question of our laying our sins on Jesus, we could never have peace with God, seeing that we do not know the extent of our sin, the depth of our guilt, the true amount of our liabilities, as God knows it. In order to have peace with God, I must know that He is satisfied. God was the offended party, the aggrieved One, and He must be satisfied. Well, blessed be His name, He is satisfied, for He Himself has found the ransom. He has laid our sins, according to His estimate of them, on the head of the divine Sin-bearer. All that was needful, not merely to meet our condition, but to satisfy His claims, vindicate His majesty, and glorify His name, He Himself has provided in the atoning death of His own Son. Thus He is satisfied, and hence He can preach to us—peace by Jesus Christ, Lord of all. The spotless Christ was judged on the cross, in our stead. God hid His face from that blessed One—turned away His countenance—closed His ear—forsook Him for the moment. And why? Because He was delivered for our offences. God forsook Him that He might receive us. He treated Him as we deserved, in order that He might treat us as He deserved. Jesus took our place in death and judgment, that we might take His place in life, righteousness, and everlasting glory.

And, now, let us ask—though we have in measure anticipated the question—for what was the precious Saviour delivered? "For our offences." For how many? For all, most surely. When Jesus hung on the cross, all the believer's offences were laid upon and imputed to Him. Yes, *all*; for, albeit they were future, so far as he is concerned, when Christ bore them on the cross, yet is there no such distinction as past, present, or future with Him who spans eternity as a moment. All our sins were laid on Jesus; He answered for them and put them away for ever, so that they are gone out of God's sight, and instead of our sins, there is nothing before God save the Christ who bore them and blotted them for ever, and was raised for our justification. Who raised Him? Even the same that delivered Him. And why did He raise Him? Because all was settled for which had been delivered. Christ glorified God in the putting away of our sins; and God glorified Christ, by raising Him from the dead and crowning Him with glory and honour. Most marvellous, most precious truth! Christ forsaken on the cross, because our sins were laid on Him. Christ crowned on the throne, because our sins are put away. "He was delivered for our offences, and raised again for our justification." Such is the true, the solid, the everlasting ground of a sinner's peace in the presence of God.

And now one word as to the question of how the sinner can have this peace for himself. The answer is as simple as God can make it. What is it? Has the sinner to do aught? Has he to be anything but what he is—a poor, lost, worthless, guilty creature? No. He has simply to believe God's word—to receive into his *heart*, not merely into his *head*, the blessed message which God sends to him—to rest in Christ—to be satisfied with that which has satisfied God. God is satisfied with Christ, without anything else whatever. Is the reader satisfied? or is he waiting for something more—something of his own—his vows and resolutions—his frames, feelings, and experiences? If so, he cannot get peace. *To be satisfied with Christ, is to have peace with God.*

> The Lord of Life in death hath lain,
>   To clear me from all charge of sin;
> And, Lord, from guilt of crimson stain
>   Thy precious blood hath made me clean.

# "RIVERS OF LIVING WATER"

"In the last day, that great day of the feast, Jesus stood and cried, saying, If any man thirst, let him come unto me and drink. He that believeth on me, as the scripture hath said, out of his belly shall flow rivers of living water." John vii. 37, 38.

The feast referred to in this lovely scripture was "The feast of tabernacles," called, at the opening of the chapter, "*The Jews'* feast." This stamped its character. It could no longer be called, as in Leviticus xxiii. "A feast of Jehovah." The Lord could not own it. It had become an empty formality—a powerless ordinance—a piece of barren routine—something in which man could boast himself while God was entirely shut out.

This is nothing uncommon. There has ever been a strong tendency in the human mind to perpetuate forms when the power is gone. No doubt power may clothe itself in a certain form; and, so long as the form is the expression of the power, it is all right and good. But the danger lies in going on with the mere outward form without a single particle of inward power. Thus it was with Israel of old; and thus it is with the professing church now. We have all to watch against this snare of the devil. He will use a positive ordinance of God as a means of deceiving the soul, and shutting out God altogether. But where faith is in lively exercise, the soul has to do with God in the ordinance, whatever it is, and thus the power and freshness are duly maintained.

The reader has, no doubt, noticed that in the opening chapters of John's Gospel, the inspired writer invariably designates the feasts as feasts of the Jews; and not only so, but we find the Lord Jesus displacing one after another of these feasts and offering Himself as an object for the heart. Thus at the opening of chapter vii. we read, "After these things Jesus walked in Galilee; for he would not walk in Jewry, because the Jews sought to kill him. Now the Jews' feast of tabernacles was at hand." Terrible anomaly! deadly delusion! Seeking to murder the Son of God, and yet keeping the feast of tabernacles! Such is religious man without God. "His brethren therefore said unto him, Depart hence, and go into Judea, that thy disciples also may see thy works that thou doest. For there is no man that doeth anything in secret, and he himself seeketh to be known openly. If thou do these things, shew thyself to the world. For neither did his brethren believe on him."

Near as His brethren were to Him, according to the flesh, they knew Him not, they believed not on Him. They would fain have Him make a display of Himself before the world. They knew not His object. He had not come from heaven in order to be gazed at and wondered after. "All the world will wonder after the beast" by-and-by; but the blessed Son of God came to serve and to give. He came to hide Himself, to glorify God, and to serve man.

He refused, therefore, to exhibit Himself at the feast. "Then Jesus said unto them, my time is not yet come; but your time is always ready. The world cannot hate you; but me it hateth, because I testify of it that the works thereof are evil. Go ye up unto this feast: I go not up yet to this feast: for my time is not yet full come. When he had said these words unto them, he abode still in Galilee. But when his brethren were gone up, then went he also up unto the feast, not openly, but as it were in secret."

And for what did He go up? He went up to serve. He went up to glorify His Father, and to be the willing Servant of man's necessity. "Now about the midst of the feast, Jesus went up into the temple and taught. And the Jews marvelled, saying, How knoweth this man letters, having never learned? Jesus answered them, saying, My doctrine is not mine, but his that sent me." Here His moral glory, as the self-hiding Servant, shines out. "My doctrine is not mine." Such was His answer to those who wondered where He got His learning. Alas! they knew Him not. His motives and His objects lay beyond the reach of carnal and worldly-minded men. They measured him by their own standard, and hence, all their conclusions were utterly false. "If any man will do his will he shall know of the doctrine, whether it be of God, or whether I speak of myself [ἀπ' ἐμαυτοῦ]. He that speaketh of himself seeketh his own glory; but he that seeketh his glory that sent him, the same is true and no unrighteousness is in him."

141

The blessed One did not speak from Himself, as if He were independent of the Father, but as One who lived in absolute and complete dependence, and in unbroken communion, drawing all His springs from the living God, doing nothing, saying nothing, thinking nothing apart from the Father.

We have the same truth with reference to the Holy Ghost, in John xvi. "Howbeit, when he the Spirit of truth is come, he will guide you into all truth; for he shall not speak of himself; but whatsoever he shall hear, that shall he speak; and he will shew you things to come." The Holy Ghost did not speak from Himself, as independent of the Father and the Son, but as One in full communion with them.

But we must turn, for a moment, to the words which form the special subject of this paper. "In the last day, that great day of the feast, Jesus stood and cried, saying, "If any man thirst, let him come unto me and drink." Here we have set before us a truth of infinite preciousness and immense practical power. The Person of Christ is the divine spring of all freshness and spiritual energy. It is in Him alone the soul can find all it really needs. It is to Him we must betake ourselves for all our personal refreshment and blessing. If, at any time, we find ourselves dull, heavy and barren, what are we to do? Make efforts to raise the tone? Nay, this will never do. What then? Let him "Come unto me and drink."

Mark the words. It is not, "Come unto me and draw." We may draw for others and be dry ourselves; but if we drink, our own souls are refreshed, and then—"Rivers of living water."

Nothing is more miserable than the restless efforts of a soul out of communion. We may be very busy; our hands may be full of work; our feet may run hither and thither; the head may be full of knowledge; but if the heart be not livingly occupied with the Person of Christ, it will, it must be, all barrenness and desolation so far as we are personally concerned; and there will, there can be, no "rivers of living water" flowing out for others. Impossible. If we are to be made a blessing to others, we must feed upon Christ for ourselves. We do not "drink" for other people, we drink to satisfy our thirst; and as we drink, the rivers flow. Shew us a man whose heart is filled with Christ, and we will shew you a man whose

142

hands are ready for work, and his feet ready to run; but unless we begin with heart communion, our running and our doing will be a miserable failure—there will be no glory to God—no rivers of living water.

Yes, reader, we must begin in the very innermost circle of our own moral being, and there be occupied, by faith, with a living Christ, else all our service will prove utterly worthless. If we want to act on others; if we would be made a blessing in our day and generation; if we desire to bring forth any fruit to God; if we would shine as lights amid the moral gloom around; if we would be a channel of blessing in the midst of a sterile desert, then, verily, we must hearken to our Lord's words in John vii. 37. We must drink at the fountain head. And what then? Drink still—drink ever— drink largely, and then the rivers must flow. If I say, "I must try and be a channel of blessing to others" I shall only prove my own folly and weakness. But if I bring my empty vessel to the fountain head and get it filled, then, without the smallest effort, the rivers will flow.

# A FRAGMENT ON WORSHIP

It is deeply important that the christian reader should understand the true character of the worship God looks for, and in which He delights. God delights in Christ; and hence it should be our constant aim to present Him to God. Christ should ever be the material of our worship, and He will be, in proportion as we are led by the Holy Ghost. How often, alas! it is otherwise with us the heart can tell. Both in the assembly and in the closet, how often is the tone low, and the spirit dull and heavy! We are occupied with self instead of with Christ; and the Holy Ghost, instead of being free to do His own proper work—which is to take of the things of Christ and shew them unto us—is obliged to occupy us with ourselves, in self-judgment, because our ways have not been right.

All this is to be deeply deplored. It demands our serious attention, both as assemblies and as individuals, in our public reunions and in our private devotions. Why is the tone of our public meetings frequently so low? Why such feebleness, such barrenness, such wandering? Why are the hymns and prayers so often wide of the true mark? Why is there so little that really deserves the name of worship? Why is there so little in our midst to refresh the heart of God?—so little that He can speak of as "My bread for my sacrifices made by fire, for a sweet savour unto me?" We are occupied with *self* and its surroundings—our wants, our weakness, our trials, our difficulties; and we leave God without the bread of His sacrifice. We actually rob Him of His due, and of that which His loving heart desires.

# SEPARATION: NOT FUSION

"Therefore, thus saith the Lord, If thou return, then will I bring thee again, and thou shalt stand before me; and if thou take forth the precious from the vile, thou shalt be as my mouth; let them return unto thee; but return not thou unto them." Jeremiah xv. 19.

The principle laid down in the foregoing passage is of the deepest possible importance to all who desire to walk with God. It is by no means a popular principle; very far from it. But this does not detract from its value in the judgment of those who are taught of God. In an evil world the popular thing is almost sure to be the wrong thing; and whatever has most of God—most of Christ—most of pure truth—is sure to be most unpopular. This is an axiom in the judgment of faith, inasmuch as Christ and the world are at opposite points of the moral compass.

Now, one of the most popular ideas of the day is fusion, or amalgamation; and all who desire to be accounted men of broad sympathies and liberal sentiments go thoroughly in for this grand object. But we hesitate not to avow that nothing can be more opposed to the revealed mind of God. We make this statement in the full consciousness of its opposition to the universal judgment of Christendom. For this we are quite prepared. Not that we court opposition; but we have long since learnt to distrust the judgment of what is called the religious world, because we have so constantly found that judgment to be diametrically opposed to the plainest teaching of holy scripture; and it is, we can truly say, our deep and earnest desire to stand with the word of God against every thing and every one; for we are well assured that nothing can abide for ever, save that which is based upon the imperishable foundation of holy scripture.

What, then, does scripture teach on the subject of this paper? Is it separation, or fusion? What was the instruction to Jeremiah in the passage quoted above? Was he told to try and amalgamate with those around him? Was he to seek to mingle the precious

145

with the vile? The very reverse. Jeremiah was taught of God first of all to return himself—to stand apart even from those who were the professed people of God, but whose ways were contrary to His mind. And what then? "I will bring thee again, and thou shalt stand before me."

Here, then, we have Jeremiah's personal path and position most clearly laid down. He was to return, and take his stand with God in thorough separation from evil. This was his bounden duty, regardless of the thoughts of men, or of his brethren. They might deem and pronounce him narrow, bigoted, exclusive, intolerant, and the like; but with that he had nothing whatever to do. His one grand business was to obey. Separation from evil was the divine rule, not amalgamation with it. The latter might seem to offer a wider field of usefulness, but mere usefulness is not the object of a true servant of Christ, but simple obedience. The business of a servant is to do what he is told, not what he considers right or good. If this were better understood, it would simplify matters amazingly. If God calls us to separation from evil, and we imagine we can do more good by amalgamation with it, how shall we stand before Him? How shall we meet Him? Will He call that good which resulted from positive disobedience to His Word? Is it not plain that our first, our last, our only duty, is to obey? Assuredly. This is the foundation, yea, it is the sum and substance of all that can really be called good.

But was there not something for Jeremiah to do in his narrow *path* and circumscribed *position*? There was. His *practice* was defined with all possible clearness. And what was it? "If thou *separate* the precious from the vile, thou shalt be as my mouth." He was not only to stand and walk in separation himself, but he was to try and separate others also. This might give him the appearance of a proselytizer, or of one whose object was to draw people over to his way of thinking. But here again he had to rise above all the thoughts of men. It was far better, far higher, far more blessed, for Jeremiah to be as God's mouth, than to stand well with his fellows. What are man's thoughts worth? Just nothing. When his breath goeth out of him, in that very hour his thoughts perish. But God's thoughts shall endure for ever. If Jeremiah had set about mingling

146

the precious with the vile, he would not have been as God's mouth; nay, he would have been as the devil's mouth. Separation is God's principle; fusion is Satan's.

It is counted liberal, large-hearted, and charitable, to be ready to associate with all sorts of people. Confederacy, association, limited liabilities, are the order of the day. The Christian must stand apart from all such things; not because he is better than other people, but because God says, "Be not unqually yoked together with unbelievers." It was not because Jeremiah was better than his brethren that he had to separate himself, but simply because he was commanded to do so by Him whose word must ever define the course, govern the conduct, and form the character of His people. And, further, we may rest assured it was not in sourness of temper, or severity of spirit, but in profound sorrow of heart and humility of mind that Jeremiah separated himself from those around him. He could weep day and night over the condition of his people; but the necessity of separation was as plain as the word of God could make it. He might tread the path of separation with broken heart and weeping eyes, but tread it he must if he would be as God's mouth. Had he refused to tread it, he would have been making himself to be wiser than God. What, though those around him, his brethren and friends, might not be able to understand or appreciate his conduct; with this he had nothing whatever to do. He might refer them to Jehovah for an explanation, but his business was to obey, not to explain or apologize.

Thus it is always. "Be ye not unequally yoked together with unbelievers: for what fellowship hath righteousness with unrighteousness? and what communion hath light with darkness? And what concord hath Christ with Belial? or what part hath he that believeth with an infidel? And what agreement hath the temple of God with idols? For ye are the temple of the living God; as God hath said, I will dwell in them, and walk in them; and I will be their God, and they shall be my people. Wherefore come out from among them, and be ye separate, saith the Lord, and touch not the unclean; and I will receive you, and will be a Father unto you, and ye shall be my sons and daughters, saith the Lord Almighty." 2 Corinthians vi. 14-18.

147

It may seem very plausible and very popular to say, "We ought not to judge other people. How can we tell whether people are believers or not? It is not for us to set ourselves up as holier than others. It is charitable to hope the best. If people are sincere, what difference does it make as to creeds? Each one is entitled to hold his own opinions. It is only a matter of views after all."

To all this we reply, God's word commands Christians to judge, to discern, to discriminate, to come out, to be separate. This being so, all the plausible arguments and reasonings that can possibly be adduced are, in the judgment of a true-hearted, single-eyed, servant of Christ, lighter by far than the small dust of the balance.

Hearken to the following weighty words from the blessed apostle Paul to his son Timothy—words bearing down with unmistakeable clearness upon all the Lord's people at this very moment: "Nevertheless, the foundation of God standeth sure, having this seal, the Lord knoweth them that are his. And *let every one that nameth the name of Christ depart from iniquity. But in a great house there are not only vessels of gold and silver, but also of wood and of earth; and some to honour, and some to dishonour. If a man purge himself from these* (the dishonourable vessels), *he shall be a vessel unto honour, sanctified, and meet for the master's use, and prepared unto every good work.*" 2 Timothy ii. 19-21.

Here we see that if any man desires to be a sanctified vessel, meet for the Master's use, and *prepared unto every good work,* he must separate himself from the iniquity and the dishonourable vessels around him. There is no getting over this without flinging God's word overboard; and surely to reject God's word is to reject Himself. His word commands me to purge myself, to depart from iniquity, to turn away from those who have a form of godliness, but deny its power.

# TWO IMPOSSIBLES

## (Hebrews vi)

There are few who have set out to follow the Lord Jesus who have not, at some time or other, gone through painful exercise of heart in connection with the opening verses of Hebrews vi. And while, in the long run, they have had no reason to regret the exercise, yet it is always needful to distinguish between the Spirit's using a scripture to search, and Satan's abusing it to stumble us. Searching is good for us. It is most healthful. We all need it, and we have to be thankful when we get it, we are so prone to be light and superficial, and to retire from anything that probes the conscience.

Still, we have not the slightest doubt that many true and earnest souls, many to whom Hebrews vi. 4-6 has no application whatever, have been stumbled and discouraged through not understanding the true force and bearing of the passage. It is to help such that we pen the following lines, for we can truly say there is no work in which we have a more intense interest than in taking up the stumbling-blocks out of the way of God's beloved people. We feel most fully assured it is work which He delights to have done, inasmuch as He has given express commandment to His servants to do it. We have just to take care lest, in our desire to remove the stumbling-blocks, we should in any wise disturb the landmarks. May the blessed Spirit, then, graciously help us to a right understanding of this sadly misunderstood passage of holy scripture!

Our special business, just now, is to inquire who are they of whom the inspired writer speaks in verses 4-6—those of whom he declares, "It is impossible to renew them again to repentance?" A correct answer to this question will remove much, if not all, of the difficulty felt in respect to this portion of the Epistle to the Hebrews; and in reaching this answer there are two things to be borne in mind—first, that in verses 1 and 2, there is not a single feature belonging to Christianity as distinct from Judaism; secondly, that in verses 4 and 5 there is not a single expression that rises to the height of the new birth, or the sealing of the Spirit.

Let us quote the apostle's words: "Therefore, leaving the principles of the doctrine of Christ," or, as the margin reads it, "The word of the beginning of Christ, let us go on to perfection; not laying again the foundation of repentance from dead works, and of faith toward God, of the doctrine of baptisms [or washings], and of laying on of hands, and of resurrection of the dead, and of eternal judgment."

Now it must be plain to the reader that the apostle could never exhort those professing christian Hebrews to "leave" anything belonging to Christianity. There is not a single fact in that glorious economy, from first to last—not a single stone in that glorious superstructure, from foundation to topstone—not a single principle in that magnificent system, from beginning to end—that we could afford to leave or dispense with for a moment. For what, let us ask, is the grand foundation of Christianity? The cross. And what are its two characteristic facts? A Man glorified in heaven, and God dwelling in man on the earth. Could we leave these? God forbid! To whom, or to what, should we go? It is impossible that we could leave or give up a single fact, feature, or principle of our glorious Christianity.

What, then, have we got in Hebrews vi. 1, 2? Simply those elements of truth contained in the Jewish system which, in so far as they possessed any permanent value, are reproduced in Christianity; but, as a system, were to be abandoned for ever. Where is there a word peculiar to Christianity in this passage? Can we not see at a glance that the apostle has Judaism before his mind? It is this he exhorts his brethren to leave, and to go on to Christianity, which he here calls "perfection."

It is a very commonly received idea that the words, "Let us go on to perfection," refer to our leaving the earlier stages of the divine life, and getting on to the higher. This we believe to be a total mistake. As to what is called "the higher christian life," there is in reality no such thing. If there be a higher life, there must be a lower one; but we know, blessed be God, that Christ is our life,

150

the life of each, the life of all; and there cannot be anything higher than that. The merest babe in Christ has as high a life as the most matured and profoundly taught member of the church of God.

No doubt there is progress in the divine life, growth in grace, faith growing exceedingly. All this we own most fully, and would charge ourselves to seek after most earnestly. But it is not the subject of Hebrews vi. 1, 2. It is not a question of going from one form in the school of Christ to another, but of leaving the school of Moses to enter fully, heartily, and intelligently, the school of Christ. It is not a question of going from one stage of christian life to another, but of abandoning Judaism to go on to Christianity. We could not abandon a single atom of Christianity without abandoning Christ Himself, for He is the foundation, the source, the centre, the spring of it all.

But the reader may feel disposed to ask, Have we not got "repentance, faith, resurrection, and eternal judgment" in Hebrews vi. 1, 2?* True, but only as elements of the Jewish system. There is not a word about "faith in our Lord Jesus Christ"—not a word about Christ at all; it is simply Judaism, to which some of the Hebrew professors were in danger of returning, but from which the apostle earnestly urges them to go on.

Let us now turn for a moment to verses 4, 5. "For it is impossible for those who were once enlightened, and have tasted of the heavenly gift, and were made partakers of the Holy Ghost, and have tasted the good word of God, and the powers of the world to come [of the coming age], if they shall fall away, to renew them again unto repentance."

Now the reader will notice that, as in verses 1, 2, we have not a single clause specially characteristic of Christianity; so, in verses 4, 5, we have not a single clause that rises to the height of the new birth, or the sealing of the Holy Ghost. A person might be all that is here spoken of, and yet never have been born again, never sealed by the Holy Ghost. How many thousands have been "enlightened" by the gospel, without being converted by it! Wherever the gospel

---

* Resurrection, as seen in Christianity, is not merely "resurrection of the dead;" but, "resurrection *from among* the dead."

has been preached, wherever the Bible has been received and read, an enlightening influence has gone forth, altogether irrespective of any saving work wrought in souls. Look, for example, at the nations of Europe since the Reformation. In all those countries that have received the Bible, we see the oral effect produced in the way of intelligence, civilisation, and refinement, apart altogether from the question of the conversion of individual souls. On the other hand, those countries which have refused the Bible exhibit the melancholy results of ignorance, moral darkness, and degradation. In a word, there may be enlightenment of the understanding without any divine work in the conscience or in the heart.

But what means the "tasting the heavenly gift?" Does not this imply the new birth? By no means. Many may have gotten a taste of the new, the heavenly, things set forth in the glorious gospel of God, and yet never have passed from death unto life, never have been broken down before God, about their sins—never have received Christ into their hearts. Tasting of the heavenly gift, and passing by new birth into the heavenly kingdom, are totally different things.

So also many were made "partakers (μετόχους) of the Holy Ghost," so as to speak with tongues, prophesy, and the like, who nevertheless were never born of the Spirit. When the Holy Ghost came down on the day of Pentecost, His presence pervaded the whole assembly. His power was felt by all, converted or unconverted. The word rendered "partakers" does not express intelligent fellowship, and this makes it all the more clear that there is not the slightest thought of new birth or sealing.

Further, as to "tasting the good word of God," do we not all know too well that unconverted people can, in a certain sense, enjoy the word of God, and have a measure of delight in hearing a full, free, gospel preached? Have we not often heard persons who furnished no sort of evidence of divine life speaking, in highly appreciative terms, of what they called the savoury doctrines of grace? There is a wide and very material difference indeed between a person tasting the good word of God, and the word of God entering the soul, in living, quickening, convicting, and converting power.

152

Finally, a person might taste "the power of the coming age"—the age when Messiah will set up His kingdom—he might heal diseases, and cast out devils—he might take up serpents, and drink poison—he might speak with tongues: he might do all these things, and yet never have been born again. "Thus"—as a recent writer has solemnly and forcibly put it—"we may fairly give the fullest force to every one of these expressions. Yet, write them out ever so largely, they fall short both of the new birth and of sealing with the Holy Ghost. There is everything, one may say, save inward spiritual life in Christ, or the indwelling seal of it. That is to say"—and, oh, may it be deeply pondered in this day of intellectual knowledge and flippant profession!—" one may have the very highest endowments and privileges, in the way both of meeting the mind, and also of exterior power; and yet all may be given up, and the man become so much the keener enemy of Christ. Indeed such is the natural result. It had been the mournful fact as to some. They had fallen away. Hence renewal to repentance is an impossibility"—declared to be so by the authoritative and conclusive testimony of the Holy Ghost—" seeing they crucify to themselves the Son of God, and put him to an open shame."

"Why impossible? The case supposed is"—not any one who ever possessed a single spark of divine life in his soul; no, nor yet any one with the very feeblest desire after Christ, or one atom of true repentance or desire to flee from the wrath to come, but that—"of persons, after the richest proof and privilege, turning aside apostates from Christ, in order to take up Judaism once more. As long as that course is pursued, repentance there cannot be. Supposing a man had been the adversary of Messiah here below"—as, for example, Paul himself, the very writer of the epistle—"there was still the opening for him of grace from on high. It was possible that the very man that had slighted Christ here below, might have his eyes opened to see and receive Christ above; but this abandoned, there is no fresh condition in which He could be presented to men. Those who rejected Christ, in the fulness of His grace, and in the height of His glory in which God had set Him as man before them"—Christ the object of fourfold testimony, His works, the Father John the Baptist, and Moses. (John v.)—"Those that rejected

153

Him, not merely on earth, but in heaven"—as attested by the Holy Ghost sent down from the ascended and glorified Man on the throne of the Majesty in the heavens—"what was there to fall back upon? What possible means to bring them to repentance after that? There is none. What is there but Christ coming in judgment?"*

Surely there is, and can be nothing else. For one who, from amid the full blaze of gospel light and privilege, could deliberately go back to the darkness of Judaism, there remains nothing but hopeless impenitence, hardness of heart, judicial blindness, and eternal judgment.

It is not, be it carefully observed, a child of God falling into sin, and getting at a distance from God. Such an one will, most surely, be brought back, and restored, though it may be through sore affliction under the chastening hand of God. It is not an anxious soul earnestly seeking the way of life and peace. It is not the case of a poor soul ignorant and out of the way. To none of these does the "impossible" of Hebrews vi. 4 apply. There is not a single anxious, earnest, soul beneath the canopy of heaven whose case is impossible. There is just one case that approaches awfully near to Hebrews vi. 4, and that is one who has gone on sinning against light, refusing to act on the plain word of God, resisting the truth —knowingly and deliberately resisting—because of the consequences of acting upon it.

This is indeed most solemn. No one can take it upon him to say at what depths of darkness, blindness, and hardness of heart, a case of this kind may arrive. It is a terrible thing to trifle with light, and to go on with what we know to be wrong, because of worldly advantage, to please friends, to avoid persecution and trial, or for any reason whatsoever. "Give glory to the Lord your God, before he cause darkness, and before your feet stumble on the dark mountains, and while ye look for light, he turn it into the shadow of death, and make it gross darkness." Jeremiah xiii. 16.

Having sounded this warning note for any whose case may need it, we close this part of our subject by presenting to any troubled soul whose eye may scan these lines, that precious word at the very

---

* "Lectures Introductory to St. Paul's Epistles," by W. Kelly.

end of the inspired volume—a word issuing forth from the very heart of God—the heart of Christ—"*Whosoever will, let him take the water of life* FREELY."

## PART II

In reading the Epistle to the Hebrews, we can hardly fail to notice the way in which the most solemn words of warning stand side by side with words of deepest comfort and consolation. Thus, for example, chapter iv. opens with, "Let us therefore *fear;*" and closes with, "Let us therefore come *boldly.*" When we think of who we are, what we are, and where we are, we have reason to fear. But when we think of God—His grace, His goodness, His tender mercy, His faithfulness—we may cherish the most fearless confidence. When we think of the world, with all its dangers, temptations, and snares, we may well be on our guard. But when we think of "the throne of grace," with its exhaustless provisions, and of our most merciful, faithful, and sympathising High Priest, we can draw nigh with holy boldness, and find an ample supply to meet our deepest need.

So also, in chapter x., we have the same striking contrast—the warning voice, and the sweet accents of comfort and encouragement. Hearken to the former. "If we sin wilfully after that we have received the knowledge of the truth, there remaineth no more sacrifice for sins, but a certain fearful looking for of judgment and fiery indignation, which shall devour the adversaries. He that despised Moses' law died without mercy under two or three witnesses; of how much sorer punishment, suppose ye, shall he be thought worthy who hath trodden under foot the Son of God, and hath counted the blood of the covenant, wherewith he was sanctified, an unholy thing, and hath done despite unto the Spirit of grace? For we know him that hath said, Vengeance belongeth unto me, I will recompense ,saith the Lord. And again, The Lord will judge his people. It is a fearful thing to fall into the hands of the living God."

How awfully solemn is all this! How searching! Should we seek to blunt the edge of the warning? God forbid! We should only see that it has its true direction, its proper application. Can it ever touch an anxious inquirer, or a true-hearted, earnest, follower of Christ? Assuredly not, save indeed that it may deepen the earnestness of the one ,and quicken the pace of the other. For only see, reader, how close the word of comfort and encouragement stands to the awful note of warning and admonition. "But call to remembrance the former days, in which, after ye were illuminated, ye endured a great fight of afflictions, partly whilst ye were made a gazing-stock, both by reproaches and afflictions; and partly whilst ye became companions of them that were so used. For ye had compassion of me in my bonds, and took joyfully the spoiling of your goods, knowing in yourselves that ye have in heaven a better and an enduring substance. Cast not away therefore your confidence, which hath great recompense of reward. For ye have need of patience, that, after ye have done the will of God, ye might receive the promise. For yet a little while, and he that shall come will come, and will not tarry. Now the just shall live by faith; but if any man draw back, my soul shall have no pleasure in him. But we are not of them that draw back unto perdition, but of them that believe to the saving of the soul."

Thus we see how the inspiring Spirit connects, in this epistle, the most precious consolation with the most solemn warning. Both are needed, and therefore both are given; and it will be our wisdom to seek to profit by both. We need never be afraid to trust scripture. If we find a difficulty, in place of puzzling over it, let us quietly wait on God for further light, meanwhile calmly resting in the assurance that no one part of the word of God can ever contradict another. All is in the most perfect harmony; the apparent discrepancies are entirely owing to our ignorance; and hence, instead of putting forth our gratuitous efforts to reconcile things, we should just allow each passage of scripture to come home in all its moral force to the heart and conscience, and produce its divinely appointed result in the formation of our character. Thus, when we read such words as these, "My sheep hear my voice, and I know them, and they follow me; and I give unto them eternal life; and *they shall never perish, neither shall any pluck them out of my hand.* My Father which gave them me is greater than all; and no

156

one is able to pluck them out of my Father's hand. I and my Father are one," it is our sweet privilege to take them in, in all their divine simplicity and heavenly clearness, and rest in them in calm confidence. There is no difficulty, no obscurity, no vagueness about them. All Christ's sheep are as safe as He can make them, as safe as He is Himself. The hand that would touch them must touch Him. They are divinely and eternally secure. Persons may imagine, or profess themselves to be, His sheep who are not so in reality; they may fall away from their mere profession, bring much reproach on the cause of Christ, cause the way of truth to be evil spoken of, and lay a stumbling-block in the way of honest inquirers, by leading them to think that true Christians can fall away, and be lost. All this may be true, but it leaves wholly untouched the precious and most comforting words of our good and faithful Shepherd, that His sheep have eternal life, and shall never —can never, perish. No passage of holy scripture can, by any possibility, contradict the plain statement of our Lord.

But then there are other passages designed to search the conscience, to make us watchful, to produce holy circumspection in our ways, to lead us to judge ourselves, to superinduce self-denial. Take the following weighty and most searching scripture: "Know ye not that they which run in a race, run all, but one receiveth the prize? So run, that ye may obtain. And every man that striveth for the mastery is temperate in all things. Now they do it to obtain a corruptible crown, but we an incorruptible. I therefore so run, not as uncertainly; so fight I, not as one that beateth the air; but I keep under my body, and bring it into subjection; lest that by any means, when I have preached to others, I myself should be a castaway." I Corinthians ix. 24-27.

Now, will any one attempt to place I Corinthians ix. in opposition to John x.? Far be the thought! What then? Why we are simply to receive both, in all their divine force, and allow them to act upon us according to the divine purpose in giving them to us —the latter on our hearts, for comfort and consolation; the former on our consciences, for admonition and warning. How terrible it would be for any one to say or to think that, because he is a sheep of Christ, he may walk in self-indulgence—because he can never

157

perish, he need not seek to keep his body under—because nothing can separate him from the love of Christ, he may give a loose rein to his desires! Surely such an one would afford most melancholy evidence that he is anything but a sheep of the flock of Christ.

But we must return to Hebrews vi., and dwell for a moment upon our second "Impossible." The first, as we have seen, had respect to man; the second has respect to God. Man, with the very highest advantages, with the very rarest privileges, with the most powerful array of evidence, will turn his back upon God and Christ; he will deliberately apostatise from Christianity, give up the truth of God, go back into darkness, and plunge into a condition, from which the Holy Ghost declares "it is impossible to renew him again to repentance."

But, as usual, in this marvellous epistle, the "strong consolation" stands in close and most gracious proximity to the awful warning. And, blessed be God, this same strong consolation is designed for us in connection with the very smallest measure of living faith in the word of God. It is not a question of great attainments in knowledge, experience, or devotedness; no, it is simply a matter of having even that measure and character of faith, and earnestness, typified by the man-slayer as he flew to the city of refuge to escape the avenger of blood. How precious is this for every true and earnest soul! The very feeblest spark of divinely-given faith secures eternal life, strong consolation, and everlasting glory, because "it is impossible for God to lie." He cannot, and will not, deny Himself, blessed for ever be His name! He has pledged His word, and added His oath, the "two immutable things;" and where is the power, human or diabolical, that can touch these two things?

We close with a passage from a volume referred to in our paper for November.

"Another point of interest which may be remarked here (1 in Heb. vi.) is the intimation at the end, compared with the beginning, of the chapter. We have seen the highest external privileges" —and they were merely external—"not only the mind of man, as far as it could, enjoying the truth, but the power of the Holy Ghost making the man, at any rate, an instrument of power"—not a subject of grace—"even though it be to his own shame and deeper condemnation afterwards. In short, man may have the utmost conceivable advantage, and the greatest external power, even of the Spirit of God Himself, and yet all come to nothing."

How solemnising! "But the very same chapter, which affirms and warns of the possible failure of every advantage, shews us the weakest faith that the whole New Testament describes coming into the secure possession of the best blessings of grace." How consolatory! How truly encouraging! "Who but God could have dictated that this same chapter should depict the weakest faith that the New Testament ever acknowledges? What can look feebler, what more desperately pressed, than a man fleeing for refuge? It is not a soul as coming to Jesus; it is not as one whom the Lord meets, and blesses on the spot; but here is a man hard pushed, fleeing for very life (evidently a figure drawn from the man-slayer fleeing from the avenger of blood), yet eternally saved and blessed according to the acceptance of Christ"—the very lowest character of faith met by the very fullest, richest, and most permanent blessing!

"There was no reality found in the persons referred to in verses 4 and 5, though so highly favoured; and hence it was, as there was no conscience before God, no sense of sin, no cleaving to Christ, that everything came to nought. But here, in the end of the chapter, there is the fruit of faith, feeble indeed, and sorely tried, but in the light that appreciates the judgment of God against sin. Hence, although it be only fleeing in an agony of soul for refuge, what is it that God gives to one in such a state? Strong consolation, and that which enters within the veil. Impossible that the Son should be shaken from His place on the throne of God. And it is as impossible that the very least and weakest believer should come to any hurt whatsoever! The weakest of saints more than conqueror is."*

Well may we exclaim, in view of all this surpassing grace, "Halleljah!" Beloved christian reader, may our whole life be spent in praising our ever blessed and most gracious Saviour-God!

---

* "Lectures Introductory to Paul's Epistles," by W. Kelly.

# "RECONCILED AND SAVED"

*"For if, when we were enemies, we were reconciled to God by the death of his Son, much more, being reconciled, we shall be saved by his life."* Romans v. 10.

If ever there was a moment in the which it was important to set forth the great foundation truths of Christianity, it is just now. The enemy is seeking, by every means in his power, to loosen the foundations of our faith—to weaken the authority of holy scripture over the heart and conscience—to introduce, in the most specious and fascinating forms, deadly error, in order to draw away the soul from Christ and His word.

It may, perhaps, be said, "This is an old story." No doubt; it is as old as the second epistle to Timothy: second epistle of Peter, and Jude. But it is a new story also; and while we do not feel it to be our work, as the conductors of "Things New and Old," to grapple, in a controversial way, with popular errors and evils, we do believe it to be our sacred duty to set forth and maintain constantly those grand, solid, fundamental truths which are our only safeguard against every form of doctrinal error and moral pravity.

Hence it is that we feel called upon, at the opening of our Volume for 1870, to draw the attention of our readers to that very weighty passage which stands at the head of this paper. It is one of the fullest and most comprehensive statements of foundation doctrine to be found within the compass of the Volume of God. Let us meditate for a little upon it.

In examining the context in which this passage stands, we find four distinct terms by which the inspired writer sets forth the condition of man, in his unconverted state. He speaks of him as *"without strength."* This is what we may call a negative term. Man is utterly powerless, wholly incapable of doing aught toward his own deliverance. He had been tried in every possible way. God had tested him and proved him, and found him absolutely good

160

for nothing. When placed in Eden, in the midst of the ten thousand delights which a beneficent Creator had poured around him, he believed the devil's lie rather than the truth of God. (Gen. iii.) When driven out of Eden, we see him pursuing a career of evil—"evil only"—evil continually—until the judgment of God falls upon the whole race, with one solitary exception—Noah and his family. (Gen. vi.-viii.) Further, when in the restored earth man is entrusted with the sword of government, he gets drunk and exposes himself to contempt in the very presence of his sons. When entrusted with the holy office of the priesthood, he offers strange fire. (Lev. x.) When entrusted with the high office of king, and enriched with untold wealth, he marries strange wives and worships the idols of the heathen. 2 Chron. xi.

Thus, wherever we trace man—the human race, we see nothing but the most humiliating failure. Man is proved to be good for nothing—"without strength."

But there is more than this. Man is "ungodly." He is not only powerless as to all that is holy and good, but also without one single moral or spiritual link with the living and true God. Examine the unrenewed heart, from its centre to its circumference, and you will not find so much as one true thought about God, or one right affection toward God. There may be a great deal that is amiable and attractive in the way of nature—much that is morally lovely in the eyes of men—many social virtues, and excellent qualities. Human nature, even in its ruins, may exhibit much of all these; just as the visible creation—this earth on which we live—displays, spite of its ruined and groaning condition, many splendid traces of the master hand that formed it.

All this is perfectly true, and perfectly obvious; and moreover, it must ever be taken into account, in dealing with the great question of man's standing and condition. There is an ultra way of speaking of the sinner's state which is much more likely to stumble and perplex the mind than to convict the conscience or break the heart. This should be carefully avoided. We should ever take account of all that is really good in human nature. If we look at the case of the rich young ruler, in Mark x., we must see that the Lord recognized something lovable in him, for we read that "Jesus beholding him, loved him," though we have no warrant whatever to suppose that there was aught of divine work in his soul, seeing that he turned his back upon Christ, and preferred the world to Him. But there was evidently something most attractive in this young man—something different indeed from those gross, coarse, and degraded forms in which human nature ofttimes clothes itself.

Now, we cannot but judge that the man who, in writing or discoursing upon the sinner's moral and spiritual state, would ignore or lose sight of those moral and social distinctions, does positive damage to the cause of truth, and neutralizes the very object which we must believe he has in view. If, for example, we approach an amiable, upright, frank, and honourable person, and, in a sweeping manner, reduce him to a dead level, or place him in the same category with a crooked, cross-grained, scheming, dishonest, contemptible character, we only drive him away in irritation and disgust. Whereas, on the other hand, if we recognize whatever is really good; if we allow—as scripture most surely does—a sufficient margin in which to set down all that is morally and socially excellent even in fallen humanity, we are, to speak after the manner of men, much more likely to gain our end, than by injudiciously ignoring those distinctions, which, inasmuch as they clearly exist, it is the height of folly to deny. Still, it holds good—and let the reader solemnly consider the weighty fact—that man—the very best, the very fairest specimen—is "without strength," and "ungodly." Nor is this all. The apostle *does* not rest in mere negatives. He not only tells us what man is *not*, but he goes on to tell us what he *is*. He gives us both sides of this great question. He not only declares that, "When we were *without strength,* in due time Christ died for the *ungodly;*" but he adds that, "God commendeth his love toward us, in that, while we were yet *sinners,* Christ died for us."

Here, then, we have the positive activity of evil—the actual energy of self-will. For, be it remembered, sin is doing our own will, in whatever line that will may travel, whatever form it may assume. It may present itself to our view in the shape of the grossest moral pravity, or it may array itself in the garb of a cultivated and refined taste; but it is self-will all the while, and self-will is sin. It may be only like the acorn—the mere seed; but the acorn contains the wide spreading oak. Thus the heart of the newly born infant is a little seed-plot in which may be found the germ of every sin that ever was committed in the world. True, each seed may not germinate or bring forth fruit; but the seed is there, and only needs circumstances or influences to unfold it. If any one be kept from gross outward sins, it is not owing to a better nature, but simply to the fact of his surroundings. All men are sinners. All by nature do their own will. This stamps their character. "All have sinned, and come short of the glory of God." From the days of fallen Adam to this moment—well nigh six thousand years, there has been but one solitary exception to this solemn and terrible rule— only One who never sinned—never did His own will, and that is the blessed Lord Jesus Christ, who, though God over all blessed for ever, yet, having become a man, He surrendered His own will completely, and did ever and only the things that pleased His Father. From the manger to the cross, He was ruled, in all things, by the will and the glory of God. He was the only perfect spotless man that ever trod this sin-stained earth—the only fair untainted sheaf that ever appeared in the field of this world—"the man Christ Jesus," who died for us "sinners"—"suffered for sins, the just for the unjust, to bring us to God."

What marvellous grace! what soul-subduing love! what amazing mercy! Oh! how it should melt these hearts of ours! Think, dear reader—think deeply of this love, this grace, this mercy. Dwell upon it until thy whole soul is absorbed in the contemplation of it. We are painfully insensible and indifferent. Indeed there is nothing more humbling than our culpable, our shameful indifference to a Saviour's love. We seem content to take salvation as the result of His cross and passion—His agony and grief—His ineffable sorrow, while, at the same time, our hearts are cold and indifferent to Him. He left the bright heavens, and came down into this dark and sinful world for us. He went down into the gloomy depths of death and the grave. He endured the hiding of God's countenance, which involved more intense anguish to His precious soul than all that men and devils, earth and hell could do—He sank in deep waters, and went down into the horrible pit and into the miry clay—all this He did for us "sinners," when we were "ungodly," and "without strength;" and yet how little we think of it! How little we dwell upon it! How little we are moved by the record of it!

The remembrance of this should humble us in the dust, before our precious Saviour-God. The hardness of our hearts in the presence of the profound mystery of the cross and passion of our Lord Christ is, if possible, a more signal and striking proof of our depravity than the sins for which He died.

But we have rather anticipated what may yet come before us in the further unfolding of our subject; and we shall close this paper with a brief reference to the fourth term by which the apostle sets forth our condition in nature. This is contained in the verse which forms our present thesis: "We were enemies." What a thought! We were not merely powerless, godless, sinful; but actually hostile —in a state of positive enmity aaginst God.

Nothing can possibly exceed this. To be the enemy of God gives the most appalling idea we can possibly have of a sinner's state. And yet such is the actual condition of the unconverted reader of these lines. He is an enemy of God. He may be amiable, polite, attractive, refined, cultivated, educated, moral, and even outwardly religious. He may occupy the very highest platform of religious profession—be a church member—a regular communicant—a worker in the vineyard—a sunday school teacher—a preacher—a minister, and all the while an enemy of God.

How awful the thought! Oh! beloved reader, do pause and consider, we beseech thee. Give this solemn question your undivided attention, just now. Do not put it aside. We appeal to thee, with all earnestness, as in the presence of Almighty God, of His Son Jesus Christ, and of the Eternal Spirit. We adjure thee, by the value of thy immortal soul, by the dread reality of the judgment seat of Christ, by all the horrors of that lake which burneth with fire and brimstone, by the worm that never dies, by the awful fact of eternity—an eternity in the gloomy shades of hell—by the unutterable agony of being separated for ever from God, from Christ, and from all that is pure and lovely—by the combined force of all these arguments, we do earnestly and affectionately beseech thee to flee, this moment, to the Saviour who stands with open arms and loving heart to receive thee. Come to Jesus! Come, now! Come, just as thou art! Only trust Him, and thou are safe—safe for ever—safe as He.

## PART II

We have, in a former volume of "Things New and Old," called the attention of our readers to the important distinction between atonement and reconciliation.* They are often confounded through lack of attention to the precise terms of holy scripture. The fact is, they are perfectly distinct, though intimately connected—distinct, as the foundation is from the building—connected, as the building is with the foundation. Atonement is the base on which reconciliation rests. Without atonement, there could not possibly be any reconciliation; but reconciliation is not atonement. The reader will do well to weigh this matter thoroughly, in the light of inspiration. It is most needful for all Christians to be clear and sound in their thoughts on divine subjects, and accurate in their way of stating them. It will invariably be found that the more spiritual any one is, the closer he will keep to the veritable language of scripture in putting forth foundation truth. Unfortunately, our most excellent Authorized Version does not help the English reader on the score of accuracy in this matter, inasmuch as we find in Romans v. 11 the word "atonement" where it ought to be "reconciliation;" and, on the other hand, we have, in Hebrews ii. 17, the word "reconciliation" where it ought to be "atonement," or "propitiation." However, the two things are perfectly distinct, and it is of real moment that the distinction should be understood and maintained.

Furthermore, we would remind the reader, that there is no foundation whatsoever in the word of God, for the idea that God needed to be reconciled to us. There is positively no such thought to be found within the covers of the Bible. It was man that needed to be reconciled to God, not God to man. Man was the enemy of

* See a series of papers, in the tenth volume of "Things New and Old," entitled, "The Ministry of Reconciliation." [See *Miscellaneous Writings of C. H. M.,* Volume IV.]

God. He was not only, as we have seen, "without strength," "ungodly," and "a sinner," but actually "an enemy."

Now it is the enemy—the alienated, the estranged one—that needs to be brought back—to be reconciled. This is plain. But God, blessed he His name! was not man's enemy, but his friend—the Friend of sinners. Such was the blessed Lord Jesus Christ, when on earth. "He went about doing good, and healing all that were oppressed of the devil, for God was with him." (Acts x.) It was His delight to do good unto all. He spent His life in doing good to those who, after all, preferred a robber and a murderer to Him, and nailed Him to a cross between two thieves. Thus, whether we look at the life or at the death of Christ, we see, in the clearest and most forcible manner, the enmity of man; the friendship, the kindness, the love of God.

But how is man to be reconciled to God? Momentous question! Let us look well to the answer. The passage of scripture which forms the theme of this article declares, in the most distinct manner, that "We are reconciled to God BY THE DEATH of his Son." (Rom. v. 10.) Nothing else could do it. The death of the cross—the atoning death—the vicarious sacrifice—the precious priceless blood of Jesus—is the necessary, the absolutely essential basis of our reconciliation to a sin-hating God. We must state this great truth in the most emphatic and unequivocal maner. Scripture is as clear and definite as possible. In order to our being reconciled to God, sin must be put away, and "without shedding of blood, there is no remission." Hebrews ix. 22.

Thus the matter stands, if we are to be taught simply by scripture. No blood-shedding, no remission—no remission, no reconciliation. Such is the divine order, and let men beware how they tamper with it. It is a very serious thing to touch the truth of God; we may rest assured that all who do so will meddle to their own hurt.

We are reconciled to God by the *death* of His Son. It is not by His incarnation—that is, His taking human nature upon Him. Incarnation could not reconcile us to God, inasmuch as it could not blot out our sins. Incarnation is not atonement. It is well to note this. There is a subtle way of playing upon the word atonement, which consists of a false division of the syllables—as though the

166

word were "at-one-ment;" and this at-one-ment is referred to the incarnation, as though, in that mysterious act, our Lord took our fallen human nature into union with Himself. Against this we solemnly warn the reader. It is fatally false doctrine. It is an effort of the enemy to displace or set aside altogether the atoning death of Christ, with all those grand foundation truths which cluster round that most precious mystery.

Is it that we do not hold, as a cardinal truth, the incarnation of the eternal Son? Nay, it forms the foundation of that great mystery of godliness of which the topstone is a glorified Man on the throne of God. "And, without controversy, great is the mystery of godliness: God was manifest in the flesh, justified in the Spirit, seen of angels, preached unto the Gentiles, believed on in the world, received up into glory." (I Tim. iii. 16.) We hold incarnation to be an integral part of the faith of a true Christian, nor could we own as a Christian any one who denied it. But it is one thing to hold a truth, and another thing altogether to displace it. It is a constant effort of Satan, if he cannot get men to reject a truth, to displace it, and in this way he gains some of his greatest apparent triumphs. Thus it is with the essential doctrine of incarnation. Assuredly, the Son of God had to become a man to die; but, then, becoming a man is one thing, and dying upon the cross is another. He might have become a man; He might have lived and laboured for three and thirty years on this earth; He might have been baptized in Jordan, and tempted in the wilderness; He might have ascended from the mount of transfiguration to that glory from which He had come, and which He had with the Father from before all worlds. At any moment, during His blessed life, He might, so far as He was personally concerned, have returned to that heaven whence He had descended. What was there to hinder Him? There was no necessity laid on Him to die, save the necessity of infinite and everlasting love. Death had no claim on Him, inasmuch as He was the sinless, spotless, holy One of God. He had not come under the federal headship of the first man. Had He done so, He would have been under the curse and wrath of God all His days, and that not vicariously, but in virtue of His connection with the first Adam. This were an open and positive blasphemy against

167

His Person. He was the Second Man the Lord from heaven, the only fair untainted grain of human wheat on which the eye of God could rest, and, as such, we repeat, He could, at any point between the manger and the cross, have returned to the bosom of the Father—that dwelling-place of ineffable love.

Let the reader seize, with clearness and power, this great truth. Let him dwell upon it. It is a truth of the very last possible importance. Jesus stood alone in this world. He was alone in the manger; alone in the Jordan; alone in the wilderness; alone on the mount; alone in the garden. All this is in perfect keeping with his own memorable words in John xii.: "Except a corn of wheat fall into the ground and die, it abideth alone; but if it die, it bringeth forth much fruit." Here is the grand point—"If it die." Unless He was to return to glory alone, He must die. If he was to have us with Him, He must die. If sins were to be remitted, He must die. If sinners were to be saved, He must die. If a new and living way was to be opened for us into the presence of God, He must die. If the veil was to be rent, He must die. That mysterious curtain remained intact when the blessed One lay in the manger of Bethlehem—and when He was baptized—and when He was anointed—and when He was tempted—and when He was transfigured—and when He was bowed in Gethsemane, sweating great drops of blood—and when he was scourged before Pontius Pilate—through all these stages of His marvellous life, the veil was unrent. There and thus it stood to bar the sinner's approach to God. Man was shut out from God, and God shut in from man; nor could all the living labours of the eternal Son—His miracles—His precious ministry—His tears, His sighs, His groans, and His prayers—His sore temptations and His untold living sorrows—not any nor all of these could have rent the veil. But the very moment that death was accomplished—we read, "The veil of the temple was rent in twain from the top to the bottom."

Such is the distinct teaching of scripture on this vital question. The death of Christ is the foundation of everything. Is it a question of life? He has given His flesh for the life of the world. Is it a question of pardon? "Without shedding of blood is no remission." Is it a question of peace? "He made peace by the blood of his cross."

Is it a question of reconciliation? "We are reconciled to God by the death of his Son." In short, it is through death we get everything—without it, nothing. It is on the ground of death, even the atoning death of Christ, that we are reconciled to God, and united, by the Holy Ghost, to the risen and glorified Head in heaven. All rests on the solid groundwork of accomplished redemption. Sin is put away; the enmity is slain; all barriers are removed; God is glorified; the law magnified; and all this by the death of Christ. "He passed through death's dark raging flood" to settle everything for us, and lay the imperishable foundation of all the counsels and purposes of the Holy Trinity.

And, now, a very few words as to the life of Christ in heaven for us. "If while we were enemies, we were reconciled to God by the death of his Son, much more, being reconciled, we shall be saved by his life." Be it carefully noted that this refers to His life after death—His life in resurrection—His life in heaven. Some would teach us that it is His life on earth—His fulfillment of the law in our room and stead. This is flatly contradicted by the very structure of the passage, and by the entire teaching of the New Testament. It is not life before death, but life after death that the apostle speaks of. In short, it is the priestly life of our blessed and adorable Lord, who ever liveth to make intercession for us. It is by this we are saved through all the difficulties and dangers, the snares and temptations of this wilderness world. We, though reconciled to God by the death of Christ, are, nevertheless, in ourselves, poor, feeble, helpless, erring creatures, prone to wander, ever liable to failure and sin, totally unable to get on for a single moment, if not kept by our great High Priest—our blessed Advocate—our Comforter. He keeps us day and night. He never slumbers nor sleeps. He maintains us continually before God in all the integrity of the position in which His death has placed us. It is impossible that our cause can ever fail in such hands. His intercession is all prevailing. "We have an Advocate with the Father, Jesus Christ the righteous." The One who bore our sins in His own body on the tree, now bears our sorrows on His heart upon the throne; and He will come again to bear the government upon His shoulders.

What a Saviour! What a Victim! What a Priest! How blessed to have all our affairs in His hand! To be sustained by such a ministry! How precious to know that the One who has reconciled us to God by His death is now alive for us on the throne; and because He lives we shall live also! All praise to His peerless name!

# "ACCEPTED" AND "ACCEPTABLE"

"He hath made us *accepted* in the beloved." (Eph. i. 6.)
"Where we labour, that whether present or absent, we may be *acceptable* to him." 2 Cor. v. 9.

The two words which form the heading of this paper, though rendered by the same word in our Authorized Version, are not at all the same. The former has respect to the person of the believer, the later to his practical ways. That refers to his standing, this to his state. It is one thing to be accepted; it is quite another to be acceptable. The former is the fruit of God's free grace to us as sinners; the latter is the fruit of our earnest labour as saints, though, most surely, it is only by grace we can do anything.

It is well that the christian reader should thoroughly understand the distinction between these two things. It will preserve him effectually from legality, on the one hand, and laxity on the other. It remains unalterably true of all believers, that God hath made them accepted in the Beloved. Nothing can ever touch this. The very feeblest lamb in all the flock stands accepted in a risen Christ. There is no difference. The grace of God has placed them all on this high and blessed ground. We do not labour to be accepted. It is all the fruit of God's free grace. He found us all alike dead in trespasses and sins. We were morally dead—far off from God, hopeless, Godless, Christless—children of wrath, whether Jews or Gentiles. But Christ died for us, and God has co-quickened, co-raised, and co-seated us in Christ, and made us accepted in Him.

This is the inalienable, eternal, standing of all, without exception, who believe in the name of the Son of God. Christ, in His infinite grace, placed Himself judicially where we were morally, and having put away our sins, and perfectly satisfied, on our behalf, the claims of divine righteousness, God entered the scene, and raised Him from the dead, and with Him all His members, as seen in His own eternal purpose, and to be called in due time, and brought into the actual possession and enjoyment of the marvellous place of blessing and privilege, by the effectual operation of the Holy Ghost.

Well, therefore, may we take up the opening words of the Epistle to the Ephesians, and say, "Blessed be the God and Father of our Lord Jesus Christ, who hath blessed us with all spiritual blessings in the heavenlies in Christ. According as he hath chosen us in him before the foundation of the world, that we should be holy and without blame before him in love; having predestinated us unto the adoption of children by Jesus Christ to himself, according to the good pleasure of his will, to the praise of the glory of his grace, wherein *he hath made us accepted in the beloved.*" All praise to His name throughout the everlasting ages!

All believers, then, are accepted—perfectly and for ever accepted —in the Beloved. God sees them in Christ, and as Christ. He thinks of them as He thinks of Him; loves them as He loves Him. They are ever before Him, in perfect acceptance in the blessed Son of His love, nor can anything, or any one, ever interfere with this their high and glorious position, which rests on the eternal stability of the grace of God, the accomplished work of His Son, and attested by the Holy Ghost sent down from heaven.

But are all believers acceptable in their practical ways? Are all so carrying themselves as that their dealings and doings will bear the light of the judgment-seat of Christ? Are all labouring to be agreeable to Him?

Christian reader, these are serious questions. Let us solemnly weigh them. Let us not turn away from the sharp edge of plain practical truth. The blessed apostle knew he was accepted. Did that make him lax, careless, or indolent? Far from it. "*We labour,*" he says, "*to be acceptable to him.*" The sweet assurance that we are accepted *in* Him is the ground of our labour to be acceptable *to* Him. 'The love of Christ constraineth us; because we thus judge, that if one died for all, then were all dead. And he died for all, that they which live should not henceforth live unto themselves, but unto him which died for them and rose again." 2 Corinthians v. 14, 15.

All this is pre-eminently practical. We are called upon, by every argument which can bear sway over the heart and conscience, to labour diligently to be acceptable to our blessed and adorable Lord. Is there aught of legality in this? Not the slightest tinge. The very reverse. It is the holy superstructure of a devoted life, erected on the solid foundation of our eternal election and perfect acceptance in a risen and glorified Christ at God's right hand. How could there be the very smallest atom of legality here? Utterly impossible. It is all the pure fruit of God's free and sovereign grace from first to last.

But ought we not, beloved christian reader, to rouse ourselves to attend to the claims of Christ as to practical righteousness? Should we not zealously and lovingly aim at giving Him pleasure? Are we to content ourselves with vapidly talking about our acceptance in Christ, while at the same time there is no real earnest care as to the acceptability of our ways? God forbid! Yea, let us so dwell upon the rich grace that shines in the acceptance of our persons, that we may be led out in diligent and fervent effort to be found acceptable in our ways.

It is greatly to be feared that there is an appalling amount of antinomianism amongst us—an unhallowed traffic in the doctrines of grace, without any godly care as to the application of those doctrines to our practical conduct. How all this is to end, it would be hard to say; but, most assuredly, there is an urgent call upon all who profess to be *accepted in Christ* to labour fervently to be *acceptable to Him*.

# RELIEF FOR A BURDENED HEART

(A Reply to an Anxious Enquirer, "E.M.")

Dear Friend,

Your letter has interested us exceedingly. Few things, indeed, lie nearer to the heart than the case of anxious and burdened spirits. The work of emancipating and soothing such is becoming, each day, more and more charming to us. Words could not convey how intensely we long to be used as God's instruments in this most delightful work. We are fully persuaded that it is a work, which lies very near the heart of Christ. How could we question this, while hearkening to such words as these, "The Spirit of the Lord is upon me, because he hath anointed me to preach the gospel to the poor; he hath sent me to heal the broken-hearted, to preach deliverance to the captives, and recovering of sight to the blind, to set at liberty them that are bruised." (Luke iv. 18.) And again "Come unto me, all ye that labour and are heavy-laden, and I will give you rest." (Matt. xi. 28.) How precious is the thought of God sending His Son, and anointing Him with the Holy Ghost, to preach glad tidings to the poor, to bring healing to the broken-hearted, sight to the blind, deliverance to the captive, liberty for the oppressed, rest for the weary! What unspeakable comfort for one who may find himself in any of these conditions!

Now, dear friend, it seems very plain that you are a weary, heavy-laden one, and as such, you are the very object for the gracious ministry of the Lord Jesus Christ; you are one of those for whom He was sent, and for whom He was anointed by the Holy Ghost. We have not the slightest doubt but that the root of the matter is in you. The very anxieties to which you give expression are, in our judgment, the evidence of a spiritual work in your soul. Not that we want you to build your peace upon this. God forbid! If all the angels in heaven, and all the men upon earth were to give expression to their confidence in your christianity, it might be a comfort and an encouragement to you, but could never form the ground of your peace, in the presence of a holy, sin-hating God. It matters little, comparatively, what men think about you: the question is, what does God think about you? He has found you out. He knows the worst about you; and yet He loves you, and gave His Son to die for you. Here is the only ground of a sinner's peace. God Himself has met your case. He has been glorified about your sins, in the death of His Son. It does not matter the least what you are. You say you are, sometimes, at a loss to know in what light to regard yourself, whether as wholly unconverted, or a backslider. The fact is, what you really want is to get to the end of yourself altogether; and when you get there, you will find God in all the fulness of His grace, as manifested in Christ; and surely to get to the end of oneself and find Christ, is the true way to find peace.

It seems to us that one special malady from which you are suffering, just now, is intense self-occupation. This is the case with thousands. It is quite true that the Spirit of God will exercise us about our condition, and cause us to judge it, but then it is only for the purpose of leading us to the very bottom of it all, so that we may find settled repose in the fulness and sufficiency of Christ. This kind of exercise is very good. We delight in seeing a soul under deep spiritual work—the deeper the better. We are of opinion that, in spiritual husbandry, the deeper the furrow the stronger the root. We do not attach much value to a superficial work in the conscience; for although it is quite true that we are not saved by any special process of exercise whether of heart or conscience, still we have frequently found that persons who had glided rapidly into a certain feeling of peace, were in danger of gliding as rapidly out of it, and becoming as miserable as they had once been happy. Sin must be seen in its sinfulness, and the sooner it is thus seen the better, so that having it really judged in the conscience, we may lay hold of a full and precious Christ, as God's answer to it all. When this is the case, the heart enjoys a more solid, abiding peace, and is not subject to those variations of which so many complain.

But, on the other hand, there is a kind of self-occupation into which Satan leads the awakened sinner for the purpose of keeping

175

him from Christ. This must be carefully guarded against. We apprehend he has entangled your feet in this snare. The style and tone of your letter quite lead us to this conclusion. We most fully enter into your case. Indeed you possess our entire sympathy. We deeply respect the feeling which leads you to absent yourself from the Lord's Table, in your present state of soul. We consider it vastly superior to the lightness, flippancy, and heartless formality with which so many approach that sacred institution. Far be it from us to pen a single line which would have the effect of emboldening you to approach the Lord's Supper in an unhappy and untruthful condition of heart and conscience. But then we want you so to apprehend the gospel of the grace of God—the full forgiveness of your sins however magnified and multiplied—your complete justification, through the death and resurrection of Christ—we want you so to see the application of all this to your own soul, as that you may be able, like the poor man in the third of Acts, to rise up from your crippled condition, and enter into the temple, leaping and walking and praising God. Be assured of it, dearly beloved, this is your privilege. There is nothing to hinder your enjoyment, this moment, save the unbelief and legality of your own spirit. The enemy would keep you occupied with yourself in order to keep you from Christ. Watch against this. It is the most hopeless, gloomy labour, to be seeking for aught in yourself. Look off unto Jesus. You will find all you want in Him. May the power of the Holy Ghost fill your whole soul with the fulness and preciousness of Christ, so that you may get into, and continue in, that holy and happy liberty which is the proper portion of every child of God.

You will further bear with us, dear E.M. when we tell you that we discern in your letter a great deal of the *legal* element. This is an evil at once hateful to the Spirit of God and subversive of your own peace and comfort. You want to get into and breathe the genial atmosphere of *free grace*—that grace which reigns through righteousness unto eternal life, by Jesus Christ our Lord. You have very unworthy thoughts of God's perfect, eternal, and unchangeable love. You seem to measure God very much by the standard of your own thoughts. You are reasoning from what you are to God, instead of *believing* what God is to you. This is a serious mistake—the mistake of many. We are all, more or less, prone to this grievous error. Very few, comparatively, *live* in the actual enjoyment of salvation by grace. There is the continual weighing of self in a legal balance. The principle of law is so deeply embedded in the heart, that nothing but the mighty power of the Spirit of God can deliver us from it, and lead us into the practical understanding of that brief, but most comprehensive statement of the apostle: "Ye are not under law; but under grace." Rom. vi.

Now, we hold it to be utterly impossible for a soul to enjoy settled peace so long as it is, in any measure, under the influence of this law-principle. There may be occasional gleams of sunshine, such as you describe in your own experience; but there never can be abiding gospel-peace, so long as a single trace of the legal element is allowed to hold sway over the conscience. Abiding peace can only flow from a deep, thorough, practical sense of free grace; and that free grace acts towards the sinner on the settled ground of accomplished atonement. Legality, on the other hand, will ever be directing the eye inward upon self—yes, ever and only upon self. It will lead us to measure our standing before God by our own progress in personal holiness, our efforts, our services, our doings, our ways, our feelings, our frames, our something or other. All this produces spiritual darkness, gloomy uncertainty, mental bondage, intense soul-torture, depression, irritability, sourness of temper. And these things again re-act most prejudicially, upon our whole moral being. They fling back their demoralizing influence upon the life and character. The harp is hung upon the willow. The hymn of joyous praise can only, as you say, be occasionally sung. The eucharistic feast—that most precious memorial of accomplished redemption—is abandoned, or if not abandoned, is *gone through*—we dare not *celebrated*—without freshness, unction, power, elevation, or depth of spiritual tone. In this way, Christ is dishonoured, the Holy Ghost is grieved, the testimony is marred, and the standard of practical christianity greatly lowered. Moreover, the enemy, finding us in this condition of soul, cuts out ample work for us, by acting, in various ways, upon our lusts and passions, which only gather strength from the very fact of our

177

being under law; for as the apostle says, "The strength of sin is the law." Thus the soul's history is summed up in two words, namely "Lust and law," or "Law and lust," and one is tossed like a ball from one to the other, until free grace comes in and gives full deliverance from both. Grace gives you power over sin; whereas law gives sin power over you. Grace keeps you in the place of continual victory; law keeps you in the place of continual defeat.

May the Lord lead you and all His people into a clearer apprehension of grace, that so your peace may flow as a river, and the fruits of righteousness abound to the praise of His name!

But we are not yet done with your letter, dear friend. We think we discern another feature in your case which tends to produce the spiritual depression of which you complain. If we mistake not, you are afflicted with a morbid or scrupulous conscience. This is a sore evil—a heavy burden—a very great trial. We deeply feel for any soul labouring under this grievous malady, for it not only affects oneself, but all with whom one comes in contact. There is a very wide difference indeed between a scrupulous conscience and a tender conscience. The former is governed by its own fears; the latter, by the word of God. That superinduces feebleness and uncertainty in all one's ways; this a holy stability and consistency. We can hardly conceive a more troublesome companion than a morbid or scrupulous conscience. It is always creating difficulties for its possessor, and placing stumbling-blocks in his way. A tender conscience, on the contrary, is invaluable. It resents only what ought to be resented. Its action is true and healthy. It does not morbidly seek out cause of trouble and defilement; but, being duly acted upon by the word of God, as applied by the Holy Ghost, it yields a true response, and thus discharges, with vigour, its divinely appointed functions.

Think, then, beloved, of all these things, and seek to watch against them, and above all, *believe* against them. Get done with self occupation, rise above your legal fears, and cast away from you the workings of a morbid conscience. Be assured of it these are three features in your case; and they are features of many a case— a self-occupied heart, a legal mind, a morbid conscience. Terrible evils! May the power of the Holy Ghost give you full deliverance

178

from these three efficient agents of the devil! May He break every chain and give you to taste the true sweetness of spiritual liberty and communion of heart with a reconciled God and Father.

Do not, any longer, harass yourself with the questions, "Am I a converted person? or am I a backslider? am I this? or am I that?" You are, in yourself, a poor lost, unworthy, good-for-nothing creature; and yet God commendeth His love toward you in that He gave His only begotten Son to bear your curse and burden on the tree. Cast yourself on His boundless love, "a sea where none can sink." See that all is done. The debt is paid. Satan is silenced. The law is magnified. Sin is put away. God is satisfied, yea, glorified. What more would you have? For what are you waiting? You may, perhaps, say to us "I know all this." You do say in your letter that you "can hardly expect to hear anything more than you have already read." Well, we want you to make your own of all this by simple, childlike faith. We want to drive you from behind every bush, and out of every legal lurking place, into the full blaze of divine and everlasting love. Cast away from you, we beseech you, dear friend, all your legal reasonings, and seek to exercise a believing mind that just takes God at His word, and takes possession, without a question, of all that He gives. We do not want to heal your wound slightly; to cry "peace, peace, when there is no peace." This would be cruelty rather than kindness. But we desire that you should "know the things which are freely given to you of God," and which are as clearly revealed in the word, as they are freely given through grace. We long to see you as happy as the gospel of the grace of God is fitted to make you. Then you will be able to sing hymns of praise, and take your seat at the table of the Lord in happy, holy, elevated communion and worship.

May the good Lord meet you in your present need! May He disperse, by the bright and blessed beams of His love, the dark cloud that has settled down upon your spirit, and fill you with all joy and peace in believing. To Him we do most affectionately commend you, praying Him to make use of what we have written, in blessing to your precious soul, and His name shall have all the praise throughout the everlasting ages.

179

# THREE PRECIOUS GIFTS

*"I give unto my sheep eternal life, and they shall never perish."*
John x.
*"The gift of God is eternal life, through Jesus Christ our Lord."*
Rom. vi.
*"He that followeth me shall not walk in darkness, but shall have the light of life."* John viii.
*"Christ shall give thee light."* Ephesians v:
*"Ye shall know the truth, and the truth shall make you free."*
John viii. 6.
*"Stand fast therefore in the liberty wherewith Christ hath made us free."* Gal. v. i.

The scriptures quoted above—and they are but a few of the many that might be adduced—teach us, very distinctly, that there are three things bestowed upon every soul that, through grace, simply and truly and heartily believes in Jesus, and these are *"Life"*— *"Light"*—and *"Liberty"*—three most precious gifts, surely—gifts in comparison with which all earthly riches, pleasures and distinctions are but as the small dust of the balance.

But there are very many who ought to be in the full and settled enjoyment of these immense privileges who actually do not know that they possess them at all, and consider it the height of presumption for any soul to think of possessing them. There are many sincere and earnest souls—truly converted persons—children of God who, through bad teaching, self-occupation or legality, are thoroughly in the dark as to the very elements of christianity—the simplest truths of the gospel. The dark atmosphere which enwraps the whole of Christendom, so obscures the light of divine truth that they really do not know where they are or what they have got. In place of life, light and liberty, they are practically in the shadow of death, in darkness and bondage. They are robbed of those three precious gifts which God, in the fulness and riches of His grace, liberally bestows upon all who believe on the name of His only-begotten Son.

Now, it is for the special purpose of helping that large and interesting class of persons who are thus robbed and spoiled, that we have penned the few inspired sentences at the head of this paper; and we affectionately entreat of such to give earnest heed to them. We are not, now, going to expound them; nor yet to enter upon a full statement of the doctrines indicated in them. Our object is rather to exhort than to expound. We want—yea, we long to see all the dear children of God in the full enjoyment of the things which are freely given to them of God in Christ.

Let all such, then, hear what our Lord Christ saith, "I give unto my sheep eternal life." "Ah! yes," some exercised soul may say; "I quite see that all Christ's sheep have eternal life; but my great, my sore—my soul-crushing difficulty is to know that I am a sheep of Christ. If only I knew that, I should count myself happy indeed."

Now this, though no doubt the language of hundreds, is a mistake. It is beginning at the wrong end. It is putting self and its feelings before Christ and His word; and, most surely, as long as any one is doing this, he must be in doubt and darkness. It is utterly impossible it can be otherwise. If it is something about myself I am called to feel or believe, in order to be saved, then, assuredly, I never can have the settled knowledge or assurance of salvation. I must have something entirely outside and independent of myself—something divinely solid—something eternally stable— some settled and absolute truth—something true in itself, apart from all my thoughts and feelngs respecting it—in short I must have God's own revelation to rest upon, or I never can know what abiding peace really is. It is the eternal truth of God, and that alone ,which forms the real basis of the soul's peace—a basis which not all the powers of earth and hell, men and devils can ever disturb. It is by believing in Christ, and not by feeling or believing something about myself ,that I get eternal life. He that believeth on the Son of God hath eternal life.

Anxious reader, do ponder this. It is of the very deepest moment. It concerns the peace and rest of your soul. We would call your earnest attention to the weighty fact that what you are called upon to believe is not something about yourself, but something about Christ. "Verily, verily, I say unto you, He that believeth on me hath everlasting life." (John vi. 47.) Do you simply and heartily believe in Jesus? Do you confide in Him? Are you thoroughly satisfied with Him? If so you have eternal life, and you should, from this moment, know it and rejoice in it. Our Lord does not say, "He that feeleth he is one of my sheep shall have eternal life." Nothing of the kind—nothing like it—nothing approaching to it. "He that believeth on me." So also, in that well-known passage in John v. "Verily, verily, I say unto you. He that *heareth* my word and believeth on him that sent me *hath* everlasting life, and shall not come into judgment, but *is passed* from death unto life."

Can aught be plainer than this? Every one who hears the word of Jesus, and believes in the One who sent Him, is the happy possessor of eternal life, and shall never come into judgment. Hence it follows that if we have not got eternal life, we do not believe on the Son of God, we have not heard His word, do not believe in God at all. Thus it stands if we are to be governed by the veritable teaching and authority of our Lord Christ. Every true believer in Jesus hath eternal life; and every one who has not eternal life is an unbeliever. So speaks the word of the living God.

But the believer should know what he possesses. Of what use or value could it be for any one to be left a large fortune in Canada, if he did not know anything about it? God would have us to know what He has freely given to us in Christ. The life is in Christ, so he that hath Christ hath the life, and he who hath not life hath not Christ. "God hath given to us eternal life, and this life is in his Son." Precious, all important word!

Nor is it otherwise with respect to the second of our "three precious gifts." As we get "life" so we get "light"—in Christ. "He that followeth me shall not walk in darkness, but shall have the light of life." God would not give us life and leave us in the dark. This would not be like Him. He has given us His Son; and, believing in Him, we get life; and, following Him, we get light—*the light of life.* Beauteous words! Words full of divine power! Enfranchising words for the soul that has been groping in darkness and the shadow of death! "The darkness is past, and the true light now shineth;" and the proper sphere for the life which we now possess is the light in which we are called and privileged to walk.

The darkness is past, the shadows are gone; the clouds are rolled away; the dim twilight has given place to the full orbed light of life streaming down into our souls, and upon our path, and enabling us to judge ourselves and our surroundings—to judge everything according to the true light that now shineth within, upon, and around us—shineth from the Father—shineth in the Son—shineth in the power of the Holy Ghost—shineth on the page of inspiration.

Finally, it follows, of blessed necessity, that as we get "life" and "light," so we get "liberty." It is all in Christ. He quickens; He enlightens; He emancipates; yea, more, He is our life, our light, our liberty. Blessed, throughout all ages, be His peerless name! "If the Son shall make you free, ye shall be free indeed." Surely, it must be so. He would not give us life and leave us in the dark. He would not give us life and leave us in bondage or slavery. No, no; such is not His way. He sets us divinely and eternally free—free from guilt and condemnation—free from the dread of wrath and judgment to come—free from the fear of death—free from the present power of sin—quite as free as from its future consequences.

May the reader lay hold of these things in simple, childlike faith, and join us in a note of fervent praise to the Giver of these "Three precious gifts."

# RESURRECTION

A correspondent requests a special notice of Phil. iii. 11. "If by any means I might attain unto the resurrection from among the dead." The point toward which the desires of the true Christian ever tend is resurrection-glory. It matters not to him by what way he is to reach that point. He longs to reach the glory, "by any means."

It may be that our friend finds difficulty in the word "if," as though it implied a doubt in the mind of the apostle as to his reaching the end in safety. We do not believe he had any such thought in his mind. The idea is simply this—he had the goal before him, and he was eagerly pressing toward it. His vision was filled with it, his heart was set on it, and as to the "means" by which he was to reach it he was quite indifferent.

It may be interesting to observe that the word which is rendered "resurrection," only occurs, so far as we are aware, in this one passage, and properly signifies "resurrection from among." The word ἀνάστασις (anastasis, resurrection) occurs about forty-two-times in the New Testament, and is applied to the broad fact of resurrection. But the word used in the eleventh verse is morally linked with the expression in Mark ix. 10, "Questioning one with another what rising from among the dead (ἐκ νεκρῶν) should mean." The disciples would have found no difficulty in the thought of resurrection as such, seeing that every orthodox Jew believed in it. But a "rising from among the dead" was something strange to them. Hence their "questioning."

Now, the proper hope of the Christian is not merely "resurrection of the dead," but "resurrection from among the dead." This makes a very material difference. It completely sets aside the idea of a general simultaneous resurrection. To speak of a resurrection from among the dead, obviously implies that all shall not rise together. Revelation xx. 5. teaches us that there will be a thousand years between the two resurrections; but it is of importance to see that

184

the very word used by the apostle to express that resurrection for which he was looking, is quite different from that usually employed to set forth the general thought of resurrection. Why is this? Simply because he meant a special thing and he therefore used a special word—a word which, as we have said, occurs only in this one place.

It is deeply solemn to remember that the Lord's people will rise from their graves and leave behind them the ashes of the wicked dead to moulder for a thousand years longer. This thought may seem to be foolishness to the natural man, but scripture teaches it, and that is quite enough for the Christian. The resurrection of the Church will be upon the same principle, and partake of the same character, as the resurrection of Christ; it will be "a resurrection from among the dead." May our hearts be set upon that glorious goal!

# THE JUDGMENT SEAT OF CHRIST

We have lately received communications from various friends, in which they earnestly seek light as to the solemn subject of the judgment seat of Christ; and as it is more than probable that many others may be exercised on the same point, we are unwilling to give it a hasty notice in our answers to correspondents.

One dear friend writes thus: "I am, at present, in a difficulty. It is this: a very dear friend has, for some time past, been very unhappy in the thought that, at the judgment seat of Christ, every secret thought and every motive of the heart will be made manifest to all there. She has no fears or doubts as to her eternal salvation, or the forgiveness of her sins; but she shrinks with horror from the thought of having the secrets of her heart manifested to all there."

Another writes as follows: "Remembering those blessed and eternally-important truths in John v. 24; I John i. 7-9, ii. 12; Heb. x. 1-17, I wish to know how you understand the following texts, which I shall transcribe in full, in order to point out the particular words to which I refer.

" 'For we must all appear before the judgment seat of Christ, that every one may receive the things done in his body, according to that he hath done, whether it be good or bad.' (2 Cor. v. 10.) 'So then every one of us shall give account of himself to God.' (Rom. xiv. 12.) 'But he that doeth wrong shall receive for the wrong he hath done: and there is no respect of persons.' Col. iii. 24, 25.

"It is on the above texts that I am anxious to be correct as to interpretation and application; and I have thought it probable that you would not regard it as trespassing on your time, if I were to ask your opinion on the subject."

We have been much interested, of late, in looking into the various reasons of the perplexity which seems to prevail in reference to the solemn subject of "The judgment seat of Christ." The very passages which our correspondent quotes are so plain, so pointed, and so definite on the question, that we have only just to take them

186

as they stand, and allow them to have their due weight upon the heart and conscience. "We must all be manifested before the judgment seat of Christ." "Every one of us must give account of himself to God." "He that doeth wrong shall receive for the wrong he hath done."

These are plain statements. Should we desire to weaken their force—to blunt their edge—to turn away their point? God forbid! We should rather seek to make a holy use of them by keeping a pressure upon nature, in all its vanities, lusts, and tempers. The Lord intended we should use them thus. He never intended that we should use them, in a legal way, to shake our confidence in Christ and his full salvation. We shall never come into judgment as to our sins. John v. 24; Rom. viii. 1; I John iv. 17, are conclusive as to that point. But then our services must come under the Master's eye. Every man's work shall be tried of what sort it is. The day will make every thing manifest. All this is very solemn, and should lead to great watchfulness and carefulness as to our works, ways, thoughts, words, motives, and desires. The deepest sense of grace, and the clearest apprehension of our perfect justification as sinners, will never weaken our sense of the deep solemnity of the judgment seat of Christ, or lessen our desire so to walk as that we may be accepted of Him.

It is well to see this. The apostle laboured that he might be accepted. He kept his body under lest he should be disapproved of. Every saint should do the same. We are already accepted *in* Christ, and as such, we labour to be accepted *of* Him. We should seek to give every truth its proper place, and the way to do this, is to be much in the presence of God, and to view each truth in immediate connection with Christ. There is always a danger of making such a use of one truth as, practically, to displace some other truth. This should be carefully guarded against. We believe there will be a full manifestation of every one and every thing before the judgment seat of Christ. Every thing will come out there. Things that looked very brilliant and praiseworthy, and that made a great noise amongst men, down here, will all be burned up as so much "wood, hay, and stubble." Things that were blazed abroad, and made use of to surround the names of men with a halo of human applause, will all be submitted to the searching action of "the fire," and, it may be, very much of them reduced to ashes. The counsels of all hearts will be made manifest. Every motive, every purpose, every design will be weighed in the balances of the sanctuary. The fire will try every man's work, and nothing will be stamped as genuine save that which has been the fruit of divine grace in our hearts. All mixed motives will be judged, condemned, and burnt up. All prejudices, all erroneous judgments, all evil surmisings concerning others—all these and such like things will be exposed and cast into the fire. We shall see things then as Christ sees them, judge them as He judges them. No one will be better pleased than myself to see all my stubble consumed. Even now, as we grow in light, knowledge, and spirituality, as we get nearer and liker to Christ, we heartily condemn many things which we once deemed all right. How much more shall we do so when we stand in the full blaze of the light of the judgment seat of Christ?

Now, what should be the practical effect of all this upon the believer? To make him doubt his salvation? To leave him in a state of uncertainty as to whether he is accepted or not? To make him question his relationship to God in Christ? Surely not. What then? To lead him to walk in holy carefulness, from day to day, as under the eye of his Lord and Master—to produce watchfulness, sobriety, and self-judgment—to superinduce faithfulness, diligence, and integrity in all his services and all his ways.

Take a simple illustration. A father leaves home for a time, and, when taking leave of his children, he appoints a certain work to be done, and a certain line of conduct to be adopted during his absence. Now, when he returns, he may have to praise some for their faithfulness and diligence, while he blames others for the very reverse. But does he disown the latter? Does he break the relationship? By no means. They are just as much his children as the others, though he faithfully points out their failure and censures them for it. If they have been biting and devouring one another, instead of doing his will; if one has been judging another's work instead of attending to his own; if there has been envy and jealousy instead of an earnest hearty carrying out of the father's intentions

188

—all these things will meet with merited censure. How could it be otherwise?

But then some, like our correspondent's friend, 'shrink with horror from the thought of having the secrets of the heart manifested to all there.' Well, the Holy Ghost declares that "The Lord will bring to light the hidden things of darkness, and make manifest the counsels of the heart: and then shall every man have praise of God." I Cor. iv. 5. He does not say to whom they shall be manifested; nor does this, in the least, affect the question, inasmuch as every true-hearted person will be far more deeply concerned about the judgment of the Master than about the judgment of a fellow-servant. Provided I please Christ, I need not trouble myself much about man's judgment. And, on the other hand, if I am more troubled about the idea of having all my motives exposed to the view of man than I am about their being exposed to the view of Christ, it is plain there must be something wrong. It proves I am occupied about *myself*. I shrink from the exposure of "my secret motives." Then it is very plain that my secret motives are not right, and the sooner they are judged the better.

And, after all, what difference would it make, though all our sins and failures were made manifest to everybody? Are Peter and David a whit less happy because untold millions have read the account of their shameful fall? Surely not. They know that the record of their sins only magnifies the grace of God, and illustrates the value of the blood of Christ, and hence they rejoice in it. Thus it is in every case. If we were more emptied of self and occupied with Christ, we should have more simple and correct thoughts about the judgment seat as well as about every thing else.

May the Lord keep our hearts true to Himself in this the time of His absence, so that when He appears we may not be ashamed before Him! May all our works be so begun, continued, and ended in Him, that the thought of having them duly weighed and estimated in the presence of His glory may not disturb our hearts! May we be constrained by the "love of Christ," not by the fear of judgment, to live unto Him who died for us and rose again! We may safely and happily leave everything in His hands, seeing He has borne our sins in His own body on the tree. We have no reason to fear, inasmuch as we know that when He shall appear, we shall be like Him, for we shall see Him as He is. The moment Christ appears we shall be changed into His image, pass into the presence of His glory, and there review the past. We shall look back from that high and holy elevation, upon our course down here. We shall see things in a different light altogether then. It may be we shall be astonished to find that many things, of which we thought a great deal down here, will be found defective up there; and, on the other hand, many little things which were done in self-forgetfulness, and love to Jesus, will be sedulously recorded, and abundantly rewarded. We shall also be able to see, in the clear light of the Master's presence, many mistakes and failures which had never before come within the range of our vision. What will be the effect of all this? Just to evoke from our hearts loud and rapturous hosannahs to the praise of Him, who has brought us through all our toils and dangers, borne with all our mistakes and failures, and assigned us a place in His own everlasting kingdom, there to bask in the bright beams of His glory, and shine in His image for ever.

We shall not dwell further on this subject, just now; but we trust sufficient has been said to relieve the minds of those dear friends who have consulted us on the point. We shall ever regard it as a happy service to communicate with our readers on any question which may happen to present difficulty to their minds. We can truly say, our desire is that the Lord would make this little Magazine a channel of help and blessing to the souls of His people everywhere, and that the name of the Lord Jesus may be magnified.

# WHAT IS A CASTAWAY?

"But I keep under my body, and bring it into subjection; lest that, by any means, when I have preached to others, I myself be a castaway." I Cor. ix. 27.

This passage has perplexed and troubled many an earnest heart. Many have argued thus, while pondering the above solemn scripture, "If such an one as Paul was uncertain as to the issue of his course, who, then, can be sure?" But was he uncertain as to the issue? By no means. The verse immediately preceding teaches us the very opposite: "I therefore so run, not as uncertainly; so fight I, not as one that beateth the air." Paul knew quite well how the whole matter was to terminate, so far as he was concerned. He could say, "I know whom (not merely what) I have believed, and am persuaded that he is able to keep that which I have committed unto him against that day." (2 Tim. i. 12.) And again, "I am persuaded, that neither death, nor life, nor angels, nor principalities, nor powers, nor things present, nor things to come, nor height, nor depth, nor any other creature, shall be able to separate us from the love of God, which is in Christ Jesus our Lord." Rom. viii. 38, 39.

These scriptures are amply sufficient to prove that Paul had not so much as a shadow of a doubt as to his eternal security. "I know" —"I am persuaded." There is nothing like doubt or uncertainty in such utterances. Ah, no! Paul knew better. His foundation was as stable as the throne of God. Whatever of certainty Christ could afford, that Paul possessed. He, surely, had not abandoned all that this world could give for a doubtful salvation—a doubtful prospect —a doubtful future. Had he done so, Festus might truly have said, "Paul, thou art beside thyself." We are fully convinced, that, so far as Paul was concerned, from the moment, in which the scales dropped from his eyes in the city of Damascus, until he was offered up in the city of Rome, his heart never once harboured a single doubt, a single fear, a single misgiving. "He was troubled on every side, yet not distressed; perplexed, but not in despair; persecuted, but not forsaken; cast down, but not destroyed." Yea, in the midst of all his conflict and trouble, he could say, "Our light affliction, which is but for a moment, worketh for us a far more exceeding and eternal weight of glory." 2 Cor. iv. 17.

Paul had no doubts or fears, as to the final issue. Neither should any one, who has truly come to Christ, inasmuch as He Himself has said, "Him that cometh to me, I will in no wise cast out." (John vi. 37.) No one, who is really cast upon Christ, will ever be cast away from Him. This is a divine axiom—a fundamental truth —an eternal reality. Christ is responsible for every lamb in the flock. The counsels of God have made Him so—the love of His own heart has made Him so—the Holy Scriptures declare Him to be so. Not one of Christ's blood-bought lambs can ever be lost, not one can ever be cast away. They are all as safe as He can make them—as safe as Himself.

But what, then, does Paul mean when he says, "Lest I myself should be a castaway?" If he does not mean to convey the idea of uncertainty, as to his personal security in Christ, what then does he mean? I believe the expression applies not to his future prospects, but his present service—not to his heavenly home, but his earthly path—not to his eternal privileges, but his present responsibilities. Paul was a servant as well as a son; and he exercised himself, and kept his body in subjection, "lest that by any means he might be disapproved of."* The body is a good servant, but a bad master; and, if not kept down, will altogether disqualify the servant of Christ for the discharge of his high and holy responsibilities. A person may be a child of God, and yet be "disapproved" as a servant of Christ. To be an efficient servant of Christ involves self-denial, self-judgment, self-emptiness, self-control. I do not become a child of God by these exercises; but, most assuredly, I shall never be a successful servant of Christ without them.

This distinction is very plain and very important. We are too prone to think, that the question of our personal security is the only one of any moment to us. This is a mistake. God has secured that;

---

* I suppose there has never been a "Nehemiah" without a "Sanballat;" or an "Ezra" without a "Rehum;" or a "Paul" without an "Alexander."

and He tells us so, in order that, with free hearts, we may run the race, carry on the warfare, fulfil the service. We do not run, fight, or work for life; we have gotten life—eternal life, ere we take a single step in the chrstian race, strike a blow in the christian warfare, or perform a single act of christian service. A dead man could not run a race; but a living man must run "lawfully," else he cannot be crowned. So, also, in reference to the servant of Christ. He must deny himself; he must keep nature down; he must keep his body in subjection, else he will be disapproved of and set aside, as a servant unfit for the Master's work, a vessel not "meet for the Master's use." A true believer can never, by any possibility, lose his relationship to Christ, or the eternal dignities and privileges connected therewith; but he can lose his present meetness for service. He may so act as to be disapproved of as a workman. Solemn thought!

We have, in the person of John Mark, an illustration of the principle laid down in I Cor. ix. 27. In Acts xiii. 5 he was counted worthy to be associated with Paul in the ministry. In Acts xv. 38 he was disapproved; and in 2 Tim. iv. 11 he was again ackowledged as a profitable servant. Now, John was as truly a child of God, a saved person, a believer in Christ, when Paul rejected him as a co-worker, as when he at first acknowledged him, and finally restored him to confidence. In no case was the question of his personal salvation raised. It was altogether a matter of fitness for service. It is very evident, that the influence of natural affection had been allowed to act on John's heart, and to unfit him, in Paul's judgment, for that great work which he, as the steward of Christ, was carrying on.

If my reader will turn to Judges vii. he will find another example, which strikingly illustrates our principle. What was the great question raised with respect to Gideon's company? Was it as to whether a man was an Israelite—a son of Abraham—a circumcised member of the congregation? By no means. What then? Simply as to whether he was a fit vessel for the service then in hand. And what was it that rendered a man fit for such service? Confidence in God, and self-denial. (See ver. 3 & 6.) Those who were fearful were rejected (v. 3). And those who consulted their own ease were rejected (v. 7). Now, the thirty-one thousand seven hundred, that were rejected, were as truly Israelites as were the three hundred that were approved; but the former were not fit servants, the latter were.

All this is easily understood. There is no difficulty, if the heart be not careful to make difficulties for itself. Many passages of the Word, which are designed to act on the conscience of the servant, are used to alarm the heart of the *child;* many that are only intended to admonish us, in reference to our *responsibility,* are used to make us question our *relationship.*

May the Lord increase in us the grace of a discerning mind, and enable us to distinguish between things that differ, so that while our hearts enter into the sweetness and tranquillizing power of those words, "Him that cometh to me, I will in no wise cast out," our conscience may also feel the solemnity of our position as servants, and recoil from every thing that might cause us to be set aside, as an unclean vessel, which the Master cannot take up and use.

May we ever remember that, while as *children of God,* we are eternally safe, yet as *servants of Christ,* we may be disapproved of and set aside.

# SELF-DENIAL

"If only we exercise a little self denial every day, we shall get on to heaven very comfortably." What a volume of wholesome practical truth in this brief utterance! The path of self-denial is the Christian's true path. "If any man," says Christ, "will come after me, let him deny himself, and take up his cross daily, and follow me." (Luke ix. 23.) Mark, it is not, "let him deny certain things belonging to himself." No, he must "deny himself;" and this is a 'daily" thing. Each morning, as we rise and enter afresh upon the pathway of daily life, we have the same grand and all-important work before us, namely, to deny self.

This hateful self will meet us at every step; for, although we know, through grace, that "our old man is crucified"—that it is dead and buried out of God's sight, still this is only as regards our standing in Christ, according to God's view of us. We know, alas! that self has to be denied, judged, and subjugated, every day, every hour, and every moment. The principle of our standing must be wrought out in practice. God sees us perfect in Christ. We are not in the flesh, but the flesh is in us, and it must be denied and kept by the power of the Spirit.

And, be it remembered, that it is not merely in its grossness that self must be denied, but in its refinement—not merely in its low habits, but in its cultivated tastes—not merely in its roughness and rudeness, but in its most polished and elegant forms. This is not always seen. It too often happens that, like Saul, we spare that which we consider "the best," and bring the edge of the sword to bear only upon "the vile and refuse." This will never do. It is self that must be denied. Yes, self, in all the length and breadth of that comprehensive. Not merely some branches, but the great parent stem—not merely some accessories of nature, but nature itself. It is a comparatively easy matter to deny certain things pertaining to self, while self is pampered and gratified all the time. I may deny my appetite to feed my religious pride. I may starve myself

195

to minister to my love of money. I may wear shabby clothes while I pride myself in sumptuous furniture and a splendid equipage. Hence, the need of being reminded that we must deny *self*.

And, oh! who can sum up all that is contained in this weighty word, self-denial? Self acts everywhere. In the closet, in the family, in the shop, in the railway carriage, in the street—everywhere, at all times, and under all circumstances. It has its tastes and its habits, its prejudices and predilections, its likings and its dislikings. It must be denied in all these. We may frequently detect ourselves liking our own image. This must be denied with uncommon decision.

Then again in matters of religion, we like those who suit us, who agree and sympathize with us, who admire our opinions or mode of propounding them. All this must be brought under the sharp edge of the knife of self-denial. If not, we may find ourselves despising some dear and honoured Christian, simply because of something which does not suit us; and, on the other hand, we shall laud to the skies some hollow, worthless character, just because of some feature which we *like*. Indeed, of all the ten thousand shapes, which self assumes, there is not one more hateful than that of religion. Clad in this garb it will make itself the centre of a *clique*, confine its affections within that narrow enclosure, and call that christian communion. Forth, from this contracted circle, it will diligently expel every one who happens to have a single disagreeable point or angle. It will obstinately refuse to accommodate itself to the scruples and infirmities of others. As to these it will not yield a single hair's breadth, while, at the same time, it will surrender any amount of truth in order to hold fellowship with its own image. All this is terrible and should be most sedulously guarded against.

If my reader will study carefully I Corinthians viii.-x., he will find a most precious lesson on the subject of self-denial. The heading of this entire section might be thus worded, "*Any length in self-denial; not an inch in surrendering truth.*" This should ever be the christian's motto. If it be merely a question of *self*, surrender *all*; if it be a question of *truth*, surrender *nothing*. "If meat make my brother to offend, I will eat no flesh while the world

196

standeth, lest I make my brother to offend." (chap. viii. 13.) Noble resolution! May we have grace to carry it out!

Again, "Though I be free from all, yet have I made myself servant unto all, that I might gain the more. . . . I am made all things to all, that I might by all means save some." (chap. ix. 19-22.) "Let no man seek his own." The very thing we are so ready to seek. "But every man another's wealth." The very last thing we feel disposed to do.

It is important and very needful to observe that when the apostle declares that he was "made all things to all," it was entirely a matter of self-denial and not of self-indulgence. He neither indulged himself, nor surrendered a single iota of the truth of God, but made himself servant to all for their good and God's glory. This is our model. May the Lord endow us with grace to imitate it! We are called to surrender not only our points and angles, prejudices and predilections, but also our personal rights for the profit of others. This is the christian's daily business, and it is as he is enabled to discharge it that he will walk in the footsteps of Jesus, and "get on comfortably to heaven."

# SELF-JUDGMENT

There are few exercises more valuable or healthful for the Christian than self-judgment. I do not mean by this the unhappy practice of looking in upon oneself for evidences of life and security in Christ. This is terrible work to be at. To be looking at a worthless self, instead of at a risen Christ, is as deplorable an occupation as we can well conceive. The idea which many Christians seem to entertain, in reference to what is called self-examination, is truly depressing. They look upon it as an exercise which may end in their discovering that they are not Christians at all. This, I repeat it, is most terrible work.

No doubt it is well for those who have been building upon a sandy foundation, to have their eyes opened to see the dangerous delusion. It is well for such as have been complacently wrapping themselves up in pharisaic robes, to have those robes stripped off. It is well for those who have been sleeping in a house on fire, to be roused from their slumbers. It is well for such as have been walking, blindfold, to the brink of some frightful precipice, to have the bandage removed from their eyes, so that they may see their danger, and retreat. No intelligent and well-regulated mind would think of calling in question the rightness of all this. But then, fully admitting the above, the question of true self-judgment remains wholly untouched. The Christian is never once taught, in the word of God, to examine himself with the idea of finding out that he is not a Christian. The very reverse is the case, as I shall endeavour to show.

There are two passages, in the New Testament, which are sadly misinterpreted. The first is in reference to the celebration of the Lord's supper: "Let a man examine himself, and so let him eat of this bread, and drink of this cup; for he that eateth and drinketh unworthily, eateth and drinketh judgment to himself, not discerning the Lord's body." (1 Cor. xi. 28, 29) Now, it is usual to apply the term "unworthily," in this passage, to persons doing the act,

198

whereas, it really refers to the manner of doing it. The apostle never thought of calling in question the christianity of the Corinthians: nay, in the opening address of his epistle, he looks at them as "the church of God which is in Corinth, sanctified in Christ Jesus, called saints" (or saints by calling). How could he use this language, in the first chapter, and, in the eleventh chapter, call in question the worthiness of these saints to take their seat at the Lord's supper? Impossible. He looked upon them as saints, and, as such, he exhorted them to celebrate the Lord's supper in a worthy manner. The question of any but true Christians being there, is never raised; so that it is utterly impossible that the word "unworthily" could apply to *persons*. Its application is entirely to the *manner*. The persons were worthy, but their manner was not; and they were called, as saints, to judge themselves as to their ways, else the Lord might judge them in their *persons*, as was already the case. In a word, it was as true Christians they were called to judge themselves. If they were in doubt as to that, they were utterly unable to judge anything. I never think of setting my child to judge as to whether he is my child or not; but I expect him to judge himself, as to his habits, else if he do not, I may have to do, by chastening, what he ought to do by self-judgment. It is because I look upon him as my child, that I will not allow him to sit at my table with soiled garments and disorderly manners.

The second passage occurs in 2 Corinthians xiii. "Since ye seek a proof of Christ speaking in me . . . examine yourselves." (Verses 3-5.) The rest of the passage is parenthetic. The real point is this. The apostle appeals to the Corinthians themselves as the clear proof that his apostleship was divine—that Christ had spoken in him—that his commission was from heaven. He looked upon them as true Christians, notwithstanding all their confusion; but, inasmuch as they were seals to his ministry, that ministry must be divine, and, hence, they ought not to listen to the false apostles who were speaking against him. Their christianity and his apostleship were so intimately connected, that to question the one was to question the other. It is, therefore, plain that the apostle did not call upon the Corinthians to examine themselves with any such idea as that the examination might issue in the sad discovery that they were not Christians at all. Quite the reverse. In truth, it is as if I were to produce a real watch to a person, and say, "Since you seek a proof that the man who made this is a watchmaker, examine it."

Thus, then, it seems plain, that neither of the above passages affords any warrant for that kind of self-examination for which some contend, which is really based upon a system of doubts and fears, and has no warrant whatever in the Word of God. The self-judgment to which I would call the reader's attention is a totally different thing. It is a sacred christian exercise, of the most salutary character. It is based upon the most unclouded confidence as to our salvation and acceptance in Christ. The Christian is called to judge self, *because he is*, and not to see *if he be*, a Christian. This makes all the difference. Were I to examine self for a thousand years, I should never find it to be aught else than a worthless, ruined, vile thing—a thing which God has set aside, and which I am called to reckon as "dead." How could I ever expect to get any comfortable evidences by such an examination? Impossible. The Christian's evidences are not to be found in his ruined self, but in God's risen Christ; and the more he can get done with the former and occupied with the latter, the happier and holier he will be. The Christian judges himself, judges his habits, judges his thoughts, words and actions, because he believes he is a Christian, not because he doubts it. If he doubts, he is not fit to judge anything. It is as knowing and enjoying the eternal stability of God's grace, the divine efficacy of the blood of Jesus, the all-prevailing power of His advocacy, the unalterable authority of the Word, the divine security of the very feeblest of Christ's sheep—it is as entering, by the teaching of God the Holy Ghost, into these priceless realities, that the true believer judges himself. The human idea of self-examination is founded upon unbelief. The divine idea of self-judgment is founded upon confidence.

But, let us never forget that we are called to judge ourselves. If we lose sight of this, nature will soon get ahead of us, and we shall make sorry work of it. The most devoted Christians have a mass of things which need to be judged, and, if they are not habitually judged, they will assuredly cut out abundance of bitter work for them. If there be irritability or levity, pride or vanity, natural indolence or natural impetuosity—whatever there be that belongs to our fallen nature, we must, as Christians, judge and subdue that thing. That which is abidingly judged will never get upon the conscience. Self-judgment keeps all our matters right and square; but, if nature be not judged, there is no knowing how, when, or where it may break out, and produce keen anguish of soul, and bring gross dishonour upon the Lord's name. The most grievous cases of failure and declension may be traced to the neglect of self-judgment in little things. There are three distinct stages of judgment, namely, self-judgment, church judgment, and divine judgment. If a man judges himself, the assembly is kept clear. If he fail to do so, evil will break out in some shape or form, and then the assembly is involved; and if the assembly fail to judge the evil, then God must deal with the assembly. If Achan had judged the covetous thought, the assembly would not have become involved. (Joshua vii.) If the Corinthians had judged themselves in secret, the Lord would not to have had to judge the assembly in public. I Cor. xi.

All this is deeply practical and soul-subduing. May all the Lord's people learn to walk in the cloudless sunshine of His favour, in the holy enjoyment of their relationship, and in the habitual exercise of a spirit of self-judgment!

# SELF-EMPTINESS

*The fulness of God ever waits upon an empty vessel.* This is a grand practical truth, very easily stated, but involving a great deal more than one might, at first sight, imagine. The entire Book of God illustrates this truth. The history of the people of God illustrates it; and the experience of each believer illustrates it. Whether we study the Book of God, or the ways of God—His ways with all—His ways with each, we have this most precious truth, that "the fulness of God ever waits on an empty vessel."

This holds good with respect to the sinner, in his first coming to Christ; and it holds good with respect to the believer, at every stage of his career, from the starting post to the goal.

I. In the first place, as regards the sinner in his first coming to Christ, what is this but the fulness of God, in redeeming love and pardoning mercy, waiting upon an empty vessel? The real matter is to get the sinner to take the place of an empty vessel. Once there, the whole question is settled. But, ah! what exercise, what struggling, what toil, what conflict, what fruitless efforts, what ups and downs, what vows and resolutions, in hundreds and thousands of cases, ere the sinner is really brought to take the place of an empty vessel, and be filled with God's salvation! How marvellously difficult it is to get the poor legal heart emptied of its legality, that it may be filled with Christ! It *will* have something of its own to lean upon and cling to. Here lies the root of the difficulty. We can never "draw water from the wells of salvation" until we come thither with empty vessels.

This is difficult work. Many spend years of legal effort ere they reach the grand moral point of self-emptiness, even in its reference to the simple question of righteousness before God. When once they have reached that point, the matter is found to be so simple that the wonder is how they could have spent so long in getting hold of it, and why they had never got hold of it before. There is never any difficulty found, when the sinner really takes the ground of self-emptiness. The question, "Who shall deliver me?" is sure to be followed by the reply, "I thank God through Jesus Christ our Lord." Rom. vii.

Now, it will always be found that the more completely the sinner gets emptied of himself, the more settled his peace will be. If self and its doings, its feelings and its reasonings, be not emptied out, there will assuredly be doubts and fears, ups and downs, wavering and fluctuation, seasons of darkness and cloudiness afterwards. Hence the vital importance of seeking to make a clean riddance of self, so that Christ, "the fulness of the Godhead bodily," may be known and enjoyed. It is the one who can most truthfully and experimentally say,

*"I'm a poor sinner and nothing at all,"*

that can also adopt as his own that additional line,

*"But Jesus Christ is my all in all."*

It is ever thus. A full Christ is for an empty sinner, and an empty sinner for a full Christ. They are morally fitted to each other; and the more I experience the emptiness, the more I shall enjoy the fulness. So long as I am full of self-confidence, so long as I am full of trust in my morality, my benevolence, my amiability, my religiousness, my righteousness, I have no room for Christ. All these things must be thrown overboard, ere a full Christ can be apprehended. It cannot be partly self and partly Christ. It must be either one or the other; and one reason why so many are tossed up and down "in dark uncertainty" is, because they are still cleaving to some little bit of self. It may be a very little bit. They may not, perhaps, be trusting in any works of righteousness that they have done; but still there is something of self retained and trusted in. It may be the very smallest possible atom of the creature—its state, its feelings, its mode of appropriating, its experiences, something or other of the creature kept in which keeps Christ out. In short, it must be so, for if a full Christ were received, a full peace would be enjoyed; and if a full peace be not enjoyed, it is only because a full Christ has not been received. This makes the matter as simple as possible.

Reader, do you fully understand this? Have you, as an empty sinner, come to Christ to be filled with His fulness, to be satisfied with His all-sufficiency, to find the solid rest of your heart and conscience in Him alone? Say, are you, now, fully satisfied with Christ? I earnestly pray you to get this point settled, now. Is Christ enough for your heart, enough for your conscience, enough for your whole moral being? See that you make earnest, real, hearty work of it now. Are you resting wholly in Christ? Which is it, Christ alone, or Christ and something else? Are you, in some secret chamber of your heart, hiding a little fragment of legality—some little atom of creature confidence—some element of self-righteousness? If so, you cannot enjoy true gospel peace. It cannot be. Gospel peace is the result of receiving a full Christ into a heart that has learnt its own emptiness. Christ is our peace. True peace is not a mere feeling in the mind. It is found in a divine, living, real Person, even Christ Himself, who, having made peace by the blood of His cross, has become our peace in the presence of God. This peace can never be disturbed, inasmuch as He who is our peace, is "the same, yesterday, to-day, and for ever." (Heb. xiii.) Were it a mere feeling in the mind, it would prove as variable as the mercury in a barometer. If I am occupied with my feelings, I am not self-emptied, and, as a consequence, I cannot know the joy and peace which flow from being occupied only with Christ, for the fulness of God ever waits upon an empty vessel.

Thus much as to the application of our thesis to the case of a sinner in his first coming to Christ.

II. Let us, now, see how it applies to a believer at every stage of his career. This is a deeply practical branch of the subject. We have very little idea at times of how full we are of self and the world. Hence it is that in one way or another, we have to be emptied from vessel to vessel. Like Jacob of old, we struggle hard, and hold fast our confidence in the flesh, until at length the source of our strength is dried up, and the ground of our confidence swept from under us, and then we are constrained to cry out,

> *"Others refuge have I none,*
> *Clings my helpless soul to Thee."*

There can be no greater barrier to our peace and habitual enjoyment of God than our being filled with self-confidence. We must be emptied and humbled. God cannot divide the house with the creature. It is vain to expect it. Jacob had the hollow of his thigh touched, in order that he might learn to lean upon God. The halting Jacob found his sure resource in Jehovah, who only empties us of nature that we may be filled with Himself. He knows that just in so far as we are filled with self-confidence, or creature-confidence, we are robbed of the deep blessedness of being filled with His fulness. Hence, in His great grace and mercy, He empties us out, that we may learn to cling, in child-like confidence, to Him. This is our only place of strength, of victory, and repose.

Some one has said, "I never was truly happy until I ceased to wish to be great." This is a fine moral truth. When we cease to wish to be *anything*, when we are content to be *nothing*, then it is we taste what true greatness—true elevation—true happiness—true peace, really is. The restless desire to be something or somebody, is destructive of the soul's tranquillity. The proud heart and ambitious spirit may pronounce this a poor, low, mean, contemptible sentiment; but ah! when we have taken our place on the forms of the school of Christ—when we have begun to learn of him who was meek and lowly in heart—when we have drunk, in any measure, into the spirit of Him who made Himself of no reputation, we then see things quite differently. "He that humbleth himself shall be exalted." The way to get up is to go down. This is the doctrine of Christ, the doctrine which fell from His lips and is inscribed on His life. "And Jesus called a little child unto him, and set him in the midst of them, and said, Verily, I say unto you, except ye be converted, and become as little children, ye shall not enter into the kingdom of heaven. Whosoever, therefore, shall humble himself as this little child, the same is greatest in the kingdom of heaven." (Matthew xviii. 2-4.) This is the doctrine of heaven—the doctrine of self-emptiness. How unlike to all that obtains down here in this scene of self-seeking and self-exaltation!

We have, in the person of John the Baptist, a fine example of one who entered, in some degree, into the real meaning of self-emptiness. The Jews sent priests and Levites from Jerusalem to ask him, "Who art thou? What sayest thou of thyself?" What was his reply? A self-emptied one. He said he was just "a voice." This was taking his true place. "A voice" had not much to glory in. He did not say, "I am one crying in the wilderness." No; he was merely "*the voice* of one." He had no ambition to be anything more. This was self-emptiness. And, observe the result. He found his engrossing object in Christ. "Again the next day after *John stood,* and two of his disciples; and looking upon *Jesus* as he *walked,* he saith, Behold the Lamb of God!" What was all this, but the fulness of God waiting on an empty vessel! John was nothing, Christ was all; and hence, when John's disciples left his side to follow Jesus, we may feel assured that no murmuring word, no accent of disappointed ambition or wounded pride escaped his lips. There is no envy or jealousy in a self-emptied heart. There is nothing touchy, nothing tenacious, about one who has learnt to take his true place. Had John been seeking his own things, he might have complained when he saw himself abandoned; but, ah! my reader, when a man has found his satisfying object in "the Lamb of God," he does not care much about losing a few disciples.

We have a further exhibition of the Baptist's self-emptied spirit in the third chapter of John. "And they came unto John, and said unto him, Rabbi, he that was with thee beyond Jordan, to whom thou barest witness, behold, the same baptizeth, and all come to him." Here was a communication quite calculated to draw out the envy and jealousy of the poor human heart. But mark the reply, the noble reply, of the Baptist: "A man can receive NOTHING, except it be given him from heaven. . . . He must increase, but I must decrease. *He that cometh from above is above all;* he that is of the earth is earthly, and speaketh of the earth: *he that cometh from heaven is* ABOVE ALL." Precious testimony this! A testimony to his own utter nothingness, and

Christ's fulness, glory, and peerless excellence! "A voice" was "nothing." Christ was "high over all."

Oh! for a self-emptied spirit—"A heart at leisure from itself"—a mind delivered from all anxiety about one's own things! May we be more thoroughly delivered from *self*, in all its detestable windings and workings! Then could the Master use us, own us, and bless us. Hearken to His testimony to John—the one who said of himself that he was nothing but a voice. "Verily I say unto you, among them that are born of women there hath not risen a greater than John the Baptist." (Matt. xi. 11.) How much better to hear this from the Master than from the servant! John said, "I am a voice." Christ said he was the greatest of prophets. Simon Magus "gave out that *himself* was some great one." Such is the way of the world—the manner of man. John the Baptist, the greatest of prophets, gave out that himself was *nothing*—that Christ was "*above all*." What a contrast!

May we be kept lowly and self-emptied, that so we may be continually filled with Christ. This is true rest—true blessedness. May the language of our hearts, and the distinct utterance of our lives ever be, "*Behold the Lamb of God.*"

# SELF-CONTROL

The word "temperance," in 2 Pet. i. 6, means a great deal more than what is usually understood by that term. It is customary to apply the expression "temperance" to a habit of moderation in reference to eating and drinking. No doubt it fully involves this, but it involves very much more. Indeed, the Greek word used by the inspired apostle, may, with strict propriety, be rendered "self-control." It gives the idea of one who has *self* habitually *well reined in*.

This is a rare and admirable grace, diffusing its hallowed influence over the entire course, character, and conduct. It not only bears directly upon one, or two, or twenty selfish *habits*, but upon *self*, in all the length and breadth of that comprehensive and most odious term. Many a one who would look, with proud disdain, upon a glutton or a drunkard, may himself fail, every hour, in exhibiting the grace of self-control. True it is that gluttony and drunkenness should be ranged with the very vilest and most demoralizing forms of selfishness. They must be regarded as amongst the most bitter clusters that grow on that widespread tree. But, then, *self* is a tree, and not a mere branch of a tree, or a cluster on a branch; and we should not only *judge* self when it works, but *control* it that it may not work.

Some, however, may ask, "How can we control self?" The answer is blessedly simple: "I can do *all* things through Christ that strengtheneth me." (Phil. iv.) Have we not gotten salvation in Christ? Yes, blessed be God, we have. And what does this wondrous word include? Is it mere deliverance from the wrath to come? Is it merely the pardon of our sins, and the assurance of exemption from the lake that burneth with fire and brimstone? It is far more than these, precious and priceless though they be. In a word, then, "salvation" implies a full and hearty acceptance of Christ as my "wisdom," to guide me out of folly's dark and devious paths, into paths of heavenly light and peace; as my "righteousness," to justify me in the sight of a holy God; as my "sanctification," to make me practically holy in all my ways; and as my "redemption," to give me final deliverance from all the power of death, and entrance upon the eternal fields of glory.

Hence, therefore, it is evident that "self-control" is included in the salvation which we have in Christ. It is a result of that practical sanctification with which divine grace has endowed us. We should carefully guard against the habit of taking a narrow view of salvation. We should seek to enter into all its fulness. It is a word which stretches from everlasting to everlasting, and takes in, in its mighty sweep, all the practical details of daily life. I have no right to talk of salvation, as regards my soul, in the future, while I refuse to know and exhibit its practical bearing upon my conduct, in the present. We are saved, not only from the guilt and condemnation of sin, but also, and as fully, from the power, the practice, and the love of it. These things should never be separated, nor will they by any one who has been divinely taught the meaning, the extent, and the power of that precious word "salvation."

Now, in presenting to my reader a few practical sentences on the subject of self-control, I shall contemplate it under the three following divisions, namely—the thoughts, the tongue, and the temper. I take it for granted that I am addressing a saved person. If my reader be not that, I can only direct him to the one true and living way, "Believe on the Lord Jesus Christ, and thou shalt be saved, and thy house." (Acts xvi.) Put your whole trust in Him, and you shall be as safe as He is Himself. This grand theme is largely dwelt upon, and variously illustrated, throughout the pages of this magazine, and to them I would refer the unconverted sinner, or the anxious inquirer, while I proceed to deal with the practical and much-needed subject of self-control.

I. And, first, as to our thoughts, and the habitual government thereof. I suppose there are few Christians who have not suffered from evil thoughts—those troublesome intruders upon our most profound retirement—those constant disturbers of our mental repose, that so frequently darken the atmosphere around us, and prevent us from getting a full, clear view upward into the bright heaven above. The Psalmist could say, "I hate vain thoughts." No wonder. They are truly hateful, and should be judged, condemned, and expelled. Some one, in speaking of the subject of evil thoughts, has said, "I cannot prevent birds from flying over me, but I can prevent their alighting upon me. In like manner, I cannot prevent evil thoughts being suggested to my mind, but I can refuse them a lodgment therein."

But how can we control our thoughts? No more than we could blot out our sins, or create a world. What are we to do? Look to Christ. This is the true secret of self-control. He can keep us, not only from the lodgment, but also from the suggestion of the evil thoughts. We could no more prevent the one than the other. He can prevent both. He can keep the vile intruders, not only from getting in, but even from knocking at the door. When the divine life is in energy—when the current of spiritual thought and feeling is deep and rapid—when the heart's affections are intensely occupied with the Person of Christ, vain thoughts do not trouble us. It is only when spiritual indolence creeps over us that evil thoughts —vile and horrible progeny!—come in upon us, like a flood; and then our only resource is to look straight to Jesus. We might as well attempt to cope with the marshalled hosts of hell, as with a horde of evil thoughts. Our refuge is in Christ. He is made unto us sanctification We can do all things through Him. We have just to bring the name of Jesus to bear upon the flood of evil thoughts, and He will, most assuredly, give full and immediate deliverance.

However, the more excellent way is, to be preserved from the suggestions of evil, by the power of pre-occupation with good. When the channel of thought is decidedly upward, when it is deep and well formed, free from all curves and indentations, then the current of imagination and feeling, as it gushes up from the deep fountains of the soul, will naturally flow onward in the bed of that channel. This, I repeat, is unquestionably, the more excellent way. May we prove it in our own experience. "Finally, brethren, whatsoever things are true, whatsoever things are venerable, whatsoever things are just, whatsoever things are lovely, whatsoever things are of good report, if there be any virtue, and if there be any praise, *think* on these things. Those things which ye have both learned and received, and heard and seen in me, do; and the God of peace shall be with you." (Phil. iv. 8, 9.) When the heart is fully engrossed with Christ, the living embodiment of all those things enumerated in verse 8, we enjoy profound peace, unruffled by evil thoughts. This is true self-control.

II. And, now, as to the tongue, that influential member, so fruitful in good, so fruitful in evil—the instrument whereby we can either give forth accents of soft and soothing sympathy, or words of bitter sarcasm and burning indignation. How deeply important is the grace of self-control in its application to such a member! Mischief, which years cannot repair, may be done by the tongue in a moment. Words, which we would give the world, if we had it, to recall, may be uttered by the tongue in an unguarded hour. Hear what the inspired apostle saith on this subject: "If any man offend not in word, the same is a perfect man, and able also to bridle the whole body. Behold, we put bits in the horses' mouths, that they may obey us; and we turn about their whole body. Behold also the ships ,which though they be so great, and are driven of fierce winds, yet are they turned about with a very small helm, whithersoever the governor listeth. Even so the tongue is a little member and boasteth great things. Behold, how great a matter a little fire kindleth! And the tongue is a fire, a world of inquity: so is the tongue among our members, that it defileth the whole body, and setteth on fire the course of nature; and it is set on fire of hell. For every kind of beasts, and of birds, and of serpents, and of things in the sea is tamed, and hath been tamed of mankind. But the tongue can no man tame; it is an unruly evil, full of deadly poison." (James iii. 2-8.)

Who, then, can control the tongue? "No man" can do it; but Christ can; and we have only to look to Him, in simple faith which implies, at once, the sense of our own utter helplessness and His all-sufficiency. It is utterly impossible that we could control the tongue. As well might we attempt to stem the ocean's tide, the mountain torrent, or the Alpine avalanche. How often, when suffering under the effects of some egregious blunder of the tongue, have we resolved to command that unruly member somewhat better next time; but, alas! our resolution proved to be like the morning cloud that passeth away, and we had only to retire and weep over our lamentable failure in the matter of self-control. Now, why was this? Simply because we undertook the matter in our own strength, or, at least, without a sufficiently deep consciousness of our own weakness. This is the cause of constant failure. We must cling to Christ as the babe clings to its mother. Not that our clinging is of any value; still we must cling. Thus, and thus alone, can we successfully bridle the tongue. And oh! let us remember, at all times, the solemn searching words of the same apostle, James, "If any one (man, woman, or child) among you seem to be religious, and bridleth not his tongue, but deceiveth his own heart, this man's religion is vain." (chap. i. 26.) These are wholesome words for a day like the present, when there are so many unruly tongues abroad. May we have grace to attend to these words! May their holy influence appear in our ways!

III. The last point to be considered is the temper, which is intimately connected with both the tongue and the thoughts. Indeed, all three are very closely linked. When the spring of *thought* is spiritual, and the current heavenly, the *tongue* is only the active agent for good, and the *temper* is calm and unruffled. Christ dwelling in the heart by faith regulates every thing. Without Him, all is worse than worthless. I may possess and exhibit the self-command of a Franklin or a Socrates, and, all the while, be wholly ignorant of the "self-control" of 2 Peter i. 6. The latter is founded on "faith;" the former on philosophy, two totally different things. We must remember that the word is *"Add to your faith."* This puts faith first, as the only link to connect the heart with Christ, the living source of all power. Having Christ, and abiding in Him, we are enabled to add "courage, knowledge, self-control, patience, godliness, brotherly kindness, charity." Such are the precious fruits that flow from abiding in Christ. But I can no more control my temper than my tongue or my thoughts; and if I set about it, I shall be sure to break down every hour. A mere philosopher, without Christ, may exhibit more self-control as to tongue and temper, than a Christian, if he abides not in Christ. This ought not to be, and would not be, if the Christian simply looked to Jesus. It is when he fails in this that the enemy gains the advantage. The philosopher without Christ, seems to succeed in the great business of self-control, only that he may be the more effectually blinded as to the truth of his condition, and carried headlong to eternal ruin. But Satan delights to make a Christian stumble and fall, only that he may thereby blaspheme the precious name of Christ.

Christian reader, let us remember these things. Let us look to Christ to control our thoughts, our tongue, and our temper. Let us "give all diligence." Let us think how much is involved. "If these things be in you and abound, they make you that ye shall neither be barren nor unfruitful in the knowledge of our Lord Jesus Christ. But he that lacketh these things is blind, and cannot see afar off, and hath forgotten that he was purged from his old sins." This is deeply solemn. How easy it is to drop into a state of spiritual blindness and forgetfulness! No amount of knowledge, either of doctrine or the letter of Scripture, will preserve the soul from this awful condition. Nothing but "the knowledge of our Lord Jesus Christ" will avail; and this knowledge is to be increased in the soul by "giving all diligence to add to our faith" the various graces to which the apostle refers in the above eminently practical and soul-stirring passage. "Wherefore the rather, brethren, give diligence to make your calling and election sure: for if ye do these things ye shall never fall: for so an entrance shall be ministered unto you abundantly into the everlasting kingdom of our Lord and Saviour Jesus Christ."

# PROVISION FOR PERILOUS TIMES

## (READ 2 TIMOTHY)

It is of the very last importance, for the servant of Christ, in all ages, to have a clear, deep, abiding, influential sense of his position, his path, his portion, and his prospects—a divinely wrought apprehension of the ground which he is called to occupy; the sphere of action which is thrown open to him; the divine provision made for his comfort and encouragement, his strength and guidance; and the brilliant hopes held out to him. There is uncommon danger of our being allured into a mere region of theory and speculation, of opinion and sentiment, of dogmas and principles. The freshness of first love is frequently lost by contact with the men and things of what may be called "the religious world." The lovely verdure of early personal christianity is often destroyed by a wrong use of the machinery of religion, if we may be allowed to use such a term.

In the kingdom of nature, it frequently happens that some stray seed has dropped into the ground, taken root, and sprung up into a tender plant. The hand of man had nothing to do with it. God planted it, watered it, and made it grow. He assigned it its position, gave it its strength, and covered it with beauteous verdure. By and by, man intruded upon its solitude and transplanted it to his own artificial enclosure, there to wither and droop. Thus it is, too often, alas! with the plants of God's spiritual kingdom. They are often injured by man's rude hand. They would be far better, if left to the sole management of the Hand that planted them. Young Christians frequently suffer immensely from not being left to the exclusive training of the Holy Ghost, and the exclusive teaching of Holy Scripture. Human management is almost sure to stunt the growth of God's spiritual plants. It is not, by any means, that God may not use men as His instruments in watering, culturing, and carng for, His precious plants. He assuredly may and does; but,

214

then, it is God's culture and care, not man's. This makes all the difference. The Christian is God's plant. The seed which produced him was divine. It was directed and planted by God's own hand, and that same hand must be allowed to train it.

Now, what is true of the individual believer is equally true of the Church, as a whole. In the First Epistle to Timothy, the Church is looked at in its original order and glory. It is there viewed as "The house of God"—"The church of the living God" —"The pillar and ground of the truth." Its officebearers, its functions, and its responsibilities, are there minutely and formally described. The servant of Christ is instructed as to the mode in which he is to conduct himself in the midst of such a hallowed and dignified sphere. Such is the character, such the scope and object of Paul's First Epistle to Timothy.

But, in the Second Epistle, we have something quite different. The scene is entirely changed. The house which, in the first epistle, was looked at in its *rule*, is here contemplated in its *ruin*. The church, as an economy set up on the earth, had, like every other economy, utterly failed. Man fails in everything. He failed amid the beauty and order of Paradise. He failed in that favoured land "that flowed with milk and honey, the glory of all lands." He failed amid the rare privileges of the gospel dispensation; and he will fail amid the bright beams of millennial glory. (Comp. Gen. iii., Judges ii., Acts xx. 29, 3 John 9, Rev. i. ii., Rev. xx. 7-9.)

The remembrance of this will help us in the understanding of 2 Timothy. It may, very properly, be termed, "a divine provision for perilous times." The apostle seems, as it were, to be weeping over the ruins of that once beautiful structure. Like the weeping prophet, he beholds "the stones of the sanctuary poured out in the top of every street." He calls to remembrance the tears of his beloved Timothy. He is glad to have even one sympathizing bosom into which to pour his sorrows. All that were in Asia had turned away from him. He was left to stand alone before Caesar's judgment seat. Demas forsook him. Alexander, the coppersmith, did him much evil. All around him, so far as man was concerned, looked gloomy and dark. He begs of his beloved Timothy to bring him his cloke, his books, and his parchments. All is strongly

215

marked. "Perilous times" are anticipated. "A form of godliness without the power"—the mantle of profession thrown over the grossest abominations of the human heart—men not able to endure sound doctrine—heaping to themselves teachers after their own lusts, having itching ears which must needs be tickled by the fabulous and baseless absurdities of the human mind. Such are the features of the Second Epistle to Timothy. Who can fail to notice them? Who can fail to see that our lot is cast in the very midst of the evils and dangers here contemplated? And is it not well to have a clear perception of these things? Why should we desire to blind our eyes as to the truth? Why deceive ourselves with vain dreams of increasing light and spiritual prosperity? Is it not better far to look the true condition of things straight in the face? Assuredly; and the rather when the selfsame epistle which so faithfully points out "the perilous times," fully unfolds the divine provision. Why should we imagine that man, under the christian dispensation, would prove a single whit better than man under all the dispensations which have gone before, or under the millennial dispensation which is yet to follow? Would not analogy, even in the absence of direct and positive proof, lead us to expect failure under this one economy as well as under all the others? If we, without exception, find judgment at the close of all the other dispensations, why should we look for aught else at the close of this? Let my reader ponder these things, and then accompany me, for a few moments, while I seek, by the grace of God, to unfold some of the divine provisions for "perilous times."

I do not attempt to expound this most touching and interesting epistle in detail. This would be impossible in an article like the present. I shall merely single out one point from each of the four chapters into which the epistle has been divided. These are, first, "unfeigned faith." (ch. i. 5.) Secondly, "the sure foundation." (chap. ii. 19). Thirdly, "the holy scriptures." (chap. iii. 15.) Fourthly, "the crown of righteousness." (chap. iv. 8.) The man who knows aught of the power of these things, is divinely provided for "perilous times."

I. And, first, as to "the unfeigned faith"—that priceless possession, the apostle says, "I thank God, whom I serve from my fore-

216

fathers with pure conscience, that without ceasing I have remembrance of thee in my prayers night and day; greatly desiring to see thee, being mindful of thy tears, that I may be filled with joy; when I call to remembrance the unfeigned faith that is in thee, which dwelt first in thy grandmother Lois and thy mother Eunice; and I am persuaded that in thee also." Here, then, we have something above and beyond every thing ecclesiastical—something which one must have, ere he is introduced to the church, and which will stand good though the church were in ruins around him. This unfeigned faith connects the soul immediately with Christ, in the power of a link which must, of necessity, be anterior to all ecclesiastical associations how important soever they may be, in their due place—a link which shall endure when all earthly associations, shall have been dissolved for ever. We do not get to Christ through the church. We get to Christ first, and then to the church. Christ is our life, not the church. No doubt, church fellowship is most valuable; but there is something above and beyond it, and it is of that something that "unfeigned faith" takes possession. Timothy had this faith dwelling in him before ever he entered the house of God. He was connected with the God of the house previous to his manifested association with the house of God.

It is well to be clear as to this. We must never surrender the intense individuality which characterizes "unfeigned faith." We must carry it with us through all the scenes and circumstances, the links and associations of our christian life and service. We must not traffic in mere church position, or build upon religious machinery, or be upborne by a routine of duty, or cling to the worthless props of sectarian sympathy or denominational predilection. Let us cultivate those fresh, vivid, and powerful affections which were created in our heart when first we knew the Lord. Let the beauteous blossom of our spring-time be succeeded, not by barrenness and sterility, but by those mellow clusters which spring from realized connection with the root. Too often, alas! it is otherwise. Too often the earnest, zealous, simple-hearted young Christian is lost in the bigoted, narrow-minded member of a sect, or the intolerant defender of some peculiar opinion. The freshness, softness, simplicity, tenderness, and earnest affection of our young days, are rarely carried forward into the advnced stages of vigorous manhood, and mature old age. Very frequently, one finds a depth of tone, a richness of experience, of moral elevation, in the early stages of the christian life which too soon gives place to a chilling formalism in one's personal ways; or a mere energy in the defence of some barren system of theology. How rarely are those words of the Psalmist realized, "They shall bring forth fruit in old age; they shall be fat and flourishing." Ps. xcii. 14.

The truth is, we all want to cultivate, more diligently, an "unfeigned faith." We want to enter, with more spiritual vigour, into the power of the link which binds us, individually, to Christ. This would render us "fat and flourishing," even in old age. "The righteous shall flourish like the palm tree; he shall grow like a cedar in Lebanon. Those that be planted in the house of the Lord, shall flourish in the courts of our God." We suffer materially by allowing what is called christian intercourse to interfere with our personal connection and communion with Christ. We are far too prone to substitute intercourse with man for intercourse with God—to walk in the footsteps of our fellow, rather than in the footsteps of Christ —to look around, rather than upward, for sympathy, support, and encouragement. These are not the fruits of "unfeigned faith." Quite the opposite. That faith is as blooming and vigorous amid the solitudes of a desert as in the bosom of an assembly. Its immediate, its all engrossing business is with God Himself. "It endures as seeing Him who is invisible." It fixes its earnest gaze upon things unseen and eternal. "It enters into that within the veil." It lives amid the unseen realities of an eternal world. Having conducted the soul to the feet of Jesus, there to get a full and final forgiveness of all its sins, through His most precious blood, it bears it majestically onward through all the windings and labyrinths of desert life, and enables it to bask in the bright beams of millenial glory.

Thus much as to this first precious item in the divine provision for "perilous times"—this "unfeigned faith." No one can ever get on without it, let the times be peaceful or perilous, easy or difficult, rough or smooth, dark or bright. If a man be destitute of this faith, deeply implanted and diligently cultivated in his for a time, by the impulses of surrounding circumstances and their soul, he must, sooner or later, break down. He may be urged on, for a time, by the impulses of surrounding circumstances and their influence. He may be propped up and borne along by his co-religionists. He may float down along the stream of religious profession. But, most assuredly, if he be not possessed of "unfeigned faith," the time is rapidly approaching when it will be all over with him for ever. The "perilous times" will soon rise to a head, and then will come the awful crisis of judgment, from which none can escape save the happy possessors of "unfeigned faith." God grant my reader may be one of these! If so, all is eternally safe.

II. We shall, now, consider, in the second place, "The sure foundation." "Nevertheless the foundation of God standeth sure, having this seal, the Lord knoweth them that are his. And let every one that nameth the name of Christ depart from iniquity." (Chap. ii. 19.) In the midst of all the "trouble," the "hardness," the "striving about words," the "profane and vain babblings," the errors of "Hymenaeus and Philetus"—in the midst of all these varied features of the "perilous times," how ineffably precious to fall back upon God's sure foundation. The soul that is built upon this, in the divine energy of "unfeigned faith," is able to resist the rapidly rising tide of evil—is divinely furnished for the most appalling times. There is a fine moral link between the unfeigned faith in the heart of man, and the sure foundation laid by the hand of God. All may go to ruin. The church may go to pieces, and all who love that church may have to sit down and weep over its ruins; but there stands that imperishable foundation, laid by God's own hand, aginst which the surging tide of error and evil may roll with all its fury, and have no effect, save to prove the eternal stability of that rock and of all who are built thereon.

"The Lord knoweth them that are his." There is abundance of false profession, but the eye of Jehovah rests on all those who belong to Him. Not one of them is, or ever can be forgotten by Him. Their names are engraven on His heart. They are as precious to Him as the price He paid for them, and that is nothing less than the "precious blood" of His own dear Son. No evil can befall them. No weapon formed against them can prosper. "The eternal God is their refuge, and underneath are the everlasting arms." What rich, what ample provision for "perilous times!" Why should we fear? Why should we be anxious? Having "unfeigned faith within, and God's foundation beneath, it is our happy privilege to pursue, with tranquillized hearts, our upward and onward way, in the assurance that all is, and shall be well.

> "I know my sheep," He cries,
> "My soul approves them well:
> Vain is the treacherous world's disguise,
> And vain the rage of hell."

It has been well remarked that the seal on God's foundation has two sides: one, bearing the inscription, "The Lord knoweth them that are his", and the other, "Let every one that nameth the name of Christ depart from iniquity." The former is as peace-giving as the latter is practical. Let the strife and confusion be ever so great —let the storm rage and the billow arise—let the darkness thicken —let all the powers of earth and hell combine, "the Lord knoweth them that are his." He has sealed them for Himself. The assurance of this is eminently calculated to maintain the heart in profound repose, let the "times" be ever so "perilous."

But, let us never forget that each one who "names the name of Christ," is solemnly responsible to "depart from iniquity" wherever he finds it. This is applicable to all true christians. The moment I see any thing that deserves the epithet of "iniquity," be it what or where it may, I am called upon to "depart from" that thing. I am not to wait till others see with me, for what may seem to be "iniquity" to one, may not seem to be so, at all, to another. Hence, it is entirely a personal question. "Let every one." The language used in this epistle is very personal, very strong, very intense. "If a man purge himself." "Flee also youthful lusts." "From such turn away." "Continue thou." "I charge thee." "Watch thou in all things, endure afflictions." "Of whom be thou ware also. "These are solemn, earnest, weighty words—words which prove, very distinctly, that our lot is cast in times when we must not lean upon the arm or gaze upon the countenance of our fellow. We must be sustained by the energy of an "unfeigned faith," and by our personal connexion with the "sure foundation." Thus shall we be able, let others do or think as they will, to "depart from iniquity"—to "flee youthful lusts"—to "turn away" from the adherents of a powerless "form of godliness," wherever we find them, and to "beware" of every "Alexander the coppersmith."* If we suffer our feet to be moved from the rock—if we surrender ourselves to the impulse of surrounding circumstances and influences, we shall never be able to make head against the special forms of evil and error in these "perilous times."

III. This introduces us, naturally, to our third point, namely, "The holy scriptures"—that precious portion of every "man of God." "But continue thou in the things which thou hast learned and hast been assured of, knowing of whom thou hast learned them; and that from a child thou hast known the holy scriptures, which are able to make thee wise unto salvation through faith which is in Christ Jesus. All scripture is given by inspiration of God, and is profitable for doctrine, for reproof, for correction, for instruction in righteousness; that the man of God may be perfect, THOROUGHLY furnished unto ALL good works." (chap. iii. 14-17.) Here, then, we have rich provision for "perilous times." A thorough knoweldge of the One from "whom we have learned"—an accurate, personal, experimental acquaintance with "holy scripture"—that pure fountain of divine authority—that changeless source of heavenly wisdom, which even a child may possess, and without which a sage must err. If a man be not able to refer all his thoughts, all his convictions, all his principles, to God as their living source—to Christ as their living centre, and to "the holy scriptures" as their divine authority, he will never be able to get on through "perilous times." A second-hand faith will never do. We must hold truth directly from God, through the medium, and on the authority of "the holy scriptures." God may use a man to show me certain things in the word; but I do not hold them from man, but from God. It is, "knowing of whom thou hast learned;" and when this is the case I am able, through grace,

---

* I suppose there has never been a "Nehemiah" without a "Sanballat;" or an "Ezra" without a "Rehum;" or a "Paul" without an "Alexander."

to get on through the thickest darkness, and through all the devious paths of this wilderness world. Inspiration's heavenly lamp emits a light so clear, so full, so steady, that its brightness is only made the more distinctly manifest by the surrounding gloom. "The man of God" is not left to drink of the muddy streams that flow along the channel of human tradition; but with the vessel of "unfeigned faith," he sits beside the limpid and ever-gushing fountain of "holy scripture," there to drink of its refreshing waters, to the full satisfaction of his thirsty soul.

It is worthy of remark that, although the inspired apostle was fully aware, when writing his first epistle, of Timothy's "unfeigned faith" and of his knowledge, from childhood's earliest dawn, of "the holy scriptures," yet he does not allude to these things until, in his second epistle, he contemplates the appalling features of the "perilous times." The reason is obvious. It is in the very midst of the perils of "the last days," that one has the most urgent need of "unfeigned faith" and "the holy scriptures." We cannot get on without them. When all around is fresh and vigorous—when all are borne onward as by one common impulse of genuine devotedness—when every heart is full to overflowing of deep and earnest attachment to the Person and cause of Christ—when every countenance beams with heavenly joy—then, indeed, it is comparatively easy to get on. But the condition of things contemplated in the Second Epistle to Timothy is the very reverse of all this. It is such, that unless one is walking closely with God, in the habitual exercise of "unfeigned faith"—in the abiding realization of the link which connects him, indissolubly, with "the foundation of God"—and in clear, unquestionable, accurate knowledge of "the holy scriptures," he must, assuredly, make shipwreck. This is a deeply solemn consideration, well worthy of my reader's undivided, prayerful attention. The time has, verily, arrived in the which each one must follow the Lord, according to his measure. "What is that to thee? Follow thou me." These words fall on the ear with peculiar power as one seeks to make his way amid the ruins of every thing ecclesiastical.

But, let me not be misunderstood. It is not that I would detract, in the smallest degree, from the value of true church fellowship, or from the divine institution of the assembly and all the privileges and responsibilities attaching thereto. Far be the thought. I believe, most fully, that christians are called to seek the maintenance of the very highest principles of communion; and moreover, we are warranted, from the epistle which now lies open before us to expect that, in the darkest times, the "purged vessel" will be able to "follow righteousness, faith, charity, peace, with them that call on the Lord out of a pure heart." (chap. ii. 22.)

All this is plain, and has its due place and value; but it, in no wise, interferes with the fact that each one is responsible to pursue a path of holy independence, without waiting for the countenance, the sympathy, the support, or the company of his fellow. True, we are to be deeply thankful for brotherly fellowship, when we can get it on true ground. Of such fellowship no words can tell the worth. Would that we knew more of it! The Lord increase it to us a hundred fold! But let us never stoop to purchase fellowship at the heavy price of all that is "lovely and of good report." May the name of Jesus be more precious to our hearts than all beside; and with all those who truly love His name our happy lot be cast on earth, as it shall be, throughout eternity, in the regions of unfading light and purity, above.

IV. And, now, one closing word as to "the crown of righteousness." "For I am now ready to be offered, and the time of my departure is at hand. I have fought a good fight, I have finished my course, I have kept the faith. Henceforth there is laid up for me a crown of righteousness, which the Lord, the righteous judge, shall give me at that day; and not to me only, but unto all them also who love his appearing." (chap. iv. 6-8). Here, the venerable pilgrim takes his stand on the summit of the spiritual Pisgah, and, with undimmed eye, surveys the bright plains of glory. He sees the crown of righteousness glittering in the Master's hand. He looks back over the course which he had run, and over the battle-field whereon he had fought—he stands on the confines of earth, and in the very midst of the ruins of that church whose rise and progress he had watched with such intense solicitude, and over whose decline and fall he had poured forth the tears of tender though disappointed affection—he fixes his eye on the goal of immortality which no power of the enemy can prevent his reaching, in tripmph; and whether it were by Caesar's axe that he was to reach that goal, or by any other means, it mattered not to one who was able to say, "I AM READY." What true sublimity! What moral grandeur! What noble elevation is here! And yet there was nothing of the ascetic in this incomparable servant, for though his vision was filled with the crown of righteousness—though he is ready to step like a conqueror into his triumphal chariot—he, nevertheless, feels it perfectly right to give minute directions about his cloke and books. This is divinely perfect. It teaches us that the more vividly we enter into the glories of heaven, the more faithfully shall we discharge the functions of earth—the more we realize the nearness of eternity, the more effectively shall we order the things of time.

Such, then, beloved reader, is the ample provision made, by the grace of God, for "the perilous times" through which you and I are now passing. "Unfeigned faith"—"The sure foundaton"—"The holy scriptures"—and "The crown of righteousness." May the Holy Ghost lead us into a deep sense of the importance and value of these things! May we love the appearing of Jesus, and earnestly look out for that cloudless morning when "the righteous judge" shall place a diadem of glory upon the brow of each one who really loves His advent!

# THE CLOSING SCENES OF
# MALACHI AND JUDE

In comparing these two inspired writings, we find many points of similarity, and many points of contrast. Both the prophet and apostle portray scenes of ruin, corruption, and apostasy. The former is occupied with the ruin of Judaism; the latter with the ruin of Christendom. The prophet Malachi, in his very opening sentences, gives, with uncommon vividness, the source of Israel's blessing, and the secret of their fall. "I have loved you, saith the Lord." Here was the grand source of all their blessedness, all their glory, all their dignity. Jehovah's love accounts for all the bright glory of Israel's past, and all the brighter glories of Israel's future. While, on the other hand, their bold and infidel challenge, "Wherein hast thou loved us?" accounts for the deepest depths of Israel's present degradation. To put such a question, after all that Jehovah had done for them, from the days of Moses to the days of Solomon, proved a condition of heart insensible to the very last degree. Those who, with the marvellous history of Jehovah's actings before their eyes, could say, "Wherein hast thou loved us?" were beyond the reach of all moral appeal. Hence, therefore, we need not be surprised at the prophet's burning words. We are prepared for such sentences as the following: "If then I be a father, where is mine honour? and if I be a master, where is my fear? saith the Lord of hosts unto you, O priests, that despise my name. And ye say, Wherein have we despised thy name?" There was the most thorough insensibility both as to the Lord's love, and as to their own evil ways. There was the hardness of heart that could say, "Wherein hast thou loved us?" and "Wherein have we wronged thee?" And all this with the history of a thousand years before their eyes—a history overlapped by the unexampled grace, mercy, and patience of God—a history stained, from first to last, with the record of their unfaithfulness, folly, and sin.

But let us hearken to the prophet's further utterances, or rather to the touching remonstrances of the aggrieved and offended God of Israel. "Ye offer polluted bread upon mine altar; and ye say, Wherein have we polluted thee? In that ye say, The table of the Lord is contemptible. And if ye offer the blind sacrifice, is it not evil? and if ye offer the lame and sick, is it not evil? offer it now unto thy governor; will he be pleased with thee, or accept thy person? saith the Lord of hosts . . . who is there even among you that would shut the doors for nought? neither do ye kindle fire on mine altar for nought. I have no pleasure in you, saith the Lord of hosts, neither will I accept an offering at your hand. For from the rising of the sun even unto the going down of the same, my name shall be great among the Gentiles; and in every place incense shall be offered unto my name, and a pure offering; for my name shall be great among the heathen, saith the Lord of hosts. But ye have profaned it, in that ye say, The table of the Lord is polluted; and the fruit thereof, even his meat, is contemptible. Ye said also, Behold, what a weariness is it! and ye have snuffed at it, saith the Lord of hosts; and ye brought that which was torn, and the lame, and the sick; thus ye brought an offering; should I accept this of your hand? saith the Lord."

Here then we have a sad and dreary picture of Israel's moral condition. The public worship of God had fallen into utter contempt. His altar was insulted; His service despised. As to the priests, it was a mere question of filthy lucre; and as to the people, the whole thing had become a perfect weariness—an empty formality—a dull and heartless routine. There was no heart for God. There was plenty of heart for gain. Any sacrifice, however maimed and torn, was deemed good enough for the altar of God. The lame, the blind, and the sick, the very worst that could be had, such as they would not dare to offer to a human governor, was laid on the altar of God. And if a door was to be opened, or a fire kindled, it must be paid for. No pay, no work. Such was the lamentable condition of things in the days of Malachi. It makes the heart sick to contemplate it.

But, thanks and praise be to God, there is another side of the picture. There were some rare and lovely exceptions to the gloomy

226

rule—some striking and beautiful forms standing out in relief from the dark background. It is truly refreshing, in the midst of all this venality and corruption, coldness and hollowness, barrenness and heartlessness, pride and stoutness of heart, to read such words as these: "Then they that feared the Lord spake often one to another; and the Lord hearkened, and heard it, and a book of remembrance was written before him for them that feared the Lord, and that thought upon his name."

How precious is this brief record! How delightful to contemplate this remnant in the midst of the moral ruin! There is no pretension, or assumption; no attempt to set up anything; no effort to reconstruct the fallen economy; no affected display of power. There is felt weakness, and looking to Jehovah; and this—be it observed and ever remembered—is the true secret of all real power. We need never be afraid of conscious weakness. It is affected strength that we have to dread and shrink from. "When I am weak, then am I strong" is ever the rule for the people of God—a blessed rule, most surely. God is to be counted upon always; and we may lay it down as a great root principle, that, no matter what may be the actual state of the professing body, individual faith can enjoy communion with God according to the very highest truth of the dispensation.

This is a grand principle to grasp and hold fast. Let the ostensible people of God be ever so sunk, individuals who judge and humble themselves before God can enjoy His presence and blessing, without let or limit. Witness the Daniels, the Mordecais, the Ezras, the Nehemiahs, the Josiahs, and Hezekiahs, and scores of others who walked with God, carried out the highest principles and enjoyed the rarest privileges of the dispensation, when all lay in hopeless ruin around them. There was a passover celebrated in the days of Josiah such as had not been known from the days of Samuel the prophet. (2 Chron. xxxv. 18.) The feeble remnant, on their return from Babylon, celebrated the feast of tabernacles, a privilege which had not been tasted since the days of Joshua the son of Nun. (Neh. viii. 17.) Mordecai, without ever striking a blow, gained as splendid a victory over Amalek as that achieved by Joshua in the days of Exodus xvii. (Esther vi. 11, 12.) In the

227

book of Daniel we see earth's proudest monarch prostrate at the feet of a captive Jew.

What do all these cases teach us? What lesson do they tell out in our ears? Simply that the humble, believing, and obedient soul is permitted to enjoy the very deepest and richest communion with God, spite of the failure and ruin of God's professing people, and the departed glory of the dispensation in which his lot is cast.

Thus it was, as we may see, in the closing scenes of Malachi. All was in hopeless ruin; but that did not hinder those who loved and feared the Lord getting together to speak about Him and to muse upon His precious name. True, that feeble remnant was not like the great congregation which assembled in the days of Solomon, from Dan to Beersheba; but it had a glory peculiar to itself. It had the divine presence in a way no less marvellous though not so striking. We are not told of any "book of remembrance" in the days of Solomon. We are not told of Jehovah's hearkening and hearing. Perhaps it may be said, there was no need. Be it so; but that does not dim the lustre of the grace that shone upon the little band in the days of Malachi. We may boldly affirm that Jehovah's heart was as refreshed by the loving breathings of that little band as by the splendid sacrifice in the days of Solomon's dedication. Their love shines out all the brighter in contrast with the heartless formalism of the professing body, and the venal corruption of the priests.

"And they shall be mine, saith the Lord of hosts, in that day when I make up my jewels; and I will spare them as a man spareth his own son that serveth him. Then shall ye return, and discern between the righteous and the wicked, between him that serveth God and him that serveth him not. For, behold, the day cometh, that shall burn as an oven; and all the proud, yea, and all that do wickedly, shall be stubble; and the day that cometh shall burn them up, saith the Lord of hosts, that it shall leave them neither root nor branch. But unto you that fear my name shall the Sun of righteousness arise with healing in his wings; and ye shall go forth, and grow up as calves of the stall. And ye shall tread down the wicked; for they shall be ashes under the soles of your feet in the day that I shall do this, saith the Lord of hosts."

228

We shall now give a hasty glance at the epistle of Jude. Here we have a still more appalling picture of apostasy and corruption. It is a familiar saying amongst us, that the corruption of the best thing is the worst corruption; and hence it is that the Apostle Jude spreads before us a page so very much darker and more awful than that presented by the prophet Malachi. It is the record of man's utter failure and ruin under the very highest and richest privileges which could be conferred upon him.

In the opening of his solemn address, the apostle lets us know that it was laid upon his heart "to write unto us of the common salvation." This would have been his far more delightful task. It would have been his joy and his refreshment to expatiate upon the present privileges and future glories wrapped up in the comprehensive folds of that precious word "salvation." But he felt it "needful" to turn from this more congenial work in order to fortify our souls aginst the rising tide of error and evil which threatened the very foundations of Christianity. "Beloved, when I gave all diligence to write unto you of the common salvation, it was needful for me to write unto you, and exhort you that ye should earnestly contend for the faith which was once delivered unto the saints." All that was vital and fundamental was at stake. It was a question of earnestly contending for the faith itself. "For there are certain men crept in unawares, who were before of old ordained to this condemnation; ungodly men, turning the grace of our God into lasciviousness, and denying the only Lord God, and our Lord Jesus Christ."

This is far worse than anything we have in Malachi. There it was a question of the law; as we read, "Remember ye the law of Moses my servant, which I commanded unto him in Horeb for all Israel, with the statutes and judgments." But in Jude it is not a question of forgetting the law, but of actually turning into lasciviousness the pure and precious grace of God, and denying the Lordship of Christ. Hence, therefore, instead of dwelling upon the salvation of God, the apostle seeks to fortify us against the wickedness and lawlessness of men. "I will therefore," he says, "put you in remembrance, though ye once knew this, how that the Lord, having saved the people out of the land of Egypt, afterward destroyed them that believed not. And the angels which kept not their first estate, but left their own habitation, he hath reserved in everlasting chains under darkness unto the judgment of the great day."

All this is most solemn; but we cannot dwell upon the dark features of this scene, space does not admit of our so doing; and besides, we rather desire to present to the christian reader the charming picture of the christian remnant given in the closing lines of this most searching scripture. As in Malachi we have, amid the helpless ruin of Judaism, a devoted hand of Jewish worshippers who loved and feared the Lord and took sweet counsel together, so in the epistle of Jude, amid the more appalling ruins of christian profession, the Holy Ghost introduces to our notice a company whom He adresses as "Beloved." These are "sanctified by God the Father, and preserved in Jesus Christ, and called." These He solemnly warns against the varied forms of error and evil which were already beginning to make their appearance, but have since assumed such awfully formidable proportions. To these He turns, with the most exquisite grace, and addresses the following exhortation, "But ye, beloved, building up yourselves on your most holy faith, praying in the Holy Ghost, keep yourselves in the love of God, looking for the mercy of our Lord Jesus Christ unto eternal life."

Here, then, we have divine security against all the dark and terrible forms of apostasy—"the way of Cain, the error of Balaam, the gainsaying of Core"—"the murmurers and complainers"—"the great swelling words"—"the raging waves"—"the wandering stars" —"having men's persons in admiration because of advantage." The "beloved" are to "build themselves up on their most holy faith."

Let the reader note this. There is not a syllable here about an order of men to succeed the apostles; not a word about gifted men of any sort. It is well to see this, and to bear it ever in mind. We hear a great deal of our lack of gift and power, of our not having pastors and teachers. How could we expect to have much gift power? Do we deserve them? Alas! we have failed, and sinned, and come short. Let us own this, and cast ourselves upon the living God who never fails a trusting heart.

230

Look at Paul's touching address to the elders of Ephesus, in Acts xx. To whom does he there commend us, in view of the passing away of apostolic ministry? Is there a word about successors to the apostles? Not one, unless indeed it be the "grievous wolves" of which he speaks, or those men who were to arise in the very bosom of the Church, speaking perverse things to draw away disciples after them. What then is the resource of the faithful? "I commend you to God, and to the word of his grace, which is able to build you up, and to give you an inheritance among all them which are sanctified."

What a precious resource! Not a word about gifted men, valuable as such may be in their right place. God forbid we should, in any way, depreciate the gifts which, spite of all the failure and sin, our gracious Lord may see fit to bestow upon His Church. But still it holds good that the blessed apostle, in taking leave of the Church, commends us not to gifted men, but to God Himself and the word of His grace. And hence it follows that, let our weakness be ever so great, we have God to look to and to lean upon. He never fails those who trust Him; and there is no limit whatsoever to the blessing which our souls may taste, if only we look to God, in humility of mind and childlike confidence.

Here lies the secret of all true blessedness and spiritual power—humility of mind, and simple confidence. There must, on the one hand, be no assumption of power; and on the other, we must not, in the unbelief of our hearts, limit the goodness and faithfulness of our God. He can and does bestow gifts for the edification of His people. He would bestow much more if we were not so ready to manage for ourselves. If the Church would but look more to Christ her living Head and loving Lord, instead of to the arrangements of men, and the appliances of this world, she would have a very different tale to tell. But if we, by our unbelieving plans, and our restless efforts to provide a machinery for ourselves, quench, and hinder, and grieve the Holy Ghost, need we marvel if we are left to prove the barrenness and emptiness, the desolation and confusion of all such things? Christ is sufficient: but He must be proved; He must be trusted; He must be allowed to act. The platform must be left perfectly clear for the Holy Ghost to display thereon the preciousness, the fulness, the all-sufficiency of Christ.

But it is precisely in this very thing we so signally fail. We try to hide our weakness instead of owning it. We seek to cover our nakedness by a drapery of our own providing, instead of confiding simply and entirely in Christ for all we need. We grow weary of the attitude of humble patient waiting, and we are in haste to put on an appearance of strength. This is our folly and our grievous loss. If we could only be induced to believe it, our real strength is to know our weakness, and cling to Christ, in artless faith, from day to day.

It is to this most excellent way that the apostle Jude exhorts the christian remnant in his closing lines. "Ye, beloved, building up yourselves in your most holy faith." These words evidently set forth the responsibility of all true Christians to be found together instead of being divided and scattered. We are to help one another in love, according to the measure of grace bestowed, and the nature of the gift communicated. It is a mutual thing—"building up yourselves." It is not looking to an order of men; nor is it complaining of our lack of gifts; but simply doing each what we can to promote the common blessing and profit of all.

The reader will notice the four things which we are exhorted to do, namely, "Building"—"Praying"—"Keeping"—"Looking." What blessed work is here! Yes, and it is work for all. There is not one true Christian on the face of the earth who cannot fulfill any or all of these branches of ministry; indeed every one is responsible so to do. We can build ourselves up on our most holy faith; we can pray in the Holy Ghost; we can keep ourselves in the love of God; and, while doing these things, we can look out for the mercy of our Lord Jesus Christ.

But, it may be asked, "Who are the 'beloved?' to whom does the term apply?" Our answer is, "To whomsoever it may concern." Let us see to it that we are on the ground of those to whom the precious title applies. It is not assuming the title, but occupying the true moral ground. It is not empty profession, but real possession. It is not affecting the name, but being the thing.

Nor does the responsibility of the christian remnant end here.

It is not merely of themselves they have to think. They are to cast a loving look and stretch forth a helping hand beyond the circumference of their own circle. "And of some have compassion, making a difference: and others save with fear, pulling them out of the fire; hating even the garment spotted by the flesh." Who are the "some?" and who are the "others?" Is there not the same beautiful undefinedness about these as there is about the "Beloved?" These latter will be at no loss to find out the former. There are precious souls scattered up and down amid the appalling ruins of Christendom, "some" of them to be looked upon with tender compassion, "others" to be saved with godly fear, lest the "beloved" should become involved in the defilement.

It is a fatal mistake to suppose that, in order to pluck people out of the fire, we must go into the fire ourselves. This would never do. The best way to deliver people from an evil position is to be thoroughly out of that position myself. How can I best pull a man out of a morass? Surely not by going into the morass, but by standing on firm ground and from thence lending him a helping hand. I cannot pull a man out of anything unless I am out myself. If we want to help the people of God who are mixed up with the surrounding ruin, the first thing for ourselves is to be in thorough and decided separation; and the next thing is to have our hearts brimfull and flowing over with tender and fervent love to all who bear the precious name of Jesus.

Here we must close; and in doing so we shall quote for the reader that blessed doxology with which the apostle sums up his solemn and weighty address. "Now unto him that is able to keep you from falling, and to present you faultless before the presence of his glory with exceeding joy, to the only wise God our Saviour, be glory and majesty, dominion and power, both now and ever. Amen." We have a great deal about "falling" in this epistle—Israel, falling—angels, falling—cities, falling; but, blessed be God, there is One who is able to keep us from falling, and it is to His holy keeping we are committed.

# THE SYMPATHY AND GRACE
# OF JESUS

(READ CAREFULLY MAT. XIV. 1-21, AND MARK VI. 30-44.)

In these two parallel scriptures we are presented with two distinct conditions of heart which both find their answer in the sympathy and grace of Jesus. Let us look closely at them; and may the Holy Ghost enable us to gather up and bear away their precious teaching!

It was, no doubt, a moment of deep sorrow to John's disciples when their master had fallen by the sword of Herod; when the one on whom they had been accustomed to lean, and from whose lips they had been wont to drink instruction, was taken from them after such a fashion. This, we may well believe, was indeed a moment of gloom and desolation to the followers of the Baptist.

But there was One to whom they could come, in their sorrow, and into whose ear they could pour their tale of grief—One of whom their master had spoken, to whom he had pointed, and of whom he had said, "He must increase, but I must decrease." To Him the bereaved disciples betook themselves, as we read, "They came and took up the body, and buried it, and went and told Jesus." (Matt. xiv. 12.) This was the very best thing they could have one. There was not another heart on earth in which they could have found such a response as in the heart—the tender, loving heart of Jesus. His sympathy was perfect. He knew all about their sorrow. He knew their loss, and how they would be feeling it. Wherefore, they acted wisely when "they went and told Jesus." His ear was ever open, and His heart ever at leisure to soothe and sympathize. He perfectly exemplified the precept afterwards embodied in the words of the Holy Ghost, "Rejoice with them that do rejoice, and weep with them that weep." (Rom. xii. 15.)

And oh! who can tell the value of genuine sympathy? Who can declare the value of having one who can really make your joys and sorrows his own? Thank God! we have such an one in the blessed Lord Jesus Christ; and although we cannot see Him with the bodily eye, yet can faith use Him in all the preciousness and power of His perfect sympathy. We can, if only our faith is simple and child-like, come from the tomb where we have just deposited the remains of some fondly-cherished object, to the feet of Jesus, and there pour out the anguish of a bereaved and desolate heart. We shall there meet no rude repulse, no heartless reproof for our folly and weakness, in feeling so deeply. No; nor yet any clumsy effort to say something suitable, an awkward effort to put on some expression of condolence. Ah! no; Jesus knows how to sympathize with a heart that is crushed and bowed down beneath the heavy weight of sorrow. His is a perfect human heart. What a thought! What a privilege to have access, at all times, in all places, and under all circumstances, to a perfect human heart! We may look in vain for this down here. Yes; look in vain, not merely in the world, but even in the church. There may, in many cases, be a real desire to sympathize, but a total lack of capacity. I may find myself, in moments of sorrow, in company with one who knows nothing about my sorrow or the source thereof. How could he sympathize? And even though I should tell him, his heart might be so occupied with other things as to have no room and no leisure for me.

Not so with the perfect Man, Christ Jesus. He has both room and leisure for each and all. No matter when, how, or with what you come, the heart of Jesus is always open. He will never repulse, never fail, never disappoint. If, therefore, we are in sorrow, what should we do? We should just do as the disciples of the Baptist did, "go and tell Jesus." This, assuredly, is the right thing to do. Let us go straight from the tomb to the feet of Jesus. He will dry up our tears, soothe our sorrows, heal our wounds, and fill up our blanks. In this way we shall be able to enter into the truth of Rutherford's words when he says, "I try to lay up all my good things in Christ, and then a little of the creature goes a great way with me." This is an experience which we may well covet. May the blessed Spirit lead us more into it!

We may now contemplate another condition of heart, as furnished by the twelve apostles, on their return from a successful mission. "And the apostles gathered themselves together unto Jesus, and told him all things, both what they had done, and what they had taught." (Mark vi. 30.) Here, we have not a case of sorrow and bereavement, but one of rejoicing and encouragement. The twelve make their way to Jesus to tell Him of their success, just as the disciples of the Baptist made their way to Him in the moment of their loss. Jesus was equal to both. He could meet the heart that was crushed with sorrow, and He could meet the heart that was flushed with success. He knew how to control, to moderate, and to direct both the one and the other. BLESSINGS FOR EVER BE UPON HIS HONOURED NAME!

"And He said unto them, Come ye yourselves apart into a desert place, and rest a while: for there were many coming and going, and they had no leisure so much as to eat." Here, then, we are conducted to a point at which the moral glories of Christ shine out with uncommon lustre, and correct the selfishness of our poor narrow hearts. Here we are taught, with unmistakable clearness, that to make Jesus the depository of our thoughts and feelings will never produce in us a spirit of haughty self-sufficiency and independence, or a feeling of contempt for others. Quite the reverse. The more we have to do with Jesus, the more will our hearts be opened to meet the varied forms of human need which may present themselves to our view from day to day. It is when we come to Jesus and empty our whole hearts to Him, tell Him of our sorrows and our joys, and cast our whole burden at His feet, that we really learn how to feel for others.

There is great beauty and power in the words, "come ye yourselves apart." He does not say, "Go ye." This would never do. There is no use in going apart into a desert place, if Jesus be not there to go to. To go into solitude without Jesus is but to make our cold, narrow hearts, colder and narrower still. I may retire from the scene around me in chagrin and disappointment, only to wrap myself up in an impenetrable selfishness. I may fancy that my fellows have not made enough of me, and I may retire in order to make much of myself. I may make myself the centre of my whole being, and thus become a cold-hearted, contracted,

236

miserable creature. But when Jesus says, "come," the case is totally different. Our finest moral lessons are learned alone with Jesus. We cannot breathe the atmosphere of His presence without having our hearts expanded. If the apostles had gone into the desert without Jesus, they would, no doubt, have eaten the loaves and fishes themselves; but having gone with Jesus they learnt differently. He knew how to meet the need of a hungry multitude, as well as that of a company of sorrowing or rejoicing disciples. The sympathy and grace of Jesus are perfect. He can meet all. If one is sorrowful, he can go to Jesus; if he is happy, he can go to Jesus; if he is hungry, he can go to Jesus. We can bring every thing to Jesus, for in Him all fulness dwells, and, blessed be His name, He never sends any one empty away.

Not so, alas! with His poor disciples. How forbidding is their selfishness when viewed in the light of His magnificent grace! "And Jesus, when He came out, saw much people, and was moved with compassion toward them, because they were as sheep not having a shepherd; and he began to teach them many things." He had gone to a desert place to give His disciples rest; but no sooner does human need present itself than the deep flowing tide of compassion rolls forth from His tender heart.

"And when the day was now far spent, his disciples came unto Him, and said, This is a desert place, and now the time is far past: send them away." What words to drop from the lips of men who had just returned from preaching the gospel! "Send them away." Ah! it is one thing to preach grace, and another thing to act it. No doubt, it is well to preach; but it is also well to act. Indeed, the preaching will be little worth if not combined with acting. It is well to instruct the ignorant; but it is also well to feed the hungry. The latter may involve more self-denial than the former. It may cost us nothing to preach; but it may cost us something to feed; and we do not like to have our private store intruded upon. The heart is ready to put forth its ten thousand objections; "What shall I do for myself? What will become of my family? We must act judiciously. We cannot do impossibilities." These, and suchlike arguments the selfish heart can urge when a needy object presents itself.

237

"Send them away." What made the disciples say this? What was the real source of this selfish request? Simply unbelief. Had they only remembered that they had in their midst the One who of old had fed "six hundred thousand footmen," for forty years in the wilderness, they would have known that He would not send a hungry multitude away. Surely the same hand that had nourished such a host for so long a time could easily furnish a single meal for five thousand. Thus faith would reason; but alas! unbelief darkens the understanding and contracts the heart. There is nothing so absurd as unbelief, and nothing which so shuts up the bowels of compassion. Faith and charity always go together, and in proportion to the growth of the one is the growth of the other. Faith opens the flood-gates of the heart and lets the tide of charity flow forth. Thus the apostle could say to the Thessalonians, "Your faith groweth exceedingly, and the charity of every one of you all toward each other aboundeth." This is the divine rule. A heart that is full of faith can afford to be charitable; an unbelieving heart can afford nothing. Faith places the heart in immediate contact with God's exhaustless treasury, and fills it with the most benevolent affections. Unbelief throws the heart in upon itself, and fills it with all manner of selfish fears. Faith conducts us into the soul-expanding atmosphere of heaven. Unbelief leaves us enwrapped in the withering atmosphere of this heartless world. Faith enables us to hearken to Christ's gracious accents, "Give ye them to eat." Unbelief makes us utter our own heartless words, "Send the multitude away." In a word, there is nothing enlarges the heart like simple faith; and nothing so contracting as unbelief. Oh! that our faith may grow exceedingly, so that our charity may abound more and more! May we reap much permanent profit from the contemplation of the sympathy and grace of Jesus!

What a striking contrast between "Send the multitude away," and, "Give ye them to eat." Thus it is ever. God's ways are not as our ways; and it is by looking at His ways that we learn to judge our ways—by looking at Him that we learn to judge ourselves. Jesus, in this lovely scene, corrects the selfishness of the disciples, first, by making them the channels through which His grace may flow to the multitude, and secondly, by making them gather up "twelve baskets full of the fragments" for themselves.

Nor is this all. Not merely is selfishness rebuked, but the heart is most blessedly instructed. Nature might say, "What need is there of the five loaves and two fishes, at all? Surely, the One who can feed such a multitude with, can as easily feed them without, such an instrumentality." Nature might argue thus; but Jesus teaches us that we are not to despise God's creatures. We are to use what we have with God's blessing. This is a fine moral lesson for the heart. "What hast thou in the house?" is the question. It is just that and nothing else that God will use. It is easy to be liberal with what we have not; but the thing is to bring out what we have, and, with God's blessing, apply it to the present need.

So also in the gathering up of the fragments. The foolish here might say, "What need of gathering up those scattered crumbs? Surely the one who has wrought such a miracle can have no need of fragments." Yes; but we are not to waste God's creatures. If in the using of the loaves and fishes we are taught not to despise any creature of God, in the gathering up of the fragments we are taught not to waste it. Let human need be liberally met, but let not a single crumb be wasted. How divinely perfect! How unlike us! Sometimes we are penurious; at other times prodigal. Jesus was never either the one or the other. "Give ye them to eat." But, "Let nothing be lost." Perfect grace! Perfect wisdom! May we adore it, and learn from it! May we rejoice in the assurance that the blessed One who manifested all this wisdom and grace is our life. Christ is our life, and it is the manifestation of this life that constitutes practical christianity. It is not living by rules and regulations, but simply having Christ dwelling in the heart by faith—Christ the source of perfect sympathy and perfect grace.

# "LOOPS OF BLUE"

## (Exod. xxvi. 4.)

In contemplating the structure of the tabernacle in the wilderness, we may observe what an important place was assigned to the "loops of blue." By means of them and the "taches of gold," the curtains were joined together, and the manifested unity of the whole structure preserved. These loops and taches might seem to be very insignificant and unimportant; but, without them, there would have been no unity. The curtains, however beautiful in themselves, would have hung apart one from the other, and thus one grand feature of the manifestation would have been lost.

Now, looking at the tabernacle as a figure of Christ, as surely we may, we can easily trace the beauty and significance of those "loops of blue and taches of gold." They typified that perfect unity and consistency in the character and ways of "the Man Christ Jesus" which were the result of His heavenly grace and divine energy. In the life of the blessed Lord Jesus, and in all the scenes and circumstances of that life, we not only see each distinct phase and feature perfect in itself, but also a perfect combination of all those phases and features, by the power of that which was heavenly and divine in Him. The curtains of the true Tabernacle were not only beautiful in themselves, but they were beautifully combined—exquisitely linked together by means of those "loops of blue and taches of gold" which can only be discerned and appreciated by those who are, in some measure, instructed in the holy mysteries of the sanctuary.

And let me add, that what is true of the Divine Living Word, is equally true of the divine written word. The spiritual student of holy scripture will readily discern the "loops of blue and taches of gold." This is only what we might expect. The Living Word is the divine embodiment of the written word; and the written word is the divine transcript of the Living Word. Hence, we may look for the same heavenly unity, the same divine consistency—

240

the same rare and exquisite combination in both the one and the other. It would be, at once, pleasant and profitable to trace, in company with my reader, the various illustrations of the loops and taches, through the word of God; but to do this fully would demand a volume; whereas, at present, I have merely time and space for a brief suggestive fragment. I should, however, like to give an example or two from the written word which may perhaps lead him to study the subject for himself.

In I Corinthians xvi. we have a very lovely and a very practical illustration of our subject. At verse 13 the apostle says, "Quit you like men, be strong." Here we have one fine feature of the christian character—that manly strength which is so desirable. But this, if taken by itself, might easily degenerate into a rough, rude, high-handed way in dealing with others, the very opposite of what we find in our divine Exemplar. Hence the Spirit in the apostle forms a loop of blue, and by means of a golden tach, links on to this manly strength, another feature which is so needful, namely, charity. "Let all your things be done with charity." Most precious combination! Strength and charity. Charity and strength. If you untie this heavenly loop, you will either have a high, haughty, inconsiderate style, or a soft, pliable, enfeebled mode of acting which will sacrifice everything for peace and quietness.

Again, look at that noble definition of pure religion, given at the close of the second chapter of James. There the apostle uses the loop and tach in order to connect together the two phases of divine religion. "To visit the fatherless and the widow in their affliction" is looped with unspotted separation from the world. In other words, active benevolence and personal holiness are inseparably linked together. Untie the loop, and what have you got? Either a sort of benevolence which can go hand in hand with the most intense spirit of worldliness; or a rigid pharisaic separation without a single generous emotion. It is only the presence of that which is heavenly and divine that can secure true unity and consistency of character. And, let it never be forgotten, that true Christianity is simply Christ reproduced, by the Holy Ghost, in the life of the Christian. Dry rules will never do; it must be Christ in all.

241

# CHRIST AND HIS YOKE

## (MATT. XI. 28-30)

"Come unto me, all ye that labour and are heavy laden, and I will give you rest. Take my yoke upon you, and learn of me; for I am meek and lowly in heart: and ye shall find rest unto your souls. For my yoke is easy, and my burden is light."

In this precious and well-known passage we have two points which are very distinct, and yet intimately connected, namely, Christ and His yoke. We have, first, coming to Christ, and its results; and, secondly, taking His yoke, and its results. "Come unto me, and I will give you rest." "Take my yoke, and ye shall find rest." These things, being distinct, should never be confounded; and, being intimately connected, should never be separated. To confound them, is to dim the lustre of divine grace; to separate them, is to infringe upon the claims of divine holiness. Both these evils should be carefully guarded against.

Many there are who hold up before the eye of the "heavy laden" sinner, the yoke of Christ as something which he must "take on" ere his burdened heart can taste of that blessed rest which Christ "gives" to "all" who simply "come unto him," just as they are. The passage before us does not teach this. It puts Christ first, and His yoke afterwards. It does not hide Christ behind His yoke, but rather places Him, in all His attractive grace, before the heart, as the One who can meet every need, remove every weight, hush every guilty fear, fill up every blank, satisfy longing desire; in a word, who is able to do as He says He will, even to "give rest." There are no conditions proposed, no demands made, no barriers erected. The simple, touching, melting, subduing, inviting, winning word is, "Come." It is not, "Go;" "Do;" "Give;" "Bring;" "Feel;" "Realize." No; it is, "Come." And how are we to "Come?" Just as we are. To whom are we to "Come?" To Jesus. When are we to "Come?" "Now."

242

Observe, then, we are to come just as we are. We are not to wait for the purpose of altering a single jot or little of our state, condition, or character. To do this, would be to "come" to some alteration or improvement in ourselves; whereas Christ distinctly and emphatically says, "Come unto me." Many souls err on this point. They think they must amend their ways, alter their course, or improve their moral condition, ere they come to Christ; whereas, in point of fact, until they really do come to Christ they cannot amend, or alter, or improve anything. There is no warrant whatever for any one to believe that he will be a single whit better, an hour, a day, a month, or a year hence, than he is this moment. And even were he better, he would not, on that account, be a wait for the purpose of altering a single jot or tittle of our state, thing as an offer of salvation, to-morrow. The word is, "To-day, if ye will hear his voice, harden not your hearts." (Heb. iii. 15.) "Behold now is the accepted time; behold, now is the day of salvation." 2 Cor. vi. 2.

There is nothing more certain than that all who have ever tried the self-improvement plan have found it an utter failure. They have begun in darkness, continued in misery, and ended in despair. And yet, strange to say, in view of the numberless beacons which are ranged before us, in terrible array, to warn us of the folly and danger of travelling that road, we are sure, at the first, to adopt it. In some way or another, self is looked to, and wrought upon, in order to procure a warrant to come to Christ. "They, being ignorant of God's righteousness, and going about to establish their own righteousness, have not submitted themselves unto the righteousness of God." (Rom. x. 3.) Nothing can possibly be a more dreary, depressing, hopeless task, than "going about to establish one's own righteousness." Indeed, the dreariness of the task must ever be commensurate with the earnestness and sincerity of the soul that undertakes it. Such an one will, assuredly, have, sooner or later, to give utterance to the cry, "O wretched man that I am!" and also to ask the question, "Who shall deliver me?" (Rom. vii. 24.) There can be no exception. All with whom the Spirit of God has ever wrought, have, in one way or another, been constrained to own the hopelessness of seeking to work out a righteousness for

243

themselves. *Christ must be all; self, nothing.* This doctrine is easily stated; but oh, *the experience!*

The same is true, in reference to the grand reality of sanctification. Many who have come to Christ for righteousness have not practically and experimentally laid hold of Him as their sanctification. Whereas He is made of God, unto us, the one as well as the other. "But of him are ye in Christ Jesus, who of God is made unto us wisdom, and righteousness, and sanctification, and redemption: that"—how deeply important, how cogent the reason! "according as it is written, He that glorieth, let him glory in the Lord." (I Cor. i. 30, 31.) The believer is just as powerless in the work of sanctification as in the work of righteousness. If it were not so, some flesh might glory in the divine presence. I could no more subdue a single lust, or trample under foot a single passion, or gain the mastery over a single temper, than I could open the kingdom of heaven, or establish my own righteousness before God. This is not sufficiently understood; and hence it is that many true Christians constantly suffer the most humiliating defeats in their practical career. They know that Christ is their righteousness, that their sins are forgiven, that they are children of God; but, then, they are sorely put about by their constant failure in personal holiness, in practical sanctification. Again and again, they enter the lists with some unhallowed desire or unsanctified temper; and, again and again, they are compelled to retire with shame and confusion of face. A person or a circumstance crossed their path yesterday, and caused them to lose their temper, and, having to meet the same to-day, they resolve to do better; but, alas! they are again forced to retreat in disappointment and humiliation.

Now, it is not that such persons may not pray earnestly for the grace of the Holy Spirit to enable them to conquer both themselves and the influences which surround them. This is not the point. They have not yet learnt *practically*, and, oh! how worthless the mere theory! that they are as completely *"without strength"* in the matter of *"sanctification"* as they are in the matter of *"righteousness,"* and, that as regards both the one and the other, Christ must be *all*; self, *nothing.* In a word, they have not yet entered into the meaning of the words, "Come unto me, and I

244

will give you rest." Here lies the source of their failure. They are as thoroughly powerless in the most trivial matter connected with practical sanctification, as they are in the entire question of their standing before God; and they must be brought to *believe* this, ere they can know the fulness of the "rest" which Christ gives. It is impossible that I can enjoy rest amid incessant defeats in my practical, daily life.

True, I can come, over and over again, and pour into my Heavenly Father's ear the humiliating tale of my failure and overthrow. I can confess my sins and find Him ever "faithful and just to forgive me my sins, and to cleanse me from all unrighteousness." (I John i. 9.) But, then, we must learn Christ as the Lord our sanctification, as well as "The Lord our righteousness;" and, moreover, it is by *faith* and not by *effort*, we are to enter into both the one and the other. We look to Christ for righteousness, because we have none of our own; and we look to Christ for practical sanctification, because we have none of our own. It needed no personal effort on our part to get righteousness, because Christ is our righteousness; and it needs no personal effort on our part to get sanctification, because Christ is our sanctification.

It seems strange that, while the inspired apostle distinctly tells us that Christ is "made of God unto us wisdom, righteousness, sanctification, and redemption," we, nevertheless, should attach the idea of personal effort to one out of the four things which he enumerates. Can we guide ourselves in the ten thousand difficulties and details of our christian course by our own wisdom or sagacity? Surely not. Ought we to make an effort? By no means. Why not? Because God has made Christ to be our 'wisdom," and therefore it is our precious privilege, having been brought to our "wits' end," to look to Christ for wisdom. In other words, when Christ says, "Come unto me," He means that we are to come unto Him for wisdom as well as for all else; and, clearly, we cannot come to Christ, and to our own efforts, at the same time. Nay, so long as we are making efforts, we must be strangers to "rest."

The same holds good with respect to "righteousness." Can we work out a righteousness for ourselves? Surely not. Ought we not to make an effort? By no means. Why not? Because God has made Christ to be unto us "righteousness," and that righteousness is "to him that worketh *not*." Rom. iv. 5.

So also in the matter of "redemption," which is put last in I Cor. i. 30, because it includes the final deliverance of the body of the believer from under the power of death. Could we, by personal effort, deliver our bodies from the dominion of mortality? Surely not. Ought we not to try? The thoughts were monstrous, yea impious. Why? Because God has made Christ to be unto us "redemption," as regards both soul and body, and He who has already applied, by the power of His Spirit, that glorious redemption to our souls, will, ere long, apply it to our bodies.

Why, then, let me ask, should "sanctification" be singled out from the precious category, and saddled with the legal and depressing idea of personal effort? If we cannot by our own efforts, get "wisdom, righteousness, and redemption," are we a whit more likely to succeed in getting "sanctification?" Clearly not. And have we not proved this, times without number? Have not our closet walls witnessed our tears and groans evoked by the painful sense of failure after failure in our own efforts to tread with steady step and erect carriage, the lofty walks of personal sanctity? Will the reader deny this? I trust not. I would fain hope he has responded to the call of Jesus, "Come unto me, all ye that labour and are heavy laden, and I will give you rest." It is vain to "labour" in our own strength, after sanctification. We must come to Jesus for that as well as for everything else. And, having come to Jesus, we shall find that there is no lust which He cannot slay, no temper that He cannot subdue, no passion that He cannot overcome. The self-same hand that has cancelled our sins, that guides us in our difficulties, and that will, by and by, deliver our bodies from the power of death, can give us complete victory over all our personal infirmities and besetments, and fill our hearts with His sacred rest.

It is, I believe, immensely important to have a clear understanding of the question of sanctification. Hundreds have gone on "labouring and heavy laden" for years, endeavouring to work out in one way or another, their sanctification; and, not succeeded to their satisfaction—for who ever did, or ever could?—they have been tempted to question if they were ever converted at all. Many, were

246

they to tell out "all the truth," could adopt as their own, the mournful lines of the poet,

> " 'Tis a point I long to know,
> Oft it causeth anxious thought,
> Do I love the Lord or no?
> Am I His or am I not?"

Such persons have clear views of gospel truth. They could, with scriptural accuracy, tell an inquirer after righteousness how, where, and when he could get it. And yet, if that self-same inquirer were to ask them about their own real state of heart before God, they could give but a sorry answer. Why is this? Simply because they have not laid hold of Christ as their sanctification, as well as their righteousness. They have been endeavoring, partly in their own strength, and partly by praying for the influences of the Holy Spirit, to stumble along the path of sanctification. They would, doubtless, deem a person very ignorant of what is called "the plan of salvation," if they found him "going about to establish his own righteousness;" but they do not see that they themselves exhibit, in another way, ignorance of that "plan" by going about to establish their own sanctification. And truly if, in the one case, it is a sorry righteousness which is wrought out, so, in the other case, it is a lame sanctification. For if it be true that "all our righteousnesses are as filthy rags," it is equally true that all our sanctifications are as filthy rags. Whatever has the word "our" attached to it must be altogether imperfect. Christ is God's righteousness, and Christ is God's sanctification. Both the one and the other are to be had by simply coming, looking, clinging, trusting to Christ. I need hardly say, it is by the power of the Spirit, and through the Holy Scriptures that Christ is applied to us, both as our righteousness and our sanctification. But all this only takes the matter more and more out of our hands, and leaves us nothing to glory in. If we could conquer an evil temper, we might indeed think ourselves clever; but as we are not asked to pick up a feather in order to add to our righteousness, or our wisdom, or our redemption, so neither are we asked to pick up a feather in order to add to our sanctification. In this, as in those, Christ is *all*; self, *nothing*. This doctrine is easily stated; but oh, *the experience!*

And, now, will any one say that the writer of this article is doing away with sanctification? If so, he may just as well say that he is doing away with "righteousness," "wisdom" or "redemption." Who will contend for *self*-righteousness, *self*-wisdom or *self*-redemption? Who but the man that contends for *self*-sanctification? Who is likely to attain and exhibit the more elevated standard of personal sanctity? Is it the man who is perpetually floundering amid his own imperfect struggles and cobweb-resolutions, or he who is daily, hourly, and momentarily clinging to Christ as his sanctification? The answer is simple. The sanctification which we get in Christ is as perfect as the righteousness, the wisdom, and the redemption. Am I doing away with "wisdom," because I say I am foolish? Am I doing away with "righteousness," because I say, I am guilty? Am I doing away with "redemption," because I say, I am mortal? Am I doing away with "sanctification," because I say, I am vile? Yes, I am doing away with all these things so far as "I" am concerned, in order that I may find them all in Christ. This is the point. All—all in Christ!

Oh! when shall we learn to get to the end of *self*, and cling simply to Christ? When shall we enter into the depth and power of those words "Come unto *me?*" He does not say, "come unto my yoke." No; but, "come unto *me*." We must cease from our own works, in every shape and form, and come to Christ,—come, *just as we are*—come, *now*. We come to Christ and get rest from and in Him before ever we hear a word about the "yoke." To put the yoke first is to displace every thing. If a "heavy laden" sinner thinks of the yoke, he must be overwhelmed by the thought of his own total inability to take it upon him or carry it. But when he comes to Jesus and enters into His precious rest, he finds the "yoke is easy and the burden light."

II. This conducts us to the second point in our subject, namely, "the yoke." It has been already observed that we must keep the two things distinct. To confound them, is to tarnish the heavenly lustre of the grace of Christ, and to put a yoke upon the sinner's neck and a burden upon his shoulder which he, as being "without strength," is wholly unable to bear. But, then, they are morally connected. All who come to Christ, must take His yoke upon them and learn of Him, if they would "find rest unto their souls." To come to Christ is one thing; to walk with Him, or learn of Him, is quite another. Christ was "meek and lowly in heart." He could meet the most adverse and discouraging circumstances with an "even so, Father." The Baptist's heart might fail amid the heavy clouds which gathered around him in Herod's dungeon; the men of that generation might refuse the double testimony of righteousness and grace, as furnished by the ministry of John and of our Lord Himself; Bethsaida, Chorazin, and Capernaum might refuse the testimony of His mighty works—a torrent of evidence which one might suppose would sweep away every opposing barrier; all these things, and many more might cross the path of the Divine Workman; but, being "meek and lowly in heart," He could say, "I thank thee, O Father—even so, Father, for so it seemed good in thy sight." His "rest" in the Father's counsels was profound and perfect; and He invites us to take His yoke, to learn of Him, to drink into His spirit, to know the practical results of a subject mind, that so we may "find rest unto our souls." A broken will is the real ground of the rest which we are to "find," after we have come to Christ. If God wills one thing, and we will another, we cannot find rest in that. It matters not what the scene or circumstance may be. We may swell a list of things, to any imaginable extent, in which our will may run counter to the will of God; but, in whatever it is, we cannot find rest so long as our will is unbroken. We must get to the end of self in the matter of will, as well as in the matter of "wisdom, righteousness, sanctification, or redemption," else we shall not "find rest."

This, my beloved reader, is deep, real, earnest, personal work. Moreover, it is a daily thing. It is a continual taking of Christ's yoke upon us, and learning of Him. It is not that we take the yoke in order to come to Christ. No; but we come to Christ first, and then, when His love fills and satisfies our souls, when His rest refreshes our spirits, when we can gaze, by faith, upon His gracious countenance, and see Him stooping down to confer upon us the high and holy privilege of wearing His yoke and learning His lesson, we find that His yoke is indeed easy, and His burden light. Unsubdued, unjudged, unmortified nature could never wear that yoke or bear that burden. The first thing is, "Come unto me, and I will give you rest." The second thing is, "Take my yoke upon you, and ye shall find rest."

We must never reverse these things—never confound them—never displace them—never separate them. To call upon a sinner to take Christ's yoke before he has gotten Christ's rest, is to place Christ on the top of Mount Sinai, the sinner at the foot of that Mount, and a dark impenetrable could between. This must not be done. Christ stands, in all His matchless grace, before the sinner's eye, and pours forth his touching invitation, "Come," and adds His heart-assuring promise, "I will give." There is no condition, no demand, "no servile work." All is the purest, freest, richest grace. Just, "come, and I will give you rest." And what then? Is it bondage, doubt, and fear? Ah! no. "Take my yoke upon you." How marvellously near this brings us to the One who has already given us rest! What a high honour to wear the same yoke with Him! It is not that He puts a grievous yoke upon our neck and a heavy burden upon our shoulder, whjch we have to carry up on the rugged sides of yon fiery Mount. This is not Christ's way. It is not thus He deals with the weary and heavy laden that come unto Him. He gives them rest. He gives them part of His yoke, and a share of His burden. In other words, He calls them into fellowship with Himself, and in proportion as they enter into this fellowship, they find still deeper and deeper rest in Him and in His blessed ways; and, at the close, He will conduct them into that eternal rest which remains for the people of God.

May the Lord enable us to enter, more fully, into the power of all these divine realities, that so His joy remain in us, and our joy may be full. There is an urgent need of a full, unreserved surrender of the heart to Christ, and a full, unreserved acceptance of Him, in all His precious adaptation to our every need. We want the whole heart, the single eye, the mortified mind, the broken will. Where these exist, there will be little complaining of doubts and fears, ups and downs, heavy days, vacant hours, restless moments, dullness and stupor, wandering and barrenness. When one has got to the end of himself, as regards wisdom, righteousness, holiness, and all beside, and when he has *really* found Christ as God's provision for ALL, then, but not until then, he will know the depth and power of that word, "REST."

"Now, then, my Lord, my Way, my Life,
Henceforth, let trouble, doubt, and strife,
   Drop off as Autumn leaves:
Henceforth, as privileged by Thee,
Simple and undistracted be,
   My soul which to thy sceptre cleaves.

At all times, to my spirit bear
An inward witness, soft and clear,
   Of Thy redeeming power:
This will instruct thy child, and fit,
Will sparkle forth what'er is meet,
   For exigence of every hour.

Thus, all the sequel is well weighed;
I cast myself upon Thine aid,
   A sea where none can sink,
Yea, in that sphere I stand, poor worm,
Where Thou wilt for Thy name perform
   Above what'er I ask or think."

# THE DIVINE ANATHEMA

"If any man love not the Lord Jesus Christ, let him be Anathema
Maranatha." I Cor. xvi. 22.

The position which this solemn anathema occupies is truly
remarkable. In the course of his lengthened epistle, the apostle
had to rebuke and correct many practical evils, and doctrinal
errors. There were divisions amongst the Corinthians. They were
puffed up for one against another. There was fornication amongst
them. They went to law one with another. There was gross dis-
order at the Lord's Supper. Some of them called in question the
grand foundation truth of the resurrection of the dead.

These were grave errors and formidable evils—errors and evils
which called forth the sharp and stern reproof of the inspired
apostle. But, be it carefully noted, that when, at the close, he
pronounces his solemn "Anathema Maranatha," it is not directed
against those who had introduced the errors or practised the evils,
but against "any man" who loves not the Lord Jesus Christ.* This,
surely, is well worthy of serious thought. The only security against
all manner of error and evil is genuine love to the Lord Jesus
Christ. A man may be so strictly moral, as that no one could put
his finger upon a single blot in his character—a single stain in his
reputation, and, underneath that strict morality, there may be a
heart as cold as ice, so far as the Lord Jesus is concerned. Again, a
man may be so marked by a spirit of noble benevolence, that his
influence is felt throughout the entire sphere in which he moves;
and, all the while, his heart may not have a single pulsation of love
to Christ. Finally, a man may possess, in the region of his understanding, a perfectly orthodox creed, and he may be devotedly
attached to the ordinances and observances of traditional religion,
and be wholly without affection for the adorable Person of the

* The word "Anathema" signifies any thing devoted to *death*; and "Maranatha" signifies the Lord cometh to *judgment*.

Lord Jesus Christ. It may even happen that all these things, namely, lofty morality, noble benevolence, sound orthodoxy, and devoted attachment to religious forms, exist in one and the same individual, and that individual be wholly void of a single spark of genuine affection for the Lord Jesus Christ, and, as a solemn and startling consequence, stand exposed to the burning Anathema of God the Holy Ghost. I may be moral, through love to *self*. I may be benevolent through love to my *fellow*. I may be orthodox, through a love of *dogmas*. I may be religious, through a love of *sect*. But none of these things can shield me from the merited judgment which is denounced by the Holy Ghost against "*any man*," no matter who or what, who "loves not the Lord Jesus Christ."

This is a deeply solemn and most seasonable word for the present moment. Let the reader deeply ponder it. Let him remember that the *only* basis for true morality—the *only* basis for divine orthodoxy —the *only* basis for "pure religion" is love to the Lord Jesus Christ, and where this love exists not, all is cold, sterile, and worthless— all exposed to death and judgment by the "Anathema Maranatha" of the Holy Ghost. If the heart be really touched with the vital spark of love to Jesus, then every effort after pure morality, every struggle against our hateful lusts, passions, and tempers, every opening of the hand of genuine, benevolence, every sound and truthful principle, every act of devotion, every pious aspiration, every fervent breathing, every outgoing of the soul, is precious to the Father—precious to the Son—precious to the Holy Ghost— all is fragrant with the perfume of that dear Name which is the theme of heaven's wonder—the centre of heaven's joy, the object of heaven's worship.

And, my beloved reader, should we not "love the Lord Jesus Christ?" Should we not hold Him dearer to our heart than all beside? Should we not be ready to surrender all for Him? Should not our bosoms swell with emotions of sincere attachment to His Person, in heaven, and His cause on earth? How could we trace Him from the bosom of the Father to the manager of Bethlehem —from the manger of Bethlehem to the cross of Calvary—and from the cross of Calvary to the throne of the majesty in the heavens—how could we "consider" Him as "the Apostle and High Priest of our profession," and not have our whole moral being brought under the mighty constraining influence of His love?

May the Holy Ghost so unfold to our souls His matchless glories and peerless excellencies, that we may "count all things but loss for the excellency of the knowledge of Christ Jesus our Lord."

> "Jesus, I love thy charming name;
>     'Tis music to mine ear,
> Fain would I sound it out so loud,
>     That earth and heaven should hear.
>
> Yes, thou are precious to my soul,
>     My transport and my trust:
> Jewels to thee are gaudy toys,
>     And gold is sordid dust.
>
> All my capacious powers can wish,
>     In thee doth richly meet:
> Nor, to mine eyes, is light so dear,
>     Nor friendship half so sweet.
>
> Thy grace still dwells upon my heart,
>     And sheds its fragrance there;
> The noblest balm of all its wounds,
>     The cordial of its care."

# THE TWO ALTARS

(Exod. xx. 24-26)

"An altar of earth thou shalt make unto me, and shalt sacrifice
thereon thy burnt offerings, and thy peace offerings, thy sheep,
and thine oxen: in all places where I record my name I will
come unto thee, and I will bless thee."

If aught could enhance the value, or add to the interest of this
passage of scripture, it is the context in which it stands. To find
such words at the close of Exodus xx. is something which must
strike the thoughtful reader. In the opening of this chapter, we
find God speaking from the top of Mount Sinai, and laying down
the law as to man's duty toward God and his duty toward his
neighbour. This law is published amid thunderings, blackness,
darkness, and tempest. "Thou shalt do this;" and "thou shalt not
do that." Such are the terms in which God speaks from the top
of the fiery mount. Thus is He compelled to erect around Himself,
and around His rights, certain barriers, in order to keep man off.
And, in the same way, has man to be kept from infringing the
rights of his fellow.

Thus much as to the opening of Exodus xx. There are no such
words here as, "I will come unto thee." Quite the reverse. The
word was, "Beware lest thou come unto me." (See Exod. xix. 12,
24.) It was impossible for man to get to God by way of law. The
barriers that were placed around that palpable mount were in-
superable to man. "By works of law shall no man living be justified." Under the law there is no possible way of access to God.
"Keep off" is the stern utterance of the entire legal system—the
expression of the very spirit and genius of the whole Mosaic
economy. Nearness and liberty are unknown under the law, and
cannot possibly be enjoyed by any one on legal ground.

Hence, then, we may safely say—and we say it with reverence—
Jehovah was not at home on the top of Mount Sinai. It was not

natural to Him to surround Himself with barriers. He was, as it were, forced into the position, by the legality of the human heart. Israel had taken upon them to say, "All that the Lord hath spoken we will do." (Exod. xix. 8.) It was this that caused Jehovah to place Himself at a distance in order that man might be tested, and the offence might abound. He had just said to the people, "Ye have seen what I did unto the Egyptians, and how I bare you on eagles' wings, and brought you unto myself. Now, therefore, if ye will obey my voice indeed, and keep my covenant, then ye shall be a peculiar treasure unto me above all people: for all the earth is mine."

To what "covenant" does He here refer? To the covenant made with Abraham—the covenant of grace. There was nothing of man's doing in this covenant. It set forth what God would do for Abraham and his seed—what He would give them, and what He would be to them. It was on the ground of this covenant that Jehovah could say to Israel, "I have brought you unto myself." But the very moment that Israel undertook to say, "All that the Lord hath spoken we will do," we hear the command issued to "set bounds about the mount," that the people might be put at a distance.

However, as we have said, all this was not according to the loving heart of the God of Israel. It did not suit His nature and character to place Himself at a distance from His people. They had compelled Him to retire within the narrow enclosures of mount Sinai, and to surround Himself with clouds and darkness, thunderings, lightnings, and tempest. Man had undertaken to do, and he must be put to the test. "The law entered that the offence might abound." And again, "By the law is the knowledge of sin."

But it is not our intention, in this short article, to dwell upon the subject of "the law." We have merely referred to it in order to bring out the striking contrast between the opening and the close of Exodus xx. It would seem as though God were in haste to come down from the top of that dreadful mountain in order to meet man at "an altar of earth"—the place of grace—the place where man's doings are displaced by God's. "An altar of earth thou shalt make unto me, and shalt sacrifice thereon thy burnt offerings, and thy peace offerings, thy sheep, and thine oxen: in all places where I record my name, *I will come unto thee, and I will bless thee.*"

What a contrast! It is as though He had said to them, "You cannot come to me, if I remain on the top of this mountain; but I will come unto you. If I remain here, I must curse you; but I will meet you at an altar of earth and bless you." Blessed be His Name, He delights not in cursing; and hence He would not record His Name on Mount Sinai, the place of distance, and darkness, where He could not come unto His people and bless them.

How blessedly all this tells out what God is! This teaching about the altar is like a ray of divine light piercing through the gloom which surrounded Mount Sinai, and shining on the spot where God would record His Name, and where He could meet His people in all the fulness of blessing.

And let the reader note the character of the offerings referred to in verse 24. We have "burnt offerings and peace offerings." Not a word about sin offerings and trespass offerings. Why is this? Surely this is the very place in which we should expect to find these latter introduced. But no. We have the burnt offering—the type of Christ surrendering Himself, in life and in death, to do the will of God; and we have the peace offering—the type of Christ as the object on which the worshipper feeds in communion with God. And not a word about the sin offering or trespass offering. Why? Is it that these are not needed? Far be the thought! They lie at the very foundation of that altar where God and the worshipper meet. The sin offering is the type of Christ bearing the judgment of God against sin. The trespass offering is the type of Christ bearing our sins in His own body on the tree. These, we repeat, form the foundation of all worship. But they are omitted in Exodus xx. 24, because we have here the nature and character of the worship in which God delights—a worship in which the soul is occupied with Christ, in the very highest aspect of His Person and work; for this is what we have in the burnt offering, wherein Christ is seen making atonement, not merely according to our need, but according to the claims of God—not merely according to the measure of the hatefulness of sin, but according to the measure of the preciousness of Christ to the heart of God.

257

What a striking contrast, then, between the opening and closing lines of Exodus xx.! What lessons are here for our hearts! What a rebuke to all our legal tendencies! We are all prone to be occupied with our *doings*, in some shape or form. Legality is natural to our hearts; and, let us remember, it was this that forced Jehovah —to speak after the manner of men—to take up the position in which we find Him in Exodus xix. and xx. Abraham did not know God in such a position. It was not as a lawgiver that God revealed Himself to the father of the faithful; but as a God of grace, as a God of promise. There were no thunderings and lightnings, no blackness, darkness, and tempest, surrounding the Blessed One when He appeared unto Abraham in Ur of the Chaldees; nor yet when He partook of his hospitality in the plains of Mamre. It was ever God's delight to have His people near Him, enjoying the precious fruits of *His grace*, and not afar off, reaping the bitter fruits of *their works*. This latter was simply the result of man's legal utterance, "All that the Lord hath spoken we will do." Up to the fatal moment in the which these words were spoken, God had been speaking and acting in the same unqualified grace toward the seed of Abraham, as He had toward that favoured patriarch himself. But when once Israel undertook *to do*, it was needful to put them thoroughly to the test; and this was done by the law.

But, it may be asked, was it not always God's purpose to give the law? Was it not necessary? Is it not designed to be the abiding rule of man's conduct—the statement of his duty to God and man—the divine summary and embodiment of his righteousness? To all this we reply, Most surely God knew from the beginning what He would do; and moreover, He, in His infinite wisdom, overruled man's legal folly, and made use of the law to raise the great question of righteousness, and prove whether it was possible for man to work out a righteousness which could be accepted. But what was the result? Did man ever get righteousness by keeping the ten commandments? Never. "By the deeds of the law shall no flesh be justified in his sight, for by law is the knowledge of sin." (Rom. iii. 20.) And again, "For as many as are of the works of the law are under the curse: for it is written, Cursed is every one that continueth not in all things which are written in the book of the law to do them. But that no man is justified by the law in the sight of God, it is evident: for the just shall live by faith." Galatians iii. 10, 11.

What, then, was the object of the law? Why was it given? And what was its effect? "The law entered that the offence might abound." (Rom. v. 20.) "Wherefore then serveth the law? It was added because of transgressions." (Gal. iii. 19.) "The law worketh wrath." Romans iv. 15.

Thus scripture answers our three questions in the plainest possible manner; and not only so, but it settles the entire law question in such a way as to remove every difficulty and every cloud from the mind that will only submit absolutely to the authority of the word.

However, when we sat down to pen this brief article, we had no thought whatever of entering on the domain of theology. It was merely our purpose to present to the heart and mind of the reader the striking lesson taught by the two altars in Exodus xx.—the altar of earth and the altar of hewn stone. In the former, we have the very spirit of the dispensation of grace; in the latter, the spirit of the dispensation of law. God wanted man to be near Him; and therefore He would have an altar of earth. In other words, man was to approach God without any efforts or doings of his own. "If thou wilt make me an altar of stone, thou shalt not build it of hewn stone [or, as the margin reads, "build them with hewing"]: for if thou lift up thy tool upon it, thou hast polluted it. Neither shalt thou go up by steps unto mine altar, that thy nakedness be not discovered thereon."

Oh! that men would only consider these things! How little are they understood! Man will be doing. He will lift up his tool in the building of his altar; and the result is, pollution. He will ascend by steps; and the result is, discovered nakedness. Thus it is, and thus it must be, because man is a sinner, and his very best works can only issue in pollution and nakedness.

But one thing is certain, God does not record His Name in any place where man's doings are set up as the basis of worship. This truth shines with heavenly lustre on every page of the sacred Volume; and it shines where we should least of all have expected to find it; namely, at the close of Exodus xx. It is something perfectly wonderful, amid the thunderings of Mount Sinai, to catch such heavenly accents as these, "In all places where I record my name *I will come unto thee, and I will bless thee.*" These are words of purest grace—words flowing from the very heart of God— words expressing the very nature and character of God. "I will come unto thee." Precious words! May they sink down into our hearts and there abide! May it be our aim and object ever to be found worshipping in that place where God records His Name, and where, instead of the nakedness and pollution which ever mark the efforts of man, we have the infinite preciousness of the grace of God, and the fulness and excellency of Christ in His Person and work!

# CLOVEN TONGUES

(Acts ii. 1-11)

It will greatly enhance the grace of this lovely passage of scripture to bear in mind what it was that rendered the cloven tongues necessary. In the eleventh chapter of Genesis, we have the inspired record of the first grand effort of the children of men to establish themselves in the earth—to form a great association, and make themselves a name. And all this, be it remembered, without God. His name is never mentioned. He was not to form any part of this proud and popular scheme. He was entirely shut out. It was not a dwelling place for God that was to be erected on the plain of Shinar. It was a city for man—a centre round which men were to gather.

Such was the object of the children of men, as they stood together on the plain of Shinar. It was not, as some have imagined, to escape another deluge. There is not a shadow of foundation in the passage for any such idea. Here are their words, "And they said, Go to, let us build us a city, and a tower whose top may reach unto heaven; and let us make us a name, lest we be scattered abroad upon the face of the whole earth." There is no thought here of escaping another flood. It is sheer imagination, without any scripture basis. The object is as plain as possible. It is precisely similar to all those great confederacies, associations, or masses of flesh, that have been formed on the earth from that day to this. The Shinar Association could vie with any association of modern times, both in its principle and object.

But it proved to be a Babel. Jehovah wrote confusion upon it. He divided their tongues and scattered them abroad, whether they would or not. In a word, divided tongues were sent as the expression of divine judgment upon this first great human association. This is a solemn and weighty fact. An association without God, no matter what its object, is really nothing but a mass of flesh,

261

based on pride, and ending in hopeless confusion. "Associate your-selves, O ye people, and ye shall be broken in pieces." (Is. viii. 9.) So much for all human associations. May we learn to keep clear of them! May we adhere to that one divine association, namely, the Church of the living God, of which a risen Christ in glory is the living Head, the Holy Ghost the living Guide, and the Word of God the living Charter!

It was to gather this blessed assembly that the cloven tongues were sent, in grace, on the day of Pentecost. No sooner had the Lord Jesus Christ taken His seat at the right hand of power, amid the brightness of heaven's majesty, than He sent down the Holy Ghost to publish the glad tidings of salvation in the ears of His very murderers. And, inasmuch as that message of pardon and peace was intended for men of various tongues, so the divine messenger came down prepared to address each "in his own tongue wherein he was born." The God of all grace made it plain—so plain that it cannot be mistaken—that He desired to make His way to each heart, with the sweet story of grace. Man, on the plain of Shinar, did not want God; but God, on the day of Pente-cost, proved that he wanted man. Blessed, for ever, be His holy Name! God had sent His Son, and man had just murdered Him; and, now He sends the Holy Ghost to tell man that there is pardon through that very blood which he had shed, for his guilt in shedding it. Matchless, marvellous, overwhelming grace! Oh! that it may sub-due our hearts, and bind us to Him who is, at once, its source, its channel, and the power of enjoyment! The grace of God has far outtopped all the enmity of man. It has proved itself victorious over all the opposition of the human heart, and all the rage of hell.

Thus, then, in Genesis xi. divided tongues were sent in judgment. In Acts ii. divided tongues were sent in grace. The blessed God of all grace would cause each one to hear of full salvation, and hear of it in those very accents in which his infant ears had hearkened to the earliest whisperings of a mother's love. "His own tongue wherein he was born." It mattered not whether the tongue were soft or harsh, refined or barbarous, the Holy Ghost would use it as the vehicle for conveying the precious message of salvation right home to the poor heart. If divided tongues had once been given to scatter in judgment, they were again given to gather in grace; not now round an earthly tower, but round a heavenly Christ; not for the exaltation of man, but for the glory of God.

Now, it is well worthy of notice, that when God was giving the law from Mount Sinai, He spoke only in one tongue and to one people. The law was carefully wrapped up in one language, and deposited in the midst of one nation. Not so the Gospel. When that was the burden, God the Holy Ghost Himself descended from heaven, in cloven tongues, to waft the soul-stirring tidings, far and wide, over the whole world, and convey them "to every creature under heaven" in the very dialect wherein he was born. This is a great moral fact. It comes down upon the heart with uncommon weight and power. When God was speaking in terms of requirement and prohibition, He confined Himself to one language; but when He was publishing the message of life and salvation, pardon and peace, through the blood of the Lamb, He spoke in every language under heaven. When man's duty was to be declared, God spoke in one dialect; but when God's salvation was to be published, He spoke in every dialect under heaven.

This, surely, tells a tale. It declares plainly which is more in harmony with the divine mind, law or grace. Blessed be His Name, He delights in grace. Law and judgment are His strange work. He has pronounced the feet of those that publish the gospel to be beautiful; whereas, of those who desired to be teachers of the law, He has said, "I would they were even cut off that trouble you." Thus His acts and His words discover the bent of His loving heart towards poor unworthy sinners. He has left nothing undone, nothing unsaid, to prove His perfect willingness to save and bless; and therefore all who die in their sins will perish without excuse, and those awful words will echo through the regions of eternal gloom, for ever and ever, "I would, but ye would not!" Reader, think of this! Are you yet in your sins? If so, we earnestly beseech you to flee, now, from the wrath to come. Accept the message of pardon, now sent to you in your own tongue wherein you were born, and go on your way rejoicing.

In conclusion, we might add, that Gen. xi., Acts ii., and Rev. vii.

9-17 form a very lovely group of scriptures. In the first, we see divided tongues sent, in *judgment;* in the second, divided tongues given in grace; and in the third, divided tongues gathered in *glory.* Well may we say, "Thy testimonies are wonderful, therefore doth my soul love them."

# ISRAEL AND THE NATIONS

## (READ PSALM LXVII)

It would greatly tend to give clearness and definiteness to missionary effort to keep fully before our minds God's original purpose in sending the gospel to the Gentiles, or nations. This we have stated in the most distinct manner in Acts xv. "Simeon hath declared," says James, "how God at the first did visit the Gentiles, to take out of them a people for his name."

Now nothing can be simpler than this. It affords no warrant whatsoever for the idea so persistently held by the professing church, namely, that the whole world is to be converted by the preaching of the gospel. Simeon knew quite well that such was not God's object in visiting the Gentiles; but simply to take out of them a people for His name. The two things are as distinct as any two things can be—indeed they stand in direct opposition. To convert all the nations is one thing; to take out of the nations a people is quite another.

The latter, and not the former, is God's present object. It is what He has been doing since the day that Simon Peter opened the kingdom of heaven to the Gentile in Acts x.; and it is what He will continue to do until the moment so rapidly approaching, in which the last elect one is gathered out, and our Lord shall come to receive His people unto Himself.

Let all missionaries remember this. They may rest assured it will not clip their wings, or cripple their energies; it will only guide their movements, by giving them a divine aim and object. Of what possible use can it be for a man to propose as the end of his labours something wholly different from that which is before the mind of God? Ought not a servant seek to do his master's will? Can he expect to please his master by running directly counter to his clearly expressed object?

Now, clearly, it is not God's purpose to convert the world by

265

the preaching of the gospel. He only means "to take out a people." True it is, blessedly true, that all the earth shall yet be filled with the knowledge of the Lord as the waters cover the sea. There is no question as to this. All scripture bears witness to it. To quote the passages would literally fill a volume. All Christians are agreed on this point,* and hence there is no need to adduce evidence.

But the question is, how is this grand and glorious result to be brought about? Is it the purpose of God to use the professing church as His agent, or a preached gospel as His instrument, in the conversion of the world? Scripture says No; and says it with an emphasis and a clearness which ought to sweep away every doubt and difficulty.

And here let it be distinctly understood that we delight in all true missionary effort. We heartily wish God's speed to every true missionary—to every one who has left home, and kindred, and friends, and all the comforts and privileges of civilized life, in order to carry the glad tidings of salvation into the dark places of the earth. And, further, we desire to render hearty thanks to God for all that has been accomplished in the fields of foreign mission; though we cannot by any means approve the mode by which the work is carried on, or the great root principle of missionary societies. We consider there is a lack of simple faith in God, and of subjection to the authority of Christ, and the guidance of the Holy Ghost. There is too much of mere human machinery, and looking to the world for aid.

But all this is beside our present mark. We are not now discussing the principle of missionary organization, or the various appliances adopted for the carrying on of missionary operation. The point with which we are occuped in this brief paper is this—will God make use of the professing church to convert the nations? We ask not, has He done so? for, were we to put the question thus, we should receive an unqualified negative from all the ends of the earth. What! Christendom convert the world! Alas! alas! she is herself the darkest moral blot in the universe of God, and a

---

* [Unfortunately, this can no longer be said, since Satan has switched his ground from the coarse "post-millenialism" to the more subtle "amillenialism." Editor].

grievous stumbling-block in the pathway of both Jew and Gentile. The professing church has been at work for eighteen long centuries; and what is the result? Let the reader take a glance at a missionary map, and he will see in a moment. Look at those patches of black, designed to set forth the dismal regions over which heathenism bears sway. Look at the red, the green, the yellow, setting forth popery, the Greek church, Mahometanism. And where is—we say not true Christianity, but even mere nominal Protestantism? That is indicated by those tiny spots of blue which, if all put together, would make but a very small fraction indeed. And as to what this Protestantism is in its best estate we need not now stop to inquire.

But, we ask, is it the revealed purpose of God to make use of the professing church in any way to convert the nations? If it be so, we admit at once that, spite of the most discouraging appearances, we must believe and hope. We freely grant that the true way in which to test any principle is not by results, but simply by the word of God.

What, then, say the scriptures on the great question of the conversation of the nations? Take, for example, the lovely psalm that stands at the head of this paper. It is but one proof among a thousand, but it is a most striking and beautiful one, and we need hardly say it perfectly harmonizes with the testimony of all scripture, from Genesis to Revelation. We cannot refrain from giving it at full length to the reader.

"God be merciful unto us, and bless us; and cause his face to shine upon us. That thy way may be known upon earth; thy saving health among all nations. Let the people praise thee, O God; let all the people praise thee. O let the nations be glad, and sing for joy: for thou shalt judge the people righteously, and govern the nations upon earth. Let the people praise thee, O God, let all the people praise thee. Then shall the earth yield her increase; and God, even our own God, shall bless us. God shall bless us, and all the ends of the earth shall fear him."

Here, then, the simple truth shines before us with remarkable force and beauty. It is when God shall have mercy upon Israel— when He shall cause His light to shine upon Zion—then, and not until then, will His way be known upon earth, His saving health among all nations. It is through Israel, and not through the professing church, that God will yet bless the nations.

That the "us" of the foregoing psalm refers to Israel, no intelligent reader of scripture needs to be told. Indeed, as we all know, the great burden of the psalms, the prophets, and the entire of the Old Testament, is Israel. There is not a syllable about the church from cover to cover of the Old Testament. Types and shadows there are in which—now that we have the light of the New Testament—we can see the truth of the church prefigured. But without that light no one could, by any possibility, find the truth of the church in Old Testament scripture. That great mystery was, as the inspired apostle tells us, *"hid"*—not in the scriptures, for whatever is contained in the scriptures in no longer hid, but revealed—but it was "hid in God;" and was not, and could not, be revealed until Christ, being rejected by Israel, was crucified, and raised from the dead. So long as the testimony to Israel was pending, the doctrine of the church could not be unfolded. Hence, although at the day of Pentecost we have the *fact of the church*, yet it was not until Israel had rejected the testimony of the Holy Ghost in Stephen that a special witness was called out in the person of Saul, to whom *the doctrine of the church* was committed. We must distinguish between the fact and the doctrine; indeed it is not until we reach the last chapter of the Acts that the curtain finally drops upon Israel; and Paul, the prisoner at Rome, fully unfolds the grand mystery of the church which from ages and generations had been hid in God, but was now made manifest. Let the reader ponder Romans xvi. 25, 26; Ephesians iii. 1-11; Colossians i. 24-27.

We cannot attempt to go fully into this glorious subject here; indeed, to refer to it at all is a digression from our present line. But we deem it needful just to say thus much, in order that the reader may fully see that Psalm lxvii. refers to Israel; and, seeing this, the whole truth will flow into his soul that the conversion of the nations stands conected with Israel, and not with the church. It is through Israel, and not through the church, that God will yet bless the nations. It is His eternal purpose that the seed of

Abraham, His friend, shall yet be pre-eminent in the earth, and that all nations shall be blessed in and through them. "Thus saith the Lord of hosts, In those days it shall come to pass, that ten men shall take hold, *out of all languages of the nations*, even shall take hold of *the skirt of him that is a Jew*, saying, We will go *with* you; for we have heard that God is with you." Zechariah viii. 23.

There is no need to multiply proofs. All scripture bears witness to the truth that God's present object is not to convert the nations, but to take out of them a people for His name; and, further, that when these nations shall be brought in—as they most assuredly shall—it will not be by the instrumentality of the church at all, but by that of the restored nation of Israel.

It would be an easy and a delightful task to prove from the New Testament, that, previous to the restoration and blessing of Israel, and therefore, *a priori*, previous to the conversion of the nations, the true church of God, the body of Christ, shall have been taken up to be for ever with the Lord, in the full and ineffable communion of the Father's house; so that the church will not be God's agency in the conversion of the Jews as a nation, any more than in that of the Gentiles. But we do not desire at this time to do more than establish the two points above stated, which we deem of much interest and importance in reference to the grand object of missionary operations. When missionary societies propose for their object the conversion of the world, they propose a palpable mistake. And when Christendom imagines that she is to be God's instrument in converting the nations, it is simply a delusion and an empty conceit. Hence, therefore, let all who go forth as missionaries see that they are ruled in their blessed work by a divine object, and, further, that they are pursuing that object in a divinely-appointed way.

# A HEART FOR CHRIST

(READ MATT. XXVI.)

In this solemn chapter, we have a great many hearts revealed. The heart of the chief priests, the heart of the elders, the heart of the scribes, the heart of Peter, the heart of Judas. But there is one heart in particular unlike all the others, and that is the heart of the woman who brought the alabaster box of very precious ointment, to anoint the body of Jesus. This woman had a heart for Christ. She may have been a very great sinner—a very ignorant sinner, but her eyes had been opened to see a beauty in Jesus which led her to judge that nothing was too costly to be spent on Him. In a word, she had a heart for Christ.

Passing over the chief priests, the elders, and the scribes, let us look for a moment at the heart of this woman in contrast with the heart of Judas and the heart of Peter.

I. Judas was a covetous man. He loved money. A very common love in every age. He had preached the gospel. He had walked in company with the Lord Jesus, during the days of His public ministry. He had heard His words, seen His ways, experienced His kindness. But, alas! though an apostle, though a companion of Jesus, though a preacher of the gospel, he had no heart for Christ. He had a heart for money. His heart was ever moved by the thought of gain. When money was in question, he was all alive. The deepest depths of his being were stirred by money. "The bag" was his nearest and dearest object. Satan knew this. He knew the special lust of Judas. He was fully aware of the price at which he could be bought. He understood his man, how to tempt him, and how to use him. Solemn thought!

Be it observed, also, that the very position of Judas made him all the more fit for Satan. His acquaintance with the ways of Christ made him a fit person to betray Him into the hands of His enemies. Head knowledge of sacred things, if the heart be not touched, renders a man more awfully callous, profane, and wicked. The chief priests and scribes in Matthew ii. had a head knowledge of the letter of Scripture, but no heart for Christ. They could at once hand down the prophetic roll and find the place where it was written, "Thou Bethlehem, in the land of Juda, art not the least among the princes of Juda; for out of thee shall come a Governor that shall rule my people Israel." (v. 6.) All this was very well, very true, and very beautiful; but, then, they had no heart for this "Governor"—no eyes to see Him—they did not want Him. They had Scripture at their fingers' ends. They would have felt ashamed, no doubt, had they not been able to answer Herod's question. It would have been a disgrace to men in their position to exhibit ignorance; but they had no heart for Christ, and hence they laid their scriptural knowledge at the feet of an ungodly king, who was about to use it, if he could, for the purpose of slaying the true heir to the throne. So much for *head-knowledge* without *heart-love*.

It is not, however, that we would make little of scriptural knowledge. Far from it. The true knowledge of Scripture must lead the heart to Jesus. But there is such a thing as knowing the letter of Scripture so as to be able to repeat chapter after chapter, verse after verse, yea, so as to be a sort of walking concordance, and, all the while, the heart be cold and callous toward Christ. This knowledge will only throw one more into the hands of Satan, as in the case of the chief priests and scribes. Herod would not have applied to ignorant men for information. The devil never takes up ignorant men, or stupid men, to act against the truth of God. No; he finds fitter agents to do his work. The learned, the intellectual, the deep-thinking, provided only they have no heart for Christ, will answer him well, at all times. What was it saved "the wise men from the east?" Why could not Herod—why could not Satan—enlist them into his service? Oh! reader, mark the reply. They had a heart for Christ. Blessed safeguard! Doubtless, they were ignorant of Scripture—they would have made but a poor hand of searching for a passage in the prophets; but they were looking for Jesus—earnestly, honestly, diligently looking for Jesus. Wherefore, Herod would fain have made use of them if he could; but they were not to be used by him. They found their way to Jesus. They did not know much about the prophet who had spoken of the "Governor;" but they found their way to the "Governor" Himself. They found Him in the Person of the babe in the manger at Bethlehem; and instead of being tools in the hands of Herod, they were worshippers at the feet of Jesus.

Now, it is not that we would commend ignorance of Scripture. By no means. People are sure to err greatly who know not the Scriptures. It was to the praise of Timothy that the apostle could say to him, "From a child thou hast known the holy Scriptures, which are able to make thee wise unto salvation;" but, then, he adds, "Through faith which is in Christ Jesus." (2 Tim. iii. 15.) The true knowledge of Scripture will always conduct us to the feet of Jesus; but mere head-knowledge of Scripture, without heart-love for Christ, will only render us the more effective agents in the hands of Satan.

Thus, in the case of the hard-hearted, money-loving Judas. He had knowledge, without a spark of affection for Christ, and his very familiarity with that blessed One made him a suitable instrument for the devil. His nearness to Jesus enabled him to be a traitor. The devil knew that thirty pieces of silver could purchase his service in the horrible work of betraying his Master.

Reader, think of this! Here was an apostle—a preacher of the gospel—a high professor; yet, underneath the cloak of profession, lay "a heart exercised in covetous practices"—a heart which had a wide place for "thirty pieces of silver," but not a corner for Jesus. What a case! what a picture! what a warning! Oh! all ye heartless professors, think of Judas! think of his course! think of his character! think of his end! He preached the gospel, but he never knew it, never believed it, never felt it. He had painted sunbeams on canvas, but he had never felt their influence. He had plenty of heart for money, but no heart for Christ. As "the son of perdition" "he hanged himself," and "went to his own place." Professing Christians, beware of head-knowledge, lip profession, official piety, mechanical religion—beware of these things, and seek to have a heart for Christ.

II. In Peter we have another warning, though of a different kind.

272

He really loved Jesus, but he feared the cross. He shrank from confessing His name in the midst of the enemy's ranks. He boasted of what he would do, when he should have been self-emptied. He was fast asleep when he ought to have been on his knees. Instead of praying he was sleeping; and, then, instead of being still, he was drawing his sword. "He followed Jesus afar off," and then "warmed himself at the high priest's fire." Finally, he cursed and swore that he did not know this gracious Master. All this was terrible! Who could suppose that the Peter of Matt. xvi. 16, is the Peter of Matt. xxvi.? Yet so it is. Man, in his best estate, is but like a sere autumn leaf. "There is none abiding." The highest position, the loudest profession, may all end in following Jesus afar off, and of basely denying His name.

It is very probable, yea, almost certain, that Peter would have spurned the thought of selling Jesus for thirty pieces of silver; and yet he was afraid to confess Him before a servant maid. He might not have betrayed Him to His enemies, but he denied Him before them. He may not have loved money, but he failed to manifest a heart for Christ.

Christian reader, remember Peter's fall, and beware of self-confidence. Cultivate a prayerful spirit. Keep close to Jesus. Keep away from the influence of this world's favour. "Keep thyself pure." Beware of dropping into a sleepy, torpid condition of soul. Be earnest and watchful. Be occupied with Christ. This is the true safeguard. Do not be satisfied with the mere avoidance of open sin. Do not rest in mere blamelessness of conduct and character. Cherish lively, warm affections toward Christ. One who "follows Jesus afar off" may deny Him before long. Let us think of this. Let us profit by the case of Peter. He himself afterwards tells us to "be sober, be vigilant; because your adversary the devil, as a roaring lion, walketh about, seeking whom he may devour: whom resist, steadfast in the faith." (I Peter v. 8, 9.) These are weighty words, coming, as they do, from the Holy Ghost, through the pen of one who had suffered so from lack of "vigilance."

Blessed be the grace that could say to Peter, before his fall, "I have prayed for thee that thy faith fail not." Mark, He does not say, "I have prayed for thee that thou mayest not fall." No; but "that thy faith fail not" when thou hast fallen. Precious, matchless grace! This was Peter's resource. He was a debtor to grace, from first to last. As a lost sinner, he was a debtor to "the precious blood of Christ"; and as a stumbling saint, he was a debtor to the all-prevailing advocacy of Christ. Thus it was with Peter. The advocacy of Christ was the basis of his happy restoration. Of this advocacy Judas knew nothing. It is only those who are washed in the blood that partake of the advocacy. Judas knew nothing of either. Hence "he went and hanged himself;" whereas Peter went forth, as a converted or restored soul, to "strengthen his brethren." There is no one so fit to strengthen his brethren as one who has himself experienced the restoring grace of Christ. Peter was able to stand before the congregation of Israel and say, "Ye denied the Holy One and the Just," the very thing he had done himself. This shows how entirely his conscience was purged by the blood and his heart restored by the advocacy of Christ.

III. And now, one word as to the woman with the alabaster box. She stands forth in bright and beauteous contrast with all. While the chief priests, elders, and scribes were plotting against Christ, "*in the palace of the high priest,* who was called Caiaphas," she was anointing His body "*in the house of Simon the leper.*" While Judas was covenanting with the chief priests to sell Jesus for thirty pieces of silver, she was pouring the precious contents of her alabaster box upon His Person. Touching contrast! She was wholly absorbed with her object, and her object was Christ. Those who knew not His worth and beauty might pronounce her sacrifice a waste. Those who could sell Him for thirty pieces of silver might talk of 'giving to the poor;" but she heeded them not. Their surmisings and murmurings were nothing to her. She had found her all in Christ. They might murmur, but she could worship and adore. Jesus was more to her than all the poor in the world. She felt that nothing was "waste" that was spent on Him. He might only be worth thirty pieces of silver to one who had a heart for money. He was worth ten thousand words to her, because she had a heart for Christ. Happy woman! May we imitate thee! May we ever find our place at the feet of Jesus, loving, adoring, admiring, and worshipping His blessed Person. May we spend and be spent in His service, even though heartless professors should deem our service a foolish "waste." The time is rapidly approaching when we shall not repent of anything done for His name's sake; yea, if there could be room for a single regret, it will be that we so faintly and feebly served His cause in the world. If, on "the morning without clouds," a single blush could mantle the cheek, it will be that we did not, when down here, dedicate ourselves more undividely to His service.

Reader, let us ponder these things. And may the Lord grant us A HEART FOR CHRIST!